International Political Economy Series

Series Editor
Timothy M. Shaw, University of Massachusetts Boston, Boston, MA, USA
Emeritus Professor, University of London, London, UK

The global political economy is in flux as a series of cumulative crises impacts its organization and governance. The IPE series has tracked its development in both analysis and structure over the last three decades. It has always had a concentration on the global South. Now the South increasingly challenges the North as the centre of development, also reflected in a growing number of submissions and publications on indebted Eurozone economies in Southern Europe. An indispensable resource for scholars and researchers, the series examines a variety of capitalisms and connections by focusing on emerging economies, companies and sectors, debates and policies. It informs diverse policy communities as the established trans-Atlantic North declines and 'the rest', especially the BRICS, rise.

NOW INDEXED ON SCOPUS!

Korbla P. Puplampu · Kobena T. Hanson ·
Peter Arthur
Editors

Sustainable Development, Digitalization, and the Green Economy in Africa Post-COVID-19

palgrave
macmillan

Editors
Korbla P. Puplampu
Department of Sociology
Grant MacEwan University
Edmonton, AB, Canada

Kobena T. Hanson
Independent Development Evaluation
African Development Bank
Abidjan, Côte d'Ivoire

Peter Arthur
Department of Political Science
Dalhousie University
Halifax, NS, Canada

ISSN 2662-2483 ISSN 2662-2491 (electronic)
International Political Economy Series
ISBN 978-3-031-32163-4 ISBN 978-3-031-32164-1 (eBook)
https://doi.org/10.1007/978-3-031-32164-1

© The Editor(s) (if applicable) and The Author(s), under exclusive license to Springer Nature Switzerland AG 2023

This work is subject to copyright. All rights are solely and exclusively licensed by the Publisher, whether the whole or part of the material is concerned, specifically the rights of translation, reprinting, reuse of illustrations, recitation, broadcasting, reproduction on microfilms or in any other physical way, and transmission or information storage and retrieval, electronic adaptation, computer software, or by similar or dissimilar methodology now known or hereafter developed.
The use of general descriptive names, registered names, trademarks, service marks, etc. in this publication does not imply, even in the absence of a specific statement, that such names are exempt from the relevant protective laws and regulations and therefore free for general use.
The publisher, the authors, and the editors are safe to assume that the advice and information in this book are believed to be true and accurate at the date of publication. Neither the publisher nor the authors or the editors give a warranty, expressed or implied, with respect to the material contained herein or for any errors or omissions that may have been made. The publisher remains neutral with regard to jurisdictional claims in published maps and institutional affiliations.

Cover credit: Rob Friedman/iStockphoto.com

This Palgrave Macmillan imprint is published by the registered company Springer Nature Switzerland AG
The registered company address is: Gewerbestrasse 11, 6330 Cham, Switzerland

Acknowledgments

Scholarship is a cooperative enterprise, and we consider it a privilege to have obtained the help of so many people and institutions in the writing of this volume. First, it is intriguing how our conversations about the place of the African continent in the global socio-political system have spawned several thoughts and reflections. These thoughts and reflections, especially in what has come to be called the post-COVID-19 world, offer material to reflect on previous discussions on digitalization and the emerging discourse on the green economy.

Second, we extend our heartfelt thanks to the contributors in this book. In our busy professional lives, you took time to respond and accommodated our timelines. Your commitment is a testament of the value of collaboration in the academy. We are particularly saddened by the untimely death of our colleague to be, Katie Mutula, a student of Vanessa Tang and Kobena Hanson, but delighted to have her contribution as part of a chapter in the book. Vanessa and Kobena, thank you for your work in training the next generation of academics in Africa.

Third, our sincere appreciation again goes to the invaluable team at Palgrave, notably Tim Shaw (Series Editor) for his critical insights which helped us to shape our focus; Anca Pusca (Senior Editor) and her colleagues Rebecca Roberts and Ananda Kumar Mariappan. Your support was vital to ensuring this project reached fruition successfully. Last but not the least, we also thank the anonymous reviewers whose constructive critique and feedback helped shape the quality and critical thoughts of the volume.

To our families, we once again say a big thanks for accommodating our occasional absences while preparing this volume. The cooperation of several people notwithstanding, any shortcomings in the book are entirely that of the editors and each individual contributor.

Contents

Part I Sustainable Development, Digitalization, and the Green Economy in Africa Post-COVID-19

1 Sustainable Development, Digitalization, and the Green Economy in Post-COVID-19 Africa 3
   Peter Arthur, Korbla P. Puplampu, and Kobena T. Hanson

2 Beyond the Rhetoric: Digitalization Policy for Resilience in Africa Post-COVID-19 13
   Korbla P. Puplampu

3 Politics Versus Reality: The African State and Governance Post-COVID-19 41
   Peter Arthur

Part II Natural Resources Governance and Socio-Economic Systems

4 Reimagining Natural Resources Governance in Africa: Is Digitalization the Game Changer? 71
   Peter Arthur

5	Assessing Extractive Natural Resources and Digitalization of Governance Initiatives in Africa: Rethinking Questions of Decline and Resilience Kobena T. Hanson and Peter Arthur	101
6	Natural Resources Management, Sovereign Wealth Fund, and the Green Economy: Digitalization, Policies, and Institutions for Sustainable Development in Africa Korbla P. Puplampu, Hosea O. Patrick, and Benjamin D. Ofori	125

Part III The Green Economy, Digitalization and The Race To 2030

7	Fostering Africa's Digital Trade in Services and Green Economy Post-COVID-19 Kobena T. Hanson, Vanessa T. Tang, and Katie M. Mutula	153
8	Green Economic Policies in Africa Abbi M. Kedir, Fama Gueye, Adama Kane, and Mahamadi Gaba	175
9	Digitalization of What We Eat and How We Think in Africa Post-COVID-19 Korbla P. Puplampu and Samuel M. Mugo	199
10	The African State, Sustainable Development, Digitalization, Green Economy in Africa Post-COVID-19 Korbla P. Puplampu, Kobena T. Hanson, Timothy M. Shaw, and Peter Arthur	227

Index	243

NOTES ON CONTRIBUTORS

Peter Arthur is an Associate Professor of Political Science and International Development Studies at Dalhousie University, Canada. His research interests focus on sub-Saharan Africa, with an emphasis on the contribution of small-scale enterprises, new regionalism, capacity development and post-conflict reconstruction, the governance of oil, and natural resources management. He has published in several journals such as *Africa Today*, *African Studies Review*, *Commonwealth and Comparative Politics*, and *Journal of Contemporary African Studies* and edited and contributed to several books including *Disruptive Technologies, Innovation and Development in Africa* and *From Millennium Development Goals to Sustainable Development Goals: Rethinking African Development*.

Mahamadi Gaba is an environmental economist and a Ph.D. candidate in climate change economics West African Science Service Center on Climate Change and Adapted Land Use (WASCAL) program at the University of Cheick Anta Diop (UCAD), Dakar, Senegal. His research interests are in natural resources, environmental economics, sustainable development, and environmental justice, with particular focus on green finance, renewable energy, and agricultural economics.

Fama Gueye is a lecturer in Economics and Sustainable Development in the Public Policy Institute (IPP) at the University of Cheikh Anta Diop of Dakar (UCAD), Senegal where she is also the deputy director of the West African Science Service Center on Climate Change and Adapted Land

Use (WASCAL) Climate Change Economics program. Her research interests include sustainable development, environmental and natural resource economics, agriculture, and econometrics.

Kobena T. Hanson is Principal Evaluation Capacity Development Officer at the African Development Bank, Cote d'Ivoire. His research focuses on capacity development, digital technology, and public policy. He is an editor/co-editor of *Disruptive Technologies, Innovation and Development in Africa* (Palgrave 2020), *From Millennium Development Goals to Sustainable Development Goals: Rethinking African Development* (Routledge 2018), Managing Africa's Natural Resources: Capacities for Development (Palgrave 2014), and has published in peer-reviewed journals such as *Environment & Planning A, GeoJournal, Journal of African Development, African Geographical Review*, and *Africa Today*.

Adama Kane is a PhD student in Climate Change Economics at the West African Science Service Center on Climate Change and Adapted Land Use (WASCAL) program at the faculty of Economics and Management at the University Cheikh Anta Diop, Dakar, Senegal and teaches refresher courses to undergraduate students in economic policy, environmental economics, natural resource economics, and rural economics. She also works at the Directorate of Planning and Economic Policies in Dakar. Her research interests include sustainable development, agriculture and food security, environmental and natural resource economics, econometrics, and economic policy.

Abbi M. Kedir is an Associate professor (Senior Lecturer) in international business in the Management School of the University of Sheffield, UK. He has provided research expertise to both government and international organizations such as the United Nations. His research work has been published in peer-reviewed international publications such as *Entrepreneurship: Theory & Practice, International Journal of Entrepreneurship and Small Business, Service Industries Journal*, and *International Journal of Entrepreneurship and Innovation*. In addition to book chapters and commissioned reports, he is on the editorial board of international journals such as *Journal of Entrepreneurial Behaviour and Research*.

Samuel M. Mugo is an Associate Professor of Chemistry at Grant MacEwan University, Canada. Dr. Mugo's research is focused on developing smart polymer nanomaterials as molecular receptors for fabricating mobile chemical analytics platforms. His research group has developed mobile sensors for use in precision agriculture, environmental monitoring, and noninvasive wearables for environmental, health, and wellness applications. The polymer nanomaterials developed in Mugo research group are also utilized for encapsulation and controlled release of biopesticide and nutraceuticals. Dr. Mugo has published his research in several academic journals including *IEEE Sensors,* and *Talanta* as well as edited books.

Katie M. Mutula (1990–2021), a Kenyan-born scholar and academic, was a PhD candidate in Economics at the University of Kwa Zulu-Natal, Durban, South Africa. With research interests in global value chains and small and medium enterprises (SMEs), Katie Mutula, by the time of her passing, had conceived and started collecting data for a book titled "The Diasporean" that would be an exposé of her experiences studying, working, and living in the diaspora for over two decades. In her memory a book project on Diaspora experiences is forthcoming undertaken by the Alternation African Scholarship Book Series. Chapter 7 in this volume, co-authored with Vanessa Tang and Kobena Hanson, her co-supervisors, is dedicated to Katie Mutula – A truly kind and warm-hearted strategic thinker and visionary.

Benjamin D. Ofori is a Senior Research Fellow at the Institute for Environment and Sanitation Studies (IESS) at the University of Ghana with research and teaching interests in local markets and domestic trade, urbanization, management of local Resources, and community livelihood especially in dam-affected areas. Dr. Ofori has contributed to edited books, technical reports and published in peer-reviewed articles in journals such as *International Journal of Development and Sustainability* and the *Journal of Geography and Regional Planning and Environment Development and Sustainability.*

Hosea O. Patrick is a Postdoctoral Fellow in Geography, Geomatics, and Environment at the University of Toronto, Mississauga, Ontario, Canada and obtained his Ph.D. in Political Science from the University of KwaZulu-Natal, South Africa. Dr. Patrick's teaching and research interests are in climate change, social and environmental justice, decolonization, peace, and conflict. He has contributed to chapters in edited volumes such as *Big Brother Naija and Popular Culture in Nigeria* and *Indigenous African Popular Music* and the Springer *Handbook of Climate Change,*

Management. He has also published in journals such as *African Insight, African Renaissance*, and *Journal of Transformation in Higher Education* and recently co-edited a special issue of the *Journal of Inclusive cities and Built Environment* on (De)-Coloniality, Autonomy, Identity, and Spatial Justice in Africa.

Korbla P. Puplampu teaches in the Department of Sociology at Grant MacEwan University, Edmonton, Canada. His research interests include the global restructuring of agriculture and higher education; the politics of identity in multicultural societies, transnational, and global citizenship. Dr. Puplampu has recent academic publications in journals such as *Journal of African Political Economy and Development, Journal of Inclusive Cities, and Built Environment* and *Social Identities*. He has co-edited and contributed to several books including *Disruptive Technologies, Innovation and Development in Africa*, and *From Millennium Development Goals to Sustainable Development Goals: Rethinking African Development*.

Timothy M. Shaw taught at Dalhousie University from 1971 to 2000 and directed the Pearson Institute, the International Development Studies department, and the Centre for Foreign Policy Studies. He has held visiting professorships in Denmark, Japan, Nigeria, South Africa, Uganda, UK, USA, Zambia, and Zimbabwe. Recently, Shaw directed the Institute of Commonwealth Studies at the University of London, the Institute of International Relations at the University of the West Indies in Trinidad and Tobago, and the Global Governance and Human Security program at the University of Massachusetts Boston, where he continues to serve as a visiting professor. He is the editor of the International Political Economy (IPE) series for Palgrave Macmillan and Springer and the IPE of New Regionalisms series for Routledge.

Vanessa T. Tang is a senior policy development consultant and lecturer in international economics at the University of KwaZulu-Natal. Dr. Tang has consulted for various organizations including most recently the KwaZulu-Natal Economic Development, Tourism and Environmental Affairs, African Development Bank, and African Union. She has published numerous papers in books, journals, and government reports on issues related to international trade, welfare, tourism, special economic zones, and regional economic integration. Her most recent co-edited books are titled *Comparative Regionalism for Development in the 21st Century:*

Insights from the Global South, published by Routledge, UK and *Development and Sustainable Growth of Mauritius*, published by Palgrave Macmillan, USA. Her latest research project addresses income inequality in the context of structural transformation, published by Oxford University Press, UK.

Acronyms

4IR	Fourth Industrial Revolution
ACBF	African Capacity Building Foundation
ACET	African Centre for Economic Transformation
AfCFTA	African Continental Free Trade Area
AfDB	African Development Bank
AI	Artificial Intelligence
AMDC	African Minerals Development Centre
AMV	African Mining Vision
ANRC	African Natural Resources Centre
APRM	African Peer Review Mechanism
AU	African Union
AUC	African Union Commission
DPI	Digital Preparedness Index
EITI	Extractive Industries Transparency Initiative
FIP	Forest Investment Program
GDP	Gross Domestic Product
GHG	Greenhouse Gases
GVCs	Global Value Chains
ICTs	Information and Communications Technologies
IFSWF	International Forum for Sovereign Wealth Fund
IIAG	Ibrahim Index of African Governance
ILO	International Labor Organization
IMF	International Monetary Fund
IoTs	Internet of Things
KPCS	Kimberly Process Certification Scheme
LCDS	Low Carbon Development Strategies

LTE	Long Term Evolution
MDGs	Millennium Development Goals
MSMEs	Micro, Small and Medium Enterprises
NREN	National Research and Education Networks
SDGs	Sustainable Development Goals
SDLO	Sustainable Development License to Operate
SLO	Social License to Operate
SSA	Sub-Saharan Africa
SWFs	Sovereign Wealth Funds
TAE	Tertiary Agricultural Education
WOAN	Wholesale Open Access Networks

List of Figures

Fig. 7.1	World Digital Services Exports, 2018–2021 (US Dollars Millions) (*Source* Authors' compilation based on UNCTAD handbook of statistics data [UNCTAD, 2023])	162
Fig. 7.2	Contributions to the total change in world services exports, 2019–2021 (percentage points) (*Source* Authors' compilation based on UNCTAD handbook of statistics data [UNCTAD, 2023])	162
Fig. 7.3	Africa's Digital Services Exports, 2018–2021 (US Dollars Millions) (*Source* Authors' compilation based on UNCTAD handbook of statistics data [UNCTAD, 2023])	163
Fig. 7.4	World and Africa's Internet Connection, 2018–2020 (Percentage of Population) (*Source* Authors' compilation based on the World Bank, World Development indicators data [WDI, 2023])	165
Fig. 7.5	Relationship Between Africa's Export Diversification and the Green Economy (*Source* Authors' compilation of the concentration index is based on UNCTAD handbook of statistics data [UNCTAD, 2023]. The Global Green Economy index is based on Dual Citizen LLC data [Dual Citizen LLC, 2023])	167

List of Boxes

Box 8.1	Less taxes for more solar	188
Box 8.2	Carbon tax: project of Senegalese carbon taxation	189
Box 8.3	Cement factory in Senegal using biomass for energy	190
Box 8.4	Positive developments emanating from COVID-19: digitization and e-commerce	190

PART I

Sustainable Development, Digitalization, and the Green Economy in Africa Post-COVID-19

CHAPTER 1

Sustainable Development, Digitalization, and the Green Economy in Post-COVID-19 Africa

Peter Arthur, Korbla P. Puplampu, and Kobena T. Hanson

INTRODUCTION AND PROBLEM

African countries recovered quickly following the 2008 global financial crisis and were on a trajectory, in most cases, to attain the UN-sponsored sustainable development goals (SDGs), Agenda 2030 and subsequently the African Union's Agenda 2063. However, the March 2020 COVID-19 global pandemic in changing the foundations of society, also revealed and clearly exposed inequalities within and among countries in both the global North and global South. While the global community concertedly

---

P. Arthur (✉)
Department of Political Science, Dalhousie University, Halifax, NS, Canada
e-mail: peter.arthur@dal.ca

K. P. Puplampu
Department of Sociology, Grant MacEwan University, Edmonton, AB, Canada
e-mail: puplampuk@macewan.ca

© The Author(s), under exclusive license to Springer Nature Switzerland AG 2023
K. P. Puplampu et al. (eds.), *Sustainable Development, Digitalization, and the Green Economy in Africa Post-COVID-19*, International Political Economy Series, https://doi.org/10.1007/978-3-031-32164-1_1

rallied in pandemic containment measures and medical research produced vaccines in record time, that is only part of the story. The fact is that the pandemic is not over. By November 2021, Omicron, a new mutation variant of the COVID-19 virus, originally identified by researchers in South Africa and subsequently in Netherlands and other countries of the world, introduced another level of uncertainty, compelling some national governments to extend social assistance programs and policy interventions on how to slow down the economic impact of the virus and begin a re-building program (*The Economist*, 2021). What is obvious is that the prevailing inequalities within and among countries raise questions of access to the vaccine and how national interests, for example, vaccine nationalism, and the lack of trust between governments and their citizens undermine the basis for any form of solidarity. Thus, this risk, which is widely acknowledged as a global problem, calls for a rethinking of solutions that is based on a global approach (Okonjo-Iweala et al., 2021; Stiglitz, 2020).

The broader policy response and implications to the COVID-19 pandemic can be characterized as follows: an unprecedented level of spending public funds to restore social safety, rising public debt, failing economic enterprises, including contractions in activities such as the hospitality sector, as well as natural resource management, specifically environmental pollution (AfDB, 2021). The depth of public spending, which highlights the role of the state in the economic and social arena, runs contrary to the prevailing neoliberal edict of a minimal role of the state in the economy and society at large.

For African states, the search for revenue to shore up the economy, including the moribund social safety system in areas such as health and education, calls for a concerted effort in revenue mobilization in the face of falling commodity prices, shrinking value of sovereign wealth funds and the changing landscape for the international financial architecture including foreign aid, even though diasporic remittances have actually increased in the past year for most African countries (AfDB, 2021; Zeufack et al., 2021). Indeed, for African policymakers, the issues are how

---

K. T. Hanson
Independent Development Evaluation, African Development Bank, Abidjan, Côte d'Ivoire
e-mail: k.hanson@afdb.org

to meet increased spending needs, contain the steep increase in public debt, and mobilize more sources of tax revenue, especially from domestic sources (Selassie & Tiffin, 2021). Analysts have identified the SDGs, innovation, and digitalization as essential pieces in the puzzle on social change and the role of disruptive technology in addressing Africa's development (Arthur et al., 2020; Duarte, 2021).

For example, while the role of natural resources to Africa's development is well known, the focus now is recalibrating the natural resource regime toward a low carbon or green economy. Two main issues are at stake: the need for African countries to be better at countering tax avoidance by many multinational companies and addressing the extent to which countries that produce the minerals, such as cobalt and manganese, required for the green economy, can handle supply and demand considerations at the heart of energy transition (Albertin et al., 2021; Valckx et al., 2021). For example, the Democratic Republic of Congo accounts for about 70% of the cobalt output and holds half of the world's reserves and South Africa is key in the global supply of manganese (ANRC, 2021). However, both countries require capable and robust institutions, regulations, and policies.

The discourse on the green economy, while by no means new, has assumed renewed urgency in ongoing discussions on global climate change in a framework of carbon inequality (Oxfam International and the Institute for European Environmental Policy, 2021). In fact, Adeleke and Josue (2019) have indicated that efforts have recently shifted to the attainment of green growth by African countries, especially the sub-Saharan Africa (SSA), which is one of the regions in the world that is lacking in terms of human quality of life and productivity. Death (2014) notes that African countries face many challenges in pursuing a transition based on sustainable development. The concept of sustainable development focuses on how to utilize resources today with an eye on the needs of future generations (Ishwaran, 2012). However, addressing these challenges is crucial since as Adeleke and Josue (2019) note, the share of clean energy, carbon dioxide (CO_2) emissions, human development index, secondary school enrollment, life expectancy at birth, and access to electricity are important green economy indicators for any significant long-term impact on poverty reduction. It is therefore not surprising that the implementation of the green economy in Tanzania, for example, has become a tool for the government, international aid donors, and businesses to continue to pursue and further strengthen a policy to 'modernize' agriculture through a focus on large-scale investments (Bergius et al., 2020).

The collective impact of resource development, the drive toward Agenda 2030, and the raging COVID-19 global pandemic offer an important framework to interrogate African development. At the same time, the current context of profound changes also presents new opportunities and examples of success stories in higher education, green businesses, and agriculture innovations as responses to the necessities borne by and the result of the COVID-19 pandemic. Against this backdrop, the fundamental questions revolve around the nature of the relationship between the ongoing COVID-19 pandemic, and digitalization. Specifically, the focus should be on how to better understand the impact of the emerging issues on inequality in Africa within a global context. Furthermore, there is the need to tease out the wider implications of whether the dynamics of the health (pandemic) and technology (digitalization) nexus demonstrate resilience or decline in critical sectors of African sociopolitical systems such as agriculture (food security), education, mining, and the environment and competitiveness as part of the digital ecosystem (Duarte, 2021).

The aim of this book is therefore to examine sustainable development in Africa post-COVID-19. Specifically, the book studies governance and digitalization from the perspective of natural environment management, climate change, the green economy, as well as agriculture and education. Digitalization supports the deepening of natural resource governance by assessing extractive practices, sovereign wealth funds, and the emerging discourse on global warming and green economic policies. This analytical exercise will better inform economic and socio-political policies and institutions for African development. The book, against the backdrop of the United Nations Agenda 2030 and the African Union Agenda 2063, offers unique insights on digitalization, governance, the green economy, and natural resource regime in Africa post-COVID-19. To attain the objectives of the book, the authors adopt a thematic approach in individual chapters with scholars from different academic backgrounds and disciplines (Political Science, Geography, Economics, Sociology, and Chemistry) based in Africa, Europe, and North America. Representing one of the most significant efforts to bring to the fore issues relating to digitalization, green economy, and natural resource governance in the post-COVID-19 period, the contributors to the book shed light on how the broader development goals of African countries as indicated in the SDGs and Agenda 2063 can be realized.

Overview of the Chapters

The book has three main thematic parts: (1) Sustainable Development, Digitalization, and the Green Economy in Africa Post-COVID-19; (2) Natural Resources Governance and Socio-Economic Systems; and (3) The Green Economy, Digitalization, and the Race to 2030. In Part I, contributors investigate approaches to digitalization and governance in the context of facilitating the socio-economic development process in African countries endowed with extractive natural resources. Part II focuses on governance in natural resource management against the backdrop of digitalization. Specifically, the chapters in this section engage with how policymakers can make use of digitalization in production, management of, and good governance in the natural resource sector, to enhance their competitiveness and address specific challenges in the extractive resource sector in Africa. The section also examines the place of natural resource wealth in the transition to the green economy and through sovereign wealth funds (SWFs). The place of sustainable development and digitalization receives attention in the chapters in the third and last section of the book. Writers in this section of the book enrich the extant literature and policy debates on matters relating to how African countries can realize their UN-sponsored SDGs Vision Agenda 2030 and Agenda 2063 of the African Union: *The Africa We Want*, which represent the framework and broad plan to transform Africa into a global powerhouse of the future. The authors also discuss the role of digitalization in aiding micro, small and medium enterprises (MSMEs) to help with the realization of SDGs, the importance of a green economy, as well as the nexus of agricultural and educational systems in the development process in Africa.

Following this introductory chapter, Chapter 2 by Korbla P. Puplampu titled "Beyond the Rhetoric: Digitalization Policy for Resilience in Africa Post-COVID-19" examines digitalization policy and the institutional regime at the continental level and in selected African countries. The chapter analyzes digitalization policies and institutions in terms of the structure and organization of the digital ecosystem, including regulatory framework with the related implications for the ownership structure, privacy, cost, and consumer protection. Chapter 3, by Peter Arthur, titled "Politics Versus Reality: The African State and Governance Post-COVID-19", focuses on the importance of good governance in the post-COVID-19 economic development efforts by African countries. The author argues that the COVID-19 global pandemic, raised not only health concerns, but also, precipitated a global economic crisis in both the formal and informal sectors (Lu et al., 2020; Nchanji, 2021). The economic shutdowns around the world to contain the virus had devastating socio-economic effects on the economies of African countries. The pandemic also exposed the importance of good governance structures including political leadership in the development process. The chapter emphasizes that having a good governance infused political leadership in place would help a country deal with the various health and economic challenges of the pandemic, facilitate and maintain a post-COVID-19 recovery. This chapter, grounded in the theory of good governance, therefore highlights the political and governance implications of COVID-19 for Africa.

In Part II of the book, which starts with Chapter 4, "Reimagining Natural Resources Governance in Africa: Is Digitalization the Game Changer?", Peter Arthur notes that natural resources, including extractives, have been a major source of economic activity for many countries, especially those in the global South. Natural resources do contribute in terms of employment generation, and growth in gross domestic product (GDP). Despite the potential of the natural resource sector for economic growth, the much-anticipated benefits have often not occurred. Considering the rise in transnational initiatives and digital technology as well as the problems associated with natural resource governance and management, the chapter examines the extent to which transnational initiatives such as Extractive Industries Transparency Initiative (EITI), Kimberly Process Certification Scheme (KPCS), and African Mining Vision (AMV) and digitalization can help manage natural resources in Africa, transform extractive industries, and address the challenges that have bedeviled the sector in Africa. Particularly, the chapter focuses on how various transnational initiatives and specific tools of digitalization could be employed to ensure that natural resources are effectively managed and governed by African countries as part of efforts to facilitate their development.

Kobena T. Hanson and Peter Arthur, in Chapter 5, titled "Assessing Extractive Natural Resources and Digitalization of Governance Initiatives in Africa: Rethinking Questions of Decline and Resilience" build on some of the issues raised by Peter Arthur in chapter four of this book by discussing the extractive resource sector in Africa, and its role as a key factor in and net contributor to growth and development. Accordingly, the chapter questions the role of digitalization of governance initiatives in Africa's extractives sector. The chapter acknowledges that digitalization has become an invaluable go-to weapon to diagnose, manage and address governance challenges facing the sector. However, meaningful transformation of Africa's extractives industry will require political will, enhanced capacity development at both the individual and institutional level, and a strong link between policymakers, regulators, and industry.

In Chapter 6, "Natural Resources Management, Sovereign Wealth Fund, and the Green Economy: Digitalization, Policies, and Institutions for Sustainable Development in Africa", Korbla P. Puplampu, Hosea O. Patrick and Benjamin D. Ofori wrap up the second part of the volume. Authors of this chapter focus on the issue of how the natural resources wealth can contribute to the transition to the green economy. In addition to an analysis of the performance of sovereign wealth funds (SWFs), the chapter also examines African countries that produce natural resources critical to the transition to the green economy, as well as the role of and how digitalization can facilitate natural resources management in terms of SWFs, and a green economy with the appropriate policies and institutions for sustainable development in Africa.

The third and concluding part of the volume, which focuses on the "The Green Economy, Digitalization, and the Race to 2030", begins with Chapter 7 titled "Fostering Africa's Digital Trade in Services and Green Economy Post-COVID-19" by Kobena T. Hanson, Vanessa T. Tang and Katie Mutula. The authors argue that COVID and its impact, coupled with the rise in digitalization have spurred on a boom in digital trade in services (aka 'servicification'). The focus of this chapter is threefold: First it discusses the green economy, stressing its contested nature and appeal. Second, how digitalization is impacting the services sector and resultant growth in digital trade in services. Third, the chapter outlines country- and region-specific examples that demonstrate the acknowledgment and acceptance by governments of the essence of digitalization to issues of servicification. The chapter specifically teases-out how digitalization is aiding micro, small and medium enterprises (MSMEs) to strategically participate in global value chains (GVCs); and concludes that if Africa seeks to leverage digitalization, then the continent will need to advance its own variety of 'servicification', and that digitalization at the national level must be anchored in the AUC's Digital Transformation Strategy for Africa.

Abbi Kedir, Fama Gueye, Adama Kane and Mahamadi Gaba, in Chapter 8, titled "Green Economy Policies in Africa", analyze, with digitalization as a backdrop, Africa's efforts toward building a green to ensure the sustainability of economic development. Acknowledging its short-term costs with long-term gains in tackling poverty even if there is resistance to it and limited commitments to green industrialization the service sector, Kedir et al., submit that green growth is not merely the management of natural resources; it also seeks to change the way we think about our environment and development. Green growth is one of the most challenging issues of our time and development actors, policymakers, and research centers have flagged its intergenerational implications for global development. The chapter draws on Senegal to contextualize the case for a green economy.

Chapter 9, titled, "Digitalization of What We Eat and How We Think in Africa Post-COVID-19", by Korbla P. Puplampu and Samuel M. Mugo, looks at the agricultural system in Africa, and its role in the political and socio-economic contours of the society. The chapter notes that contemporary systems of agricultural organization, from production to marketing and consumption, including value chain dimensions, are critical areas of study in Africa. Equally significant are the systems of education that produce the necessary and required knowledge to sustain agricultural organization systems. Against the background of surveillance capitalism, specifically digitalization, the chapter discusses the relationship between agricultural and educational systems in Africa and how that link is mediated by digitalization.

In the concluding chapter, "The African State, Sustainable Development, Digitalization, Green Economy in Africa Post-COVID-19", Korbla P. Puplampu, Kobena T. Hanson, Timothy M. Shaw and Peter Arthur draw out specific lessons from the chapters in the volume. They adopt a forward-looking or aspirational posture in wrapping up the contents of the preceding chapters in terms of theory, public policies on sustainable development, digitalization, the green economy, and the post-COVID-19 African landscape. Weaving together the broad themes and arguments in the preceding chapters, this chapter identifies and states areas of agreement and divergence in terms of sustainable development, digitalization, and the green economy. It also synthesizes and presents policy suggestions and institutional prerequisites gleaned from specific chapters of the book. Finally, relevant and keen observations and remarks, even from a comparative perspective, are also properly situated, with the concluding thoughts required for the race to UN Agenda 2030 in a post-COVID-19 Africa.

Concluding Remarks

The main goals and objectives of this book, which has a wide range of theoretical paradigms and perspectives, are to investigate and outline how African countries can chart a course of development that can help them address contestations that emerged from the COVID-19 pandemic. Overall, adding to the emerging literature on digitalization, natural resource governance, and the green economy post-COVID-19, the book provides new insights, suggestions, and perspectives on how African countries can facilitate their development process in the post-COVID-19 period. Contributors to the book, making use of various theoretical paradigms as well as cases and comparative approaches, highlight how countries in Africa can make use of digitalization to reach their SDG and Agenda 2063 goals. Additionally, the book has shown the various challenges that can derail these development goals and draws on relevant examples to demonstrate how these could be overcome in order for African countries to come out stronger in the post-COVID-19 period.

References

Adeleke, O., & Josue, M. (2019). Poverty and green economy in South Africa: What is the nexus? (Nsiah, C., Eds.). *Cogent Economics & Finance, 7*(1). https://doi.org/10.1080/23322039.2019.1646847

African Development Bank (AfDB). (2021). *African economic outlook 2021 from debt resolution to growth: The road ahead for Africa*. African Development Bank.

African Natural Resources Centre (ANRC). (2021). *Rare Earth Elements (REE)—Value chain analysis for mineral based industrialization in Africa*. African Development Bank.

Albertin, G., Devlin, D., & Yontcheva, B. (2021). *Countering tax avoidance in Sub-Saharan Africa's mining sector*. https://blogs.imf.org/2021/11/05/countering-tax-avoidance-in-sub-saharan-africas-mining-sector/. Retrieved January 6, 2022.

Arthur, P., Hanson, K. T., & Puplampu, K. P. (2020). *Disruptive technologies, innovation and development in Africa*. Palgrave Macmillan.

Bergius, M., et al. (2020). Green economy, degradation narratives, and land-use conflicts in Tanzania. *World Development, 129.* https://doi.org/10.1016/j.worlddev.2019.104850

Death, C. (2014). The green economy in South Africa: Global discourses and local politics. *Politikon, 41*(1), 1–22.

Duarte, C. (2021, March). Africa goes digital. *Finance and Development,* 18–20.

Ishwaran, N. (2012). After Rio+20: Translating words in action. *Environmental Development, 4,* 184–185. https://doi.org/10.1016/j.envdev.2012.09.006

Lu, Y., Wu, J., Peng, J., & Lu, L. (2020). The perceived impact of the COVID-19 epidemic: Evidence from a sample of 4807 SMEs in Sichuan Province China. *Environmental Hazards, 19*(4), 323–340.

Nchanji, E. B. (2021). Immediate impacts of COVID-19 pandemic on bean value chain in selected countries in sub-Saharan Africa. *Agricultural System, 188,* 103034.

Okonjo-Iweala, N., Summers, L. H., & Shanmugaratnam, T. (2021, December). Rethinking multilateralism for pandemic era. *Finance and Development,* 5–9.

Oxfam International and the Institute for European Environmental Policy. (2021). *Carbon inequality in 2030.* Oxfam GB for Oxfam International.

Selassie, A. A., & Tiffin, A. (2021). *The Policymaker's Trilemma.* https://blogs.imf.org/2021/05/12/the-policymakers-trilemma/. Retrieved January 6, 2022.

Stiglitz, J. (2020, September). Conquering the great divide. *Finance and Development, 57*(3), 17–19.

The Economist. (2021, December 11). Graphic detail The Omicron variant, 89.

Valckx, N., Stuermer, M., Senevirante, D., & Prasad, A. (2021). *Metals demand from energy transition may top current global supply.* https://blogs.imf.org/2021/12/08/metals-demand-from-energy-transition-may-top-current-global-supply/

Zeufack, A. G., Calderon, C., Kambou, G., Kubota, M., Korman, V., Canales, C. C., & Aviomoh, H. E. (2021, April). COVID-19 and the future of work in Africa: Emerging trends in digital technology adoption in Africa's Pulse, No. 23. *World Bank.* https://doi.org/10.1596/978-1-4648-1714-4. License: Creative Commons Attribution CC BY 3.0 IGO.

CHAPTER 2

Beyond the Rhetoric: Digitalization Policy for Resilience in Africa Post-COVID-19

Korbla P. Puplampu

INTRODUCTION

The COVID-19 global pandemic has several lessons for the global community. While the nature and magnitude of the lessons varied in specific parts of the world, the enduring theme in every part of the world has been social inequality. In the global North, many governments abandoned the neoliberal mantra of a minimal state in the economic sphere by revamping the social safety system with significant investments in the redistribution of resources to workers who lost their jobs. The governments, following the policies on restrictions on the mobility of citizens, also provided financial support to businesses for lost income. Since the level of investment was contingent on the existence of fiscal space, governments in the global South were confronted with several structural challenges.

K. P. Puplampu (✉)
Department of Sociology, Grant MacEwan University, Edmonton, AB, Canada
e-mail: puplampuk@macewan.ca

© The Author(s), under exclusive license to Springer Nature Switzerland AG 2023
K. P. Puplampu et al. (eds.), *Sustainable Development, Digitalization, and the Green Economy in Africa Post-COVID-19*, International Political Economy Series, https://doi.org/10.1007/978-3-031-32164-1_2

In the particular case of the African sub-region, several governments have been operating under high public debt and limited fiscal capacity. This situation is the result of several persistent and interrelated factors: weak internal revenue mobilization systems, an over-bloated and often politically inspired government expenditure, including out of proportion remuneration for the political class, and excessive focus on consumption at the expense of production. Thus, many African countries were, once again, at the mercy of international financial institutions and global partners for financial infusion and political leaders faced the reality of their steady lack of foresight and planning in, for example, creating a health care system that is resilient and can address the needs of their citizens. As OXFAM (2022: 3) argues, "Africa was poorly prepared to face a pandemic, with 52% of its citizens lacking access to healthcare, 83% lacking access to social protection and 52% of workers having no formal labour rights." This means the absence of any meaningful social or welfare system that citizens can draw on in times of drastic economic changes to minimize the impact of social inequality. Beyond the common theme of social inequality, another enduring theme from the COVID-19 pandemic for the global community was nations to have existing, appropriate, and capable policy and institutions (ACBF and IsDB, 2021; UNDP, 2022).

One useful reference point before and during the COVID-19 crisis has been technological innovation, specifically communication, information, and digitalization in an era of globalization. Although technological innovations have been part of larger social development since the post-second war, the significant improvements in communication and information technologies at the dawn of the twenty-first century solidified the relationship between technological innovations and globalization. Global, continental, and national authorities have therefore identified technological innovation as a critical component of the development puzzle for the African sub-region (AUC/OECD, 2021). From the global dimension, the ongoing focus is on the UN-sponsored SDGs in the context of Agenda 2030 (UNDP, 2015). At the continental level, the African Union's (AU) Agenda 2063 continues to inspire respective African governments (AUC, 2015). The underlying problem is that before the onset of the global pandemic in 2020, the African continent was "only halfway towards achieving the SDG goals and targets by 2030" (African Union et al., 2022: 10). While there is no doubt that the COVID-19 pandemic has negatively impacted the pace toward the 2030 agenda, the prevailing hope is that digitalization and innovation have the potential to fast-track advancement with robust policies and institutions.

There are several studies on digitalization and how it can underpin business practices in the public sector and innovation for development (Abugre et al., 2021; Arthur et al., 2020; Amankwah-Amoah, 2019; Mavhunga, 2017). In the public and business sectors, Abugre et al. (2021) address the role of digital processes in key areas such as the management of public programs, human resource development, and the supply chain system. Arthur et al. (2020) draw attention to the disruptive nature of technology and how digitalization and innovation can contribute to the larger African development effort. They stress and demonstrate how the relationship between digitalization and innovation, to anchor development, would require policy and institutions as well as capacity and political leadership. Bearing in mind the fact that agriculture, for example, occupies a central role in the political, economic, and social spheres in Africa, the relationship between digitalization and innovation in agricultural development has been the focus of several studies (Puplampu & Essegbey, 2018, 2020). While agriculture formerly occupied a sizeable part of the economy, in terms of the number of people involved in agricultural production, transformation of the sector, and the value-chain dynamics have changed the size of direct and indirect labor contributions in agricultural production and service-related processes. The key now is to pursue steps that can "attract investment in human and physical capital, particularly in the fields of digitalization and green technology" (Zeufack et al., 2022: 38). The role of green technology, by default, also implies an examination of natural resources management regime in Africa within a context of digitalization and innovation (Andrews et al., 2022).

While there are studies on the policy and institutional framework of digitalization, few focus on innovation and capacity building in the post-COVID-19 African context. However, there are several reasons to examine innovation and capacity building in post-COVID-19 Africa. First, the pandemic was fought and won by technological innovations. Second, technological innovations in communication made it possible for economic and other socio-political processes to carry on when many systems had to provide their services in an online format. Third, the pandemic revealed the importance of planning for today and tomorrow in terms of policy, institutions, infrastructure, and a regulatory regime.

Finally, the pandemic exposed and established a renewed significance of the state in society.

This chapter examines the digitalization policy and institutional regime at the continental level and in selected African countries. The analysis deals with the required and sufficient conditions for a sustainable digital landscape in Africa. The chapter investigates and offers viable suggestions, drawing from both the global North and global South, on digitalization to better contextualize the post-COVID-19 world in Africa as part of the wider effort toward the United Nation-sponsored Agenda 2030 and the African Union Agenda 2063. The chapter has four sections. Section "Digitalization, Innovation, Capacity Building, and COVID-19: A Theoretical Overview" presents conceptual and theoretical insights on digitalization, innovation, and capacity building. In section "Digitalization, Science, and Innovation in Africa: A Survey", the focus shifts to a survey of the digitalization and innovation terrain in Africa, by drawing on African countries with an emphasis on policy and institutions. Section "Digitalization and Capacity Building in Africa Post-COVID-19" engages in a discussion and the final section presents a summary, policy considerations, and concluding remarks.

DIGITALIZATION, INNOVATION, CAPACITY BUILDING, AND COVID-19: A THEORETICAL OVERVIEW

Digitalization is an umbrella term for the changes involving information and communication technologies (ICTs), the subsequent improvements in interconnectivity, and the intensity of networking made possible by these technologies. These changes are most visible in areas such as artificial intelligence, the Internet of Things (IoTs), robotics, and the broader changes of work in the Fourth Industrial Revolution (4IR) (AUC/OECD, 2021; Choi et al., 2019; Hanson & Puplampu, 2018; Hanson & Tang, 2020; IMF, 2020). The 4IR, compared to previous Industrial Revolutions, has specific dimensions like velocity, scope, and impact (AfDB and KOAFEC, 2019). In terms of velocity, it is unfolding at a constantly and exceptionally quick rate, and its manifestations range from big data analytics, bioengineering, and blockchain, to the use of drones as part of the internet of things (IoTs).

There has been a significant increase in the average number of internet users in Africa with an increase per 100 population from almost 12 in 2011 to 39 in 2018 (African Union et al., 2022: 58). The same source states that even though this represents a 225-percent increase in Internet usage, it is still comparatively low compared to South-Eastern Asia, Latin America and the Caribbean, and the rest of the world. This is because the African sub-region is "catching up" from a distant starting point and any attempt to leapfrog will depend on several factors. One main factor is the impact of the technological impetus of digitalization on innovation and the subsequent implications for political, economic, socio-cultural, and the environment (Abdulai, 2022; Arthur et al., 2020; Vyas-Doorgapersad, 2022).

Innovation draws on existing technological and scientific processes to create new and novel products and usage. Louis et al. (2017: 151) conceptualize innovation in terms of creating or enhancing material and immaterial artifacts with the sole purpose of improving society and identified three types of innovation. These are incidental, institutional, and strategic. Incidental, as the name implies, occurs as an unintended outcome, while institutional is intentional and takes place through organized forms of research, basic and applied, undertaken by public and private entities. Strategic innovation is not planned, but flows out from a systemic approach, is often coordinated by the public sector and is intentional in terms of attaining specific goals. The important point to stress is that the three types of innovation are interrelated and interactive in nature. In the case of the African continent, institutional and strategic forms of innovation are significant in the discourse on human development (UNDP, 1990).

As the UNDP (1990: 9) stated more than three decades ago, people "are the real wealth of a nation. The basic objective of development is to create an enabling environment for people to live long, health, and creative lives." One aspect of the enabling environment, especially in the context of both the United Nations-sponsored Millennium Development Goals (MDGs) and Sustainable Development Goals (SDGs), Goal 8 and Goal 17 respectively, is a partnership in the development process (UNDP, 2003, 2015). As a process and a relationship, partnership invites participation and cooperation among the actors or entities in the development agenda. In discussions on global development and partnership, the distinction is always the relationship between the global South and the global North, a relationship that has historical and contemporary orientations.

The main actors in the historical and contemporary relationship between the global South, specifically in the case of the African continent, the focus of this chapter, and the global North have been multilateral institutions like the World Bank and the International Monetary Fund (IMF) and groups like the Organization for Economic Cooperation and Development (OECD) and South-South Cooperation (SSC). The World Bank (WB) and the International Monetary Fund, for example, offered policy prescriptions ranging from poverty alleviation, support for infrastructure development, building institutions for democratic governance, structural adjustment policies to post-conflict resolution. If the goal of the global partnership is human development, then the outcomes of the partnerships between the African continent and global institutions and groups have been inconclusive (Hagmann & Reyntjens, 2016; Mentan, 2010). Underlying the myriad reasons for the inconclusive outcomes are complex external and internal political and socio-economic considerations, including ideological and geopolitical issues, indeed, structural factors. Thus, many African countries continue to occupy the lower sections of the human development index (UNDP, 2022). The role of the African state in setting the enabling environment becomes an important imperative for innovation, particularly the institutional and strategic forms. Institutional and strategic forms of innovation can also be best attained in the implied link between digitalization and innovation as synergistic parts of product development to improve the human condition, especially in the post-COVID-19 era.

The World Health Organization (WHO) acknowledged COVID-19 and declared it as a global pandemic on 20th January 2020 and 12th March 2020, respectively. By March 2020, most African countries had declared various kinds of emergencies, locally and nationally, and shifted into high-gear restrictive measures (ACBF and IsDB, 2021). Even though COVID-19, was first and foremost a health problem, because of the holistic nature of health, the pandemic affected political, economic, and social sectors of every African country (ACBF and IsDB, 2021). From the political context, many African states instituted border control measures aimed at stemming migration from both continental Africa and beyond. With restrictions on mobility, the other impact of the global pandemic was in the economic arena. When COVID-19 shut down businesses, there were significant economic contractions between 2020 and 2021 as well as significant variations within several countries and across regions on the continent (AfDB, 2022). The consequences include the fact that governments experienced shortfalls in tax revenue. The political and economic difficulties led to social issues, especially with the introduction of measures like social distancing. The African Union et al. (2022: 12) stated that about thirty-three African states are "debt vulnerable" and the situation was compounded by COVID-19, as governments accumulated more debt in response to the pandemic relief with dwindling financial outlets. The general impact of COVID-19, digitalization, and innovation, in the political and socio-economic spheres in the post-COVID-19 environment, provides the best background for remarks on the concept of capacity building.

The African Capacity Building Foundation (ACBF) is a specialized agency of the African Union and the leading institution on capacity development on the continent. Following ACBF (2011: 30–31), capacity:

> comprises the ability of people, organizations and society as a whole to manage their affairs successfully; and that is the process by which people, organizations and society as a whole unleash, strengthen, create adapt and maintain capacity over time. Capacity is also better conceptualized when answering the question: capacity for what? Capacity for individuals, organizations and societies to set goals and achieve them; to budget resources and use them for agreed purposes; and to manage the complex processes and interactions that typify a working political and economic system. Capacity is most tangibly and effectively developed in the context of specific development objectives such as delivering services to poor people; instituting education, public service and health care reform; improving the investment climate for small and medium enterprises, empowering local communities to better participate in public decision-making processes; and promoting peace and resolving conflict.

Attaining development in a post-pandemic era requires a focus on the central role of technological innovations in the resolution of the pandemic and sustained businesses in the online environment. There is also the need to, the neoliberal call for a minimal state notwithstanding, pay renewed attention to the African state as the primary site for policy planning today and its role in the region's development discourse (Puplampu, 2014).

An issue in capacity development is how to harness both internal and external resources to attain specific goals. At the height of the COVID-19 pandemic, several governments and firms on the continent depended on digital technologies to interact with their citizens and clients in various socio-economic activities (ITU, 2021a; Zeufack et al., 2020). For example, Kenya used an app called Msafari for contact tracing. In Ghana, Zipline put drones and robots into service in picking up test samples from rural areas for delivery to medical laboratories located in large cities such as Accra and Kumasi. In Tanzania, learning systems went online through the Shule Direct learning platform, while the Government of Togo used the Novissi platform to pay social welfare recipients. Against this background, the interest is how these practices can be scaled up with the necessary policies and institutions in other areas of the economy post-COVID-19.

Policies and institutions in the post-COVID-19 world must be analyzed based on instances of decline, resilience, adaptation, and/or in transformation (Halpin, 2005: 20–22). The decline in capacity is about the diminishing significance of national policy and institutions in view of the changing role of the nation-state in the global era with the increasing significance of multilateral institutions. The resilience posture demonstrates the primacy of state policy and institutions, even if in a "more complex and multi-level world, and that associative processes of governance remain important in assisting national economic sectors to adapt to global change" (Halpin, 2005: 21). This suggests options for partnership and other forms of cooperation between the state and private sector institutions.

The adaptation and/or transformation thesis is about the capacity of institutions to "not merely adapt to new conditions, but fundamentally transform their existing structures, roll-over into new structures" by actors within and beyond the nation-state (Halpin, 2005: 22). Resilience, adaptation, and trends toward transformation signify capacity building of both policies and institutions. COVID-19, as argued earlier, impacted all aspects of African society, from political, economic to social relations. These problems in the COVID-19 era reiterate a call to pay attention to the nexus between digitalization and innovation, a relationship that is integral to policies and institutions on science and technology in Africa.

DIGITALIZATION, SCIENCE, AND INNOVATION IN AFRICA: A SURVEY

Digitalization, science, and innovation have almost become buzzwords in discussions on transformation and change in Africa. Consequently, both global and continental development institutions have outlined specific documents that seek to help initiate relevant policies and establish institutions that can best deepen the role of the buzzwords. At the global level, the main policy framework is the United Nations-sponsored Sustainable

Development Goals (SDGs) (2015–2030) (UNDP, 2015). Unlike the preceding Millennium Development Goals (2000–2015), the SDGs' 17 set of goals focused on critical aspects of human development in both the global North and global South. Relevant SDGs for the African continent and relevant to this chapter include SDG 1 (poverty), SDG (zero poverty), SDG 8 (decent work and economic growth), SDG 9 (industry innovation and infrastructure), SDG 10 (reduced inequalities) and SDG 17 (partnership).

At the continental level, the UN SDGs align with two specific policy documents from the African Union, first, the *Science, Technology and Innovation Strategy for Africa 2024* (STISA) and the second, *Agenda 2063—The Africa We Want*. The first policy document sets out some priority areas for the continent such as the eradication of hunger and achieving food security, prevention and control of diseases, and wealth creation. These priority areas are based on pillars such as building and upgrading the research infrastructure, enhancing the caliber of professionals, promoting entrepreneurship, innovation and finally creating an enabling environment for science, technology, and innovation development. The policy document also recognized the integrated nature of the areas of priority, the pillars and stressed the ability of science, technology, and innovation "to impact across critical sectors such as agriculture, energy, environment, health, infrastructure development, mining … among others" (STISA, 2014: 10).

The second policy document, *Agenda 2063, The Africa We Want*, also articulates seven main aspirational principles. For example, the agenda called for steps toward the creation of a prosperous Africa that is based on inclusive growth and sustainable development, specifically through job creation and investments in science, technology, research, and innovation. Cognizant of the global dimensions of the development process, Agenda 2063 also called for improved infrastructure on the continent, steps toward a high standard of living, quality of life, sound health based on environmental sustainability, climate resilient economics, and working with development partners in global affairs while taking full responsibility to generate sufficient finances for the region's development (AUC, 2015). There is no argument about the pivotal role that ICTs can play in the post-COVID-19 world and on the road to both Agenda 2030 and Agenda 2063.

As ITU (2021a) argues, ICTs would be critical in the post-COVID-19 world because, on one hand, at the height of the global pandemic, essential and nonessential human activities went online, and the case of African countries was no different as stated earlier. ICT networks were key in testing, tracking systems on COVID-19 and in managing vaccine inventories. Thus, the online world or ecosystem became the anchor for political, economic, and social relations. On the other hand, COVID-19 also revealed significant gaps in terms of access to technology, consequently, the increasing need to explore, among other things, the structure and organization of the digital ecosystem in terms of the regulatory framework with the related implications for the ownership structure, privacy, cost, and consumer protection. The structure and organization of the digital system in several African countries, like that in other parts of the world, take inspiration from both continental and global initiatives. ICTs and digitalization are therefore consistent with both the African Union Agenda 2063 and the UN-sponsored SDGs.

The digital ecosystem in Africa is situated in the environment of neoliberal globalization and its focus on market processes, with significant forms of support from development partners, such as India (Bharti Airtel and Tata) and China and local actors (NEPAD and UN, 2015). China, for instance, provided significant ICT infrastructure to several African countries (Wang et al., 2020). China, from an initial support to the Democratic Republic of Congo's (DRC) telecom sector in 2001, by 2012, has invested in various ICT projects in African countries as diverse as Ghana (2003), Sierra Leone (2005), Lesotho (2007), Tanzania (2009) while between 2000 and 2014, Nigeria, Ethiopia, and Zimbabwe received over 50% of the continent's communication aid package (NEPAD and UN, 2015: 54–55; Wang et al., 2020: 1506).

Other notable telecommunications companies operating in Africa include Vodafone, a UK-based company with operations in Ghana, South Africa, and Egypt; Orange, which is owned by France Télécom and active in Botswana, Cameroon, Senegal, and Togo; and Beeline, the Russian network, with operations in Algeria, Burundi, Central African Republic, and Zimbabwe. In addition to the foreign actors, one notable actor, in terms of being an African-based telecoms company is MTN. The company is based in South Africa and has established itself as a global telecommunications company, providing communication services in several countries in Africa and the Middle East (Bick et al., 2011; Sutherland, 2015). The argument is that these telecommunication companies are key to the digitalization and capacity building dimensions of development in Africa in a post-COVID-19 world. Digitalization will be centered on policies that are well geared to advance the development agenda in different spheres of the African political and socio-economic spheres or the digital economy. Financialization has been a common target, as part of the digital market economy. In e-commerce, companies like Jumia and Kilimall have been prominent in Nigeria and Kenya, respectively (Ademuyiwa & Adeniran, 2020: 13). Trends in other sectors of the digital economy, for example, in the area of taxation are yet to be adequately attained (Arthur et al., 2022). Put differently, though digitalization and innovations have the potential to transform socio-economic systems, there must be certain necessary and sufficient conditions.

Subsequently, several African countries, with an eye to establish these necessary and sufficient conditions to maximize the benefits from digitalization and innovations, have outlined policies and institutions. The discussion will offer brief remarks on the following countries: Kenya, Rwanda, and South Africa. The point of departure for Kenya and ICT is the Kenya Vision 2030 policy framework (Republic of Kenya, 2007). The Vision had the goal to create and position the country as a globally competitive country by 2030. Anchored by three pillars: political, economic, and social, the Vision was set on foundations such as infrastructure, science, technology, and innovation and public service reform. Kenya, according to the World Bank ICT Competitiveness in Africa report, is one of the leading ICT countries on the continent (Chevrolier et al., 2014). In attaining that leading position, the Kenya ICT Board (KICTB), as the state entity in charge of ICT in Kenya, introduced ICT policy as a central plank in the national development agenda and legitimized the 2006 National ICT policy.

The ICT policy reiterated the need to leverage technology for the human development of Kenyans in areas such as payment systems and access to government services (Banga & te Velde, 2018). In terms of payment systems, the digitalization policy placed the country at the forefront of tax design and revenue administration, specifically mobile payment systems through the pioneering M-Pesa and a national retail system that has subsequently elevated financial inclusion in Kenya (Abdulhamid, 2020; Ndung'u, 2019). Safaricom, a telecommunications company, and Commercial Bank of Africa, a commercial bank in Kenya, spearheaded the evolution of M-Pesa from a person-to-person transaction to a full-blown digital financial platform. Safaricom, as a private actor, is dominant in the mobile money market and digital economy in Kenya (Chevrolier et al., 2014). The public service reform foundations of Kenya Vision 2030 led to the automation of tax administration in 2013 with the introduction of iTax, which can capture direct and indirect tax transactions in real time (Rukundo, 2020). The digital infrastructure for tax administration turned out to be a significant tool during COVID-19 for Kenya and made it possible for the Kenya Revenue Authority to grant relief to taxpayers on issues such as the extension of tax filing deadlines and tax waiver to different categories of taxpayers (Dushime, 2020).

According to ITU (2021a: 25) Rwanda, like most African states was slow to liberalize the mobile sector. Thus, before 2006 there was a monopoly when Rwandatel which then became the second mobile operator after the liberalization of the sector. Tigo launched its services in Rwanda in 2009, but the company was later acquired by Airtel. Meanwhile, the Rwandatel license was canceled in 2011 and left the Rwanda market with two dominant players, Airtel and MTN. The government set out to address the duopoly with the wholesale open access networks (WOAN) in a public-private partnership agreement with Korea Telecom to install 4G LTE (Long-Term Evolution) (ITU, 2022: 24). Rwanda, in 2019 launched the Digital Ambassador Program (DAP) with the target of training 5,000 youth and sending them all over the country to provide digital skills training to 5 million people. As a program, DAP brought about greater community outreach to increase participation and was linked to other programs like mobile money, device and service charge affordability, and national content (ITU, 2022: 15).

The country, drawing on several existing policies, for example, the Smart Rwanda Master Plan (2015–2020), the National Broadband Policy (2013), the National Cyber Security Policy (2015), and the National Strategy for Transformation (NSTI), and the ICT Sector Strategic Plan (2017–2024) launched the National Broadband Policy and Strategy in 2022. The policy strategy with an end goal of 2050 seeks to leverage digital transformation through high-quality broadband for economic growth and prosperity (Republic of Rwanda, 2022). The policy articulated six objectives: increase access to affordable and quality broadband services, upscale the capacity and research of broadband networks, develop skills and increase value-perception for digital services, enhance infrastructure competition, promotion of broadband as a catalyst for innovation and a regulatory framework. Rwanda, like Kenya, also leveraged digitalization for tax administration, because it introduced a digital tax administration in 2013 and offered businesses extensions on tax deadlines during the 2020 global pandemic (Dushime, 2020; Rukundo, 2020).

The South African National Integrated ICT Policy White Paper of 2016 integrated and replaced several earlier documents such as the Electronic Communications Act of 2005 and the White Papers on Telecommunications of 1996. Firmly placed within the context of the South African National Development Plan, the ICT Policy White Paper stressed the following objectives: equality, accessibility, social development, economic growth, investment, user protection, privacy and security, innovation and competition, transparency and accountability, environmental production, technology neutrality and, finally, open access (Republic of South Africa, 2016). These broad-range objectives, in terms of vision and principles, are grounded on both the UNDP Agenda 2030 and the African Union 2063. Although South Africa was one of the African countries to embark on the early liberalization of the telecommunication market, the country continues to grapple with the duopoly of Vodacom and MTN (ITU, 2021a: 26; 2022: 78). The South African government, in view of increasing public agitations over data price introduced a WOAN with the hope to transition the users from 4G LTE to 5G (ITU, 2022: 26).

South Africa, like the other two countries, harnessed the benefits of digitalization in tax administration during COVID-19. This is because in 2014, South Africa, with an eye on the global trends in digital commerce, adopted the principle of tax services and intangibles that originated beyond its national border as a way to increase revenue mobilization (Rukundo, 2020: 24). The result was the ability of South Africa to introduce measures to minimize the tax burden on businesses during COVID-19 (CIAT/IOTA/OECD, 2020: 27).

Kenya made strides in ICT based on policy and institutional imperatives. That does not mean the absence of growing pains in the ICT landscape in Kenya. Rather, together with the cases of Rwanda and South Africa, the major issues that African countries are confronted with in terms of digitalization and the development discourse can be better interrogated in terms of capacity building in Africa post-COVID-19. In broad terms, this calls for establishing an appropriate regulatory regime that can, in turn, address ownership structure, privacy, and cost of data consumer protection. These are some of the ingredients for a sustainable digitalized socio-economic landscape and capacity development in post-COVID-19 Africa.

DIGITALIZATION AND CAPACITY BUILDING IN AFRICA POST-COVID-19

The extent to which digitalization and capacity building would shore up African development in the post-COVID-19 era is contingent on several factors. One issue is the situatedness of ICT policy and institutions. The structure and organizational dynamics of the ICT architecture in any country often has several other institutions, both state and non-state, but the policy is often located in one state ministry. Even though the ICT policy is situated or embedded in one ministry, the practical implications and import of the policy would require a holistic and integrated approach that involves several other state and non-state actors and the civil society at large. That means, the ICT sector ministry, in a context where resources are always scarce, would have to compete with other ministries for operational resources, even though the operationalization of the ICT policy would cut across several other ministries. The politics of resource allocation and the possibility of siege or turf mentalities by government bureaucrats cannot be ruled out when it comes to the practical implications and actualizing ICT policy and institutions in national development. This was the case in the long search for biotechnology policy in Ghana (Puplampu, 2010). The issue is also not simply one of proclaiming policies and establishing institutions since Ghana had a plethora of policies and institutions on biotechnology, but without a viable policy, institutions cannot deliver on their mandate, which is an essential aspect of capacity building and national development. So, for example, the Parliament of Ghana passed the National Vaccine Institute Bill on February 14, 2023 (African Union and Africa CDC, 2023a). The stated objective of the bill is to allow the country to produce its own vaccines with the institute playing the role of a coordinator in the development of vaccines in Ghana. However, given the lengthy period it took to enact a biosafety bill in Ghana, the question is whether the vaccine institute will be established in good time on the principles of capacity building and with the requisite resources to deliver on its mandate.

Another related concern is that capacity requires intentional empowerment of communities and their participation in public policy discourse and the decision-making process (ACBF, 2011: 31). State actors often grant non-state actors, specifically, non-profit limited space to participate and their deliberations are not taken seriously taken to shape policy outcome in ICT in Africa and that practice is part of the "deficit model" (Collins & Evans, 2002). This model assumes that any form of critical comments by non-state actors and the civil society at large is borne out of a lack of knowledge and the implied view that knowledgeable experts in charge of initiating neutral ICT policies and operationalizing institutions should be trusted (Collins & Evans, 2002). Put differently, the space for participation often created for non-state actors in technology-related dialogue is often non-existent and borders on tokenism. However, given the crucial role of digitalization and ICTs in contemporary society, it would be desirable to recast the notion of participation in a context of governance in digitalization policy and institutions in Africa.

Therefore, the digital ecosystem in African countries must engage in a paradigm shift and adopt an inherently holistic framework, in view of the post-COVID-19 world, especially with the arrival of Fifth Generation (5G) technology. COVID-19 laid bare increases in inequality "because current governance and regulatory frameworks and their implementing mechanisms are failing to deliver more equitable outcomes. As the pace of digital transformation accelerates, formulating an effective regulatory approach therefore becomes a defining moment" (ITU, 2021b: 36). This is the reason for the significance of the framework called collaborative regulation (ITU, 2021b). As a model it is fundamentally holistic, seeks to bring together policymakers and the industry with the sole aim "to tackle the issues related to the digital transformation and the digital economy" (ITU, 2021b: 37). With most African countries at Generation 1 (G1) and Generation 2 (G2) the consequence of a collaborative framework cannot be overemphasized. By 2019, there were few African countries with Generation 4 (G4) technology (Senegal, Rwanda, Nigeria, and Uganda), with Senegal and Rwanda moving closer to Generation 5 (G5) to join Kenya and South Africa that have launched G5 technology (ITU, 2021b: 41; Ngila, 2022). Although, several other countries including Ethiopia, Botswana, Egypt, Gabon, Lesotho, Madagascar, Mauritius, Nigeria, Senegal, Seychelles, Uganda, and Zimbabwe are testing or deploying 5G, there are barriers, specifically spectrum capacity that has given rise to delays (Ngila, 2022). The need to address the infrastructural deficit is necessary to improve the taxation and the digital economy as was stated earlier in the case of Kenya.

The trajectory to collaborative regulation and the transition to 5G based on capacity building should also address concerns like the cost of data and consumer protection, since ICT prices are the least affordable in Africa compared to the Arab States region (ITU, 2021a: 15). The issue of affordability, framed within the Broadband Commission target of 2%, was favorable only in Mauritius and Gabon with the Democratic Republic of Congo being prohibitively expensive (ITU, 2021a: 16). Without affordable prices, the likely outcome is further increases in the gap between urban and rural areas or rich and poor, trends that do not bode well for attaining the promises of digitalization for national development.

In the same breath, the collaborative framework and price points are necessary and sufficient conditions in what Ademuyiwa and Adeniran (2020: 18) conceptualized as the digital preparedness index (DPI) which is "the set of enablers that facilitate a country's adoption, use and local development of digital technologies. These factors include soft and hard digital infrastructure such as broadband internet, telecommunication infrastructure, social and economic amenities, broader macroeconomic conditions, business environment, and legal and institutional frameworks guiding business operations." According to Ademuyiwa and Adeniran (2020) the index has five prerequisites: education and skills; infrastructural readiness; business dynamism and environment; regulatory framework and government effectiveness; and macroeconomic fundamentals. The value on the DPI depends on the relationship among several sectors and institutions since each indicator becomes, as forcefully stated by the Africa Digital Transformation Action Plan (2022–2026), meaningful only from a holistic perspective (AfDB, 2022).

A case in point is the complex relations among education and skills, infrastructural readiness, and the regulatory framework. Education and skills are about the acquisition of knowledge from educational institutions, including innovation and research units. However, the acquisition of education and skills will be dependent on the infrastructural capacity of the learning institution and that also calls for insights into the regulatory framework since that becomes critical in capacity, access, and equity considerations. The capacity question, in this context, is about the role of state actors in discharging their digitalization mandate. Nigeria, for example, embarked upon the deregulation, liberalization, and privatization of the telecommunication sector in the late 1990s and established the Nigeria Communications Commission (NCC) as the state regulatory entity (Ojo, 2017). NCC made it possible to restructure then state-owned

Nitel and the subsequent arrival of China's Huawei and Zhongxing Telecommunications Equipment Corporation (ZTE), France's Alcatel, South Africa's MTN, Kuwait's Zain, India's Bharti Airtel, and Globacom, as the sole Nigerian private company, in the market for mobile phone services.

Yet, it took the Nigerian government a rather long time to formalize the country's telecom privatization effort because African countries struggle when it comes to awarding contracts. The issue is that many African countries "often prefer non-competitive methods such as direct contracting or sole sourcing to avoid the time-consuming process of supplier selection" (OECD/ACET, 2020: 27). The problem is that the lack of competitive bidding "can lead to a downward spiral of bribes, collusion, bid rigging and fraud. These practices can result in low quality infrastructure as well as rebidding that may require twice the time initially planned for a project" (OECD/ACET, 2020: 27). An underlining obstacle is always the nature of the digital aid package to African countries.

Take the case of Ethiopia's telecom (Ethio-Telecom) and its relationship with ZTE and Huawei, two Chinese-based telecommunications companies. The government of Ethiopia awarded a contract first to ZTE and later to Huawei to expand the country's telecommunication network, with credit facilities from China's Export-Import Bank and the China Development Bank (Dalton, 2014). Any credit or aid package is conditional, irrespective of its source. Even though China maintains there are "no-strings-attached" to its package, that argument only seems to apply when the selected company to carry the funded project is a Chinese company. In other words, the use of "Chinese partners as implementers of projects funded through concessionary loans [like the case with Ethio-Telecom] essentially results in a form of 'tied aid'" (Gagliardone & Geall, 2014: 4). The lack of competition or local capacity in awarding the contract, based on the aid package from China, led to operational difficulties that raised questions about corruption, quality of work and other concerns with ZTE's work in Ethiopia (Dalton, 2014; Gagliardone & Geall, 2014).

Perhaps, improving the digitalization policy and institutional capacity can be attained through e-governance, beginning with the public sector and then to the private sector (Abugre et al., 2021). Democratic governance, among other things, is about transparency, accountability, and fairness. Technological driven processes in the public policy regime would make it possible for policymakers to acquire timely and accurate data in their decision-making processes. However, the success of e-governance, as part of wider democratic government initiatives, requires several political and socio-cultural processes, especially how these systems consolidate transparency and fairness in the delivery of and access to public services (Arthur, 2020; Tchao et al., 2017). The African countries, like Kenya and South Africa, that are pursuing digitalization in an intentional and strategic manner are those that, for example, are also broadening the basis of revenue mobilization (ACBF, 2015; Arthur et al., 2022). The state's attempt to manage COVID-19 required fiscal capacity, and revealed the urgent need to mobilize internal sources of revenue. That argument is that the digital economy provides one useful strategy to strengthen public revenue efforts in post-COVID-19 Africa.

Another measure of digital preparedness is the impact of the regulatory framework on access and equity. Equity and consumer protection are two related concepts that cannot be ruled out in any discussions on digitalization and the nature of the country's digital preparedness. This is because "the availability of telecommunication services across society, including geographically remote places and socio-economically disadvantaged groups, is fundamental for achieving social inclusion and improving access to opportunity and services" (ITU, 2022: 1). This is also one of the main reasons for government involvement in the digital marketplace since private actors will shy away from certain areas of society if the market conditions are not to their satisfaction, particularly in terms of returns on their investment. As ITU (2022: 131) points out "a large majority of people in many African countries are still unable to afford the cost of mobile devices or data and national exclusive licensing framework predominantly used across the continent. To overcome the divide in digital adoption, governments made efforts to redress digital inequality during lockdowns through spectrum allocations and mandatory price reductions or data lifelines." Indeed, the fact that some African governments had to improve access to digital services at the height of the global pandemic is revealing from a capacity building perspective. It demonstrates the importance of planning in such a way that existing institutions can perform their role on a continuous basis, not only in times of an emergency like COVID-19.

The impact of the digital divide can be analyzed in the case of children and most children in Africa, specifically in poorer families, have almost non-existent access to the internet, compared to their counterparts in the global North (ITU, 2022: 139). This initial social class deficit, if not rectified in later years by the school system, has the potential to affect learning outcomes in the future. Furthermore, expanded access could unleash significant outcomes for the private sector, from small businesses to farmers in their operational strategies (African Union et al., 2022: 107). In view of the value of digitalization in society, access to digital services in the context of private sector actors would require some form of government or public support. In the fiscal space that most African governments occupy, government support to the private sector to enlarge access becomes a daunting task. To leverage the rapid pace of digitalization would therefore require some form of collaboration between the public and private sectors in the future (Global Connectivity Report, 2022: 107). The working relationship between the Independent Communications Authority of South Africa and private sector applicants for temporary spectrum licenses during COVID-19 can serve as a model for the relationship between public and private sectors in the post-COVID-19 world (ITU, 2022: 128).

Ademuyiwa and Adeniran (2020: 20–21), based on an analysis of the digital preparedness index, arrived at two major conclusions on digitalization and innovation. First, several African countries have significantly low levels of preparedness for digitalization, mainly because of deficits in education and skills as well as infrastructure. It is possible to argue that improvements can occur in view of the leapfrogging traits of technology. However, there are no guarantees that will occur, since improvements in education and skills and infrastructure have a long gestation period and are not like light switches that can be instantly turned on. The contention here is that consistent and painstaking planning is necessary to build and maintain capacity. The second conclusion is the "uneven and skewed" performance of several African countries (Ademuyiwa & Adeniran, 2020: 21). While there are some countries like Mauritius, South Africa, Seychelles, and Morocco with higher levels of preparedness, a sizeable number of countries are mostly below average. The variation in preparedness suggests "that as digitalization proceeds, many African countries risk missing out on the full benefits of digitalization, or they risk getting stuck in low value-added activities of the digital sector while serving as markets for finished products. This missed opportunity may result in a repeat of Africa's experience with the industrialization phase of the twentieth century" (Ademuyiwa & Adeniran, 2020: 21).

Policy Options and Conclusion

This chapter examined digitalization and capacity development in Africa post-COVID-19. Digitalization can be likened to a freight train and as a moving target, its destination and journey are contingent on several factors, both necessary and sufficient. While national governments are quick to announce policy pronouncements, the question of institutional capacity remains of significant concern. This is because of the nature of the actors and the emerging ecosystem of digitalization in Africa, especially since most of the actors are foreign in orientation. That suggests from the repatriation of their profits to project-driven initiatives, many African countries will not have the ability to capture the commanding heights implied in digitalization and its role in the emerging digital economy. In effect, the existence of structural and systemic issues will affect the competitiveness of the national digital industry (Ademuyiwa & Adeniran, 2020). For the African context, with an already small market, even with the importance of digitalization, the following suggestions are significant.

First, a regional approach as the basis for a continental orientation is a useful suggestion (Ademuyiwa & Adeniran, 2020; Hanson, 2015; ITU, 2021a, 2021b). With several regional economic communities on the continent, including the East African Community, Southern African Development Community; Economic Community of West African States, each community can adopt a common strategy based on their unique circumstances. Through inter-regional orientation and activities, a continental approach can be developed, and the nascent African Continental Free Trade Area (AfCFTA) used as leverage to create a larger entity in terms of market size. Still, at the continental level, the role of professional-oriented organizations that can serve as an anchor for the wider continent would be a step in the right direction. For example, the African Capacity Building Foundation (ACBF), as the specialized agency of the African Union on capacity building, can coordinate with its regional offices in pushing the frontiers of capacity-infused policies and institutions Africa. One organization that showcased the value of the continental approach during the COVID-19 pandemic was the Africa Centres for Disease Control and Prevention. The organization's advocacy and research agenda, drawing on digitalization and core principles like expertise, innovation and collaboration, can serve as a useful reminder of how African countries can better plan for any future pandemic and approach health and socio-economic challenges based on science (African Union and Africa CDC, 2022, 2023).

Second, the role of the African state in the region's digitalization drive requires a retooling process. COVID-19 underscored the primacy of the state as the site for national development. It was national governments that took charge of addressing the needs of their citizens during the pandemic. That singular role, often in concert, with external entities calls for careful or systematic planning in each African country and an integrative or coordinating capacity at the continental level. The need to nurture homegrown capable institutions that have the required resources is long overdue. ACBF and IsDB (2021: 56–57), identified several health and socio-economic lessons for capacity development from COVID-19. From a health perspective, one major lesson is the need for viable institutional structures, sustainability of the health supply chain, and being proactive and systematic with collaborative systems from the national, to the regional and global levels. These ingredients, when grounded in a robust institutional framework that is infused with digitalization beyond the level of rhetoric, will create resilient and transformative institutions for the future.

As ACBF and IsDB (2021: 57) cogently state, the foremost socio-economic lessons from the global pandemic for Africa is the lack of "a functioning social protection scheme, or that they still have a lot of work to do to reach a significant number of the vulnerable populations in need of social protection." Again, as the case of Togo showed, any future attempt to provide social assistance to the population requires functional and up-to-date databases for citizens who qualify for such programs. Here again, digitalized systems provide a useful example. The general lesson is that African countries need a strong system "for planning, programming, and budgeting capacities to be reinforced on the continent, as well as capacity to build and maintain financial resilience, and the leadership capacity to anticipate, plan and ensure readiness and preparedness for future pandemics when they occur" (ACBF and IsDB, 2021: 57). Such an environment has the greatest potential in mobilizing civil society in the quest of using digitalization as leverage in the national and continental development agenda. This is one way for Africa, beyond platitudes, to claim the promise of digitalization in the twenty-first century.

References

Abdulai, A. (2022). A new green revolution (GR) or neoliberal entrenchment in agri-food systems? Exploring narratives around digital Agriculture (DA) food systems, and development in sub-Sahara Africa. *The Journal of Development Studies, 58*(8), 1588–1604. https://doi.org/10.1080/00220388.2022.2032673

Abdulhamid, N. A. (2020). Disruptive technology, mobile money, and financial mobilization in Africa: M-Pesa as Kenya's solution to global financial exclusion? In P. Arthur et al. (Eds.), *Disruptive technologies, innovation and development in Africa* (187–202). Palgrave Macmillan. https://doi.org/10.1007/978-3-030-40647-9_9

Abugre, J. B., Osabutey, E. L. C., & Sigué, S. P. (Eds.). (2021). *Business in Africa in the era of digital technology: Essays in Honour of Professor William Darley*. Palgrave Macmillan. https://doi.org/10.1007/978-3-030-70538-1

Ademuyiwa, I., & Adeniran, A. (2020, July). *Assessing digitalization and data governance issues in Africa* Centre for International Governance Innovation (CIGI Papers No. 244). https://www.cigionline.org/sites/default/files/documents/no244_0.pdf

African Capacity Building Foundation (ACBF). (2011). *African capacity indicators 2011—Capacity development in fragile states*. African Capacity Building Foundation.

African Capacity Building Foundation (ACBF). (2015). *Africa capacity report 2015—Capacity imperatives for domestic resource mobilization in Africa*. African Capacity Building Foundation.

African Capacity Building Foundation (ACBF) and Islamic Development Bank (IsDB). (2021). *Capacity imperatives of pandemic responses: Building resilient health systems and ensuring socio-economic transformation in Africa*. The African Capacity Building Foundation.

Africa Centres for Disease Control and Prevention. (2022). *Strategic Plan 2022–2026 Africa CDC digital transformation strategy, Addis Ababa, Africa Centres for Disease Control and Prevention*. Africa Union and Africa Centres for Disease Control and Prevention.

Africa Centres for Disease Control and Prevention. (2023a). *Africa CDC digital transformation strategy, Addis Ababa, Africa centres for disease control and prevention*. Africa Union and Africa Centres for Disease Control and Prevention.

Africa Centres for Disease Control and Prevention. (2023b). *Africa CDC saving lifes and livelihoods Addis Ababa, Africa centres for disease control and prevention*. Africa Union and Africa Centres for Disease Control and Prevention.

African Development Bank (AfDB). (2022). *African economic outlook 2022*. African Development Bank

African Development Bank (AfDB) and Korea Africa Economic Cooperation (KOAFEC). (2019). *Potential of the fourth Industrial revolution in Africa Study Report unlocking the potential of the fourth industrial revolution in Africa*. African Development Bank.

African Union (AU) and Africa Centres for Disease Control and Prevention (Africa CDC). (2023). *Digital transformation strategy—Empowering people. Strengthening health systems*. African Union and Africa Centres for Disease Control and Prevention.

African Union Commission (AUC). (2014). *Science, technology and innovation strategy for Africa 2024*. AUC.

African Union Commission (AUC). (2015). *The Agenda 2063: The Africa we want*. The African Union Commission.

African Union Commission and Organization for Economic Cooperation and Development (AUC/OECD). (2021). *Africa's development dynamics 2021: Digital transformation for quality jobs*. AUC, OECD Publishing. https://doi.org/10.1787/0a5c9314-en

African Union, United Nations Economic Commission for Africa, African Development Bank, and United Nations Development Programme. (2022). *2020 Africa Sustainable Development Report: Towards recovery and sustainable development in the decade of action*. African Union, United Nations Economic Commission for Africa, African Development Bank, and United Nations Development Programme.

Amankwah-Amoah, J. (2019). Technological revolution, sustainability, and development in Africa: Overview, emerging issues, and challenges. *Sustainable Development, 27*(5), 910–922.

Andrews, N., Grant, J. A., & Ovadia, J. S. (Eds.). (2022). *Natural resource-based development in Africa panacea or Pandora's box?* University of Toronto Press.

Arthur, P. (2020). Disruptive technologies, democracy, governance and national elections in Africa: Back to the future? In P. Arthur et al. (Eds.), *Disruptive technologies, innovation and development in Africa* (pp. 17–38). Palgrave Macmillan. https://doi.org/10.1007/978-3-030-40647-9_2

Arthur, P., Hanson, K. T., & Puplampu, K. P. (Eds.). (2020). *Disruptive technologies, innovation and development in Africa*. Palgrave Macmillan. https://doi.org/10.1007/978-3-030-40647-9

Arthur, P., Hanson, K. T., & Puplampu, K. P. (2022). Revenue mobilization, taxation and the digital economy in post-COVID-19 Africa. *Journal of African Political Economy and Development, 1*, 1–12.

Banga, K., & te Velde, D. W. (2018). *Digitalisation and the future of manufacturing in Africa*. Overseas Development Institute.

Bick, G., Luiz, J., & Townsend, S. (2011). MTN South Africa: One group, one vision, one brand. *Emerald Emerging Markets Case Studies, 1*, 1. https://doi.org/10.1108/20450621111126765

Chevrolier, N., Ewing, J., Leenderste, M., Quigless, M., & Verghese, T. (2014). *ICT competitiveness in Africa (English)*. World Bank Group. http://docume nts.worldbank.org/curated/en/431511468193130115/ICT-competitiven ess-in-Africa

Choi, J., Drux, M., & Usman, Z. (2019). *The future of work in Africa harnessing the potential of digital technologies for all*. World Bank.

CIAT/IOTA/OECD. (2020). *Tax administration responses to COVID-19: Measures taken to support taxpayers*. OECD. https://read.oecd-ilibrary.org/view/?ref=12612647829c4rprb3y&title=Tax_administration_responsestoC OVID-9_Measures_taken_to_support_taxpayers

Collins, H. M., & Evans, R. (2002). The third wave of science studies: Studies of expertise and experience. *Social Studies of Science, 32*(2), 235–296.

Dalton, M. (2014). Telecom deal by China's ZTE, Huawei in Ethiopia faces criticism for Ethiopians, a Chinese Telecom Project Changes Lives but Draws Scrutiny. *The Wall Street Journal*. https://www.wsj.com/articles/telecom-deal-by-china8217s-zte-huawei-in-ethiopia-faces-criticism-1389064617

Dushime, A. (2020, April 21). Rethinking tax in Africa to respond to COVID-19. *The World Economic Forum COVID Action Platform*. https://www.weforum.org/agenda/2020/04/rethinking-tax-in-africa-to-respond-to-covid-19/

Gagliardone, I., & Geall, S. (2014, April). *China in Africa's media and telecommunications: Cooperation, connectivity and control Norwegian Peacebuilding Resource Centre*. Expert Analysis.

Hagmann, T., & Reyntjens, F. (Eds.). (2016). *Aid and authoritarianism in Africa: Development without democracy*. Nordic Africa Institute and Zed Books.

Halpin, D. (2005). Agricultural interest groups and global challenges: Decline and resilience. In D. Halpin (Ed.), *Surviving global change? Agricultural interest groups in comparative perspective* (pp. 1–28). Ashgate.

Hanson, K. T. (Ed.). (2015). *Contemporary regional development in Africa*. Ashgate Publishing.

Hanson, K. T., & Puplampu, K. P. (2018). The internet of things and the sharing economy: Harnessing the possibilities for Africa's sustainable development goals. In K. T. Hanson, K. P. Puplampu, & T. M. Shaw (Eds.), *From millennium development goals to sustainable development goals: Rethinking African development* (pp. 133–151). Routledge.

Hanson, K. T., & Tang, V. T. (2020). Perspectives on disruptive innovations and Africa's services sector. In P. Arthur et al. (Eds.), *Disruptive technologies, innovation and development in Africa* (pp. 255–271). Palgrave Macmillan.

International Monetary Fund (IMF). (2020). *Regional economic outlook, Sub-Saharan Africa: COVID-19: An unprecedented threat to development*. IMF.

International Telecommunication Union (ITU). (2021a). *Digital trends in Africa—Information and Communication technology trends and developments in the Africa region 2017–2020*. International Telecommunication Union.
International Telecommunication Union (ITU). (2021b). *Digital competition policy and regulations in the Africa and Arab States regions*. International Telecommunication Union.
International Telecommunication Union (ITU). (2022). *Global Connectivity Report 2022*. International Telecommunication Union.
Louis, G. E., Nazemi, N., & Remer, S. (2017). Innovation for Development: Africa. In C. C. Mavhunga (Ed.), *What do science, technology, and innovation mean from Africa?* (pp. 151–167). The MIT Press.
Mavhunga, C. C. (Ed.). (2017). *What do science, technology, and innovation mean from Africa?* The MIT Press.
Mentan, T. (2010). *The state in Africa: An analysis of impacts of historical trajectories of global capitalist expansion and domination in the continent*. Michigan State University Press.
Ndung'u, N. (2019). *Taxing mobile phone transactions in Africa: Lessons from Africa* (Policy Brief). Africa Growth Initiative at Brookings.
NEPAD and UN. (2015). *Infrastructure development: Within the context of Africa's cooperation with new and emerging development partners*. AUDA-NEPAD Agency.
Ngila, F. (2022). *Which countries have rolled out 5G in Africa?* Quartz. https://qz.com/africa/2168658/which-countries-have-rolled-out-5g-in-africa
OECD/ACET. (2020). *Quality infrastructure in 21st century Africa: Prioritising, accelerating and scaling up in the context of PIDA (2021–30)*.
Ojo, T. (2017). Political economy of Huawei's market strategies in the Nigerian telecommunication market. *International Communication Gazette, 79*(3), 317–332. https://doi.org/10.1177/1748048516689182
OXFAM. (2022, February). *Africa's extreme inequality crisis building back fairer after Covid-19*. The Commitment to Reducing Inequality Index: Africa Briefing.
Puplampu, K. P. (2010). Bureaucratic politics and the search for biotechnology policy in Ghana. In K. P. Puplampu & W. J. Tettey (Eds.), *The public sphere and the politics of survival: Voice, sustainability and public policy in Ghana* (pp. 182–211). Woeli Publishing Services.
Puplampu, K. P. (2014). The shifting boundaries of the African state in agricultural institutions and policies in an era of globalization. In E. Shizha & A. A. Abdi (Eds.), *Indigenous discourses on knowledge and development in Africa* (pp. 215–227). Routledge.
Puplampu, K. P., & Essegbey, G. O. (2018). From MDGs to SDGs: The policy and institutional dynamics of African agriculture. In K. Hanson, K. P. Puplampu, & T. M. Shaw (Eds.), *From millennium development goals*

to sustainable development goals: Rethinking African development (53–73). Routledge.

Puplampu, K. P., & Essegbey, G. O. (2020). Agricultural research and innovation: Disruptive technologies and value chain development in Africa. In P. Arthur et al. (Eds.), *Disruptive technologies, innovation & development in Africa* (pp. 39–61). Palgrave.

Republic of Kenya. (2007). *Kenya Vision 2030*. Government of Kenya.

Republic of Rwanda. (2022). *The national broadband policy and strategy*. Ministry of ICT and Innovation.

Republic of South Africa. (2016). *National Integrated ICT Policy White Paper of 2016*. Department of Telecommunications and Postal Services.

Rukundo, S. (2020, January). *Addressing the challenges of taxation of the digital economy: Lessons for African countries* (ICTD Working Paper 105). The International Centre for Tax and Development at the Institute of Development Studies.

Sutherland, E. (2015). MTN: A South African mobile telecommunications group in Africa and Asia. *Communication, 41*(4), 471–505. https://doi.org/10.1080/02500167.2015.1100645

Tchao, E. T., Keelson, E., Aggor, C., & Amankwa, G. A. M. (2017). e-Government services in Ghana—Current state and future perspective. In *2017 International Conference on Computational Science and Computational Intelligence (CSCI)* (pp. 624–631). https://doi.org/10.1109/CSCI.2017.108

United Nations Development Programme (UNDP). (1990). *Human Development Report 1990: Concept and measurement of human development*. UNDP.

United Nations Development Programme (UNDP). (2003). *Human Development Report 2003 Millennium Development Goals: A Compact among nations to end human poverty*. Oxford University Press.

United Nations Development Programme (UNDP). (2015). *Sustainable development goals*. UNDP.

United Nations Development Programme (UNDP). (2022). *Human Development Report, 2021–2022—Uncertain times, unsettled lives Shaping our future in a transforming world*. United Nations Development Programme.

Vyas-Doorgapersad, S. (2022). The use of digitalization (ICTs) in achieving sustainable development goals. *Global Journal of Emerging Market Economies, 14*(2), 265–278. https://doi.org/10.1177/09749101211067295

Wang, R. F., Bar, F., & Hong, Y. (2020). ICT aid flows from China to African countries: A communication network perspective. *International Journal of Communication, 14*, 1498–1523.

Zeufack, A. G., Calderon, C., Kabundi, A., Kubota, M., Korman, V., Raju, D., Abreha, K. G., Kassa, W., & Owusu, S. (2022, April). *Africa's Pulse, No. 25.* World Bank. https://doi.org/10.1596/978-1-4648-1871-4. License: Creative Commons Attribution CC BY 3.0 IGO.

Zeufack, A. G., Calderon, C., Kambou, G., Djiofack, C. Z., Kubota, M., Korman, V., & Cantu, C. C. (2020, April). *Africa's Pulse, No. 21.* World Bank. https://doi.org/10.1596/978-1-4648-1568-3. License: Creative Commons Attribution CC BY 3.0 IGO.

CHAPTER 3

Politics Versus Reality: The African State and Governance Post-COVID-19

Peter Arthur

INTRODUCTION

The COVID-19 global pandemic in the first quarter of 2020 and the shutdowns worldwide to contain the virus raised not only health concerns but also, a global economic crisis (Lu et al., 2020; Nchanji, 2021). The pandemic led to the cessation of business operations for both formal and informal businesses (Lu et al., 2020; Nchanji, 2021), and created the most unprecedented social, political, and economic disruption and shock wave to the entire world, with ripple effects and global vulnerabilities (Khambule, 2022). According to Fox and Signé (2020), Sub-Saharan Africa (SSA) experienced a 3.3% contraction of gross domestic product (GDP) in 2020 for the subcontinent, with the tourism industry in Africa among the hardest-hit sectors and over 40 million people were forced into poverty (Fox & Signé, 2020). Aside from the negative economic consequences, some African leaders also continue to exhibit an increasing lack

---

P. Arthur (✉)
Department of Political Science, Dalhousie University, Halifax, NS, Canada
e-mail: peter.arthur@dal.ca

© The Author(s), under exclusive license to Springer Nature Switzerland AG 2023
K. P. Puplampu et al. (eds.), *Sustainable Development, Digitalization, and the Green Economy in Africa Post-COVID-19*, International Political Economy Series, https://doi.org/10.1007/978-3-031-32164-1_3

of commitment to good governance and that was exacerbated because of the COVID-19 pandemic. For example, the 2022 Ibrahim Index of African Governance (IIAG)[1] showed that progress on good governance performance stalled or slowed down in the latter half of the decade on the African continent. Delapalme (2021) indicates that while in 2019, over 6 in 10 of Africa's citizens lived in a country where governance was better than in 2010, average year-on-year governance performance fell for the first time since 2010. Given the governance challenges that have often been a feature of many African countries, the COVID-19 pandemic further highlighted the importance of having a good and effective governance system in place that would help deal with the various health and economic challenges, as well as facilitate and maintain a post-COVID-19 recovery.

Against this backdrop, this chapter, grounded in the theory of good governance, reviews the governance implications of the impact of COVID-19 for Africa. There are several studies showing that countries with good governance generally exhibited better control of COVID-19 (Alon et al., 2020; Baris & Pelizzo, 2020; Bunyavejchewin & Sirichuanjun, 2021; Chien & Lin, 2020; Kusumasari et al., 2022; Nabin et al., 2021). This chapter therefore examines the capacity to act and analyze the extent to which the governance systems and institutions among African countries can assist in their recovery post-COVID-19.

The chapter, as part of the ongoing attempt to situate the role of good governance in the effective management of the affairs of a country, argues that the COVID-19 pandemic has presented the best opportunity that good governance structures are a vital tool in navigating various crises, including health-related ones. The study also demonstrates the significance of a good governance system that is characterized by accountability and efficiency, various institutional structures including political leadership in promoting socioeconomic development and addresses health-related challenges in the post-COVID-19 period. The chapter is structured as follows: the first section discusses the concept of good governance, its main elements, and principles. In section "Good Governance & Public Policy in Africa", good governance and public policy

---

[1] The IIAG has been published since 2007. It measures governance performance in four categories (foundations for economic opportunity; human development; security and rule of law; and participation, rights and inclusion) and 88 indicators across 54 African countries (Mo Ibrahim Foundation, 2022).

making as they pertain to Africa are discussed. Section "Good Governance and COVID-19 in Africa: An Analysis" analyzes the relationship between COVID-19 response and good governance in Africa. The final section discusses how some of the existing challenges associated with the promotion of good governance in Africa can be addressed in the post-COVID period.

Theorizing Good Governance: An Overview

Before discussing and addressing the issues raised above, the broader theoretical literature on good governance is examined in this chapter to serve as the basis on which analysis and conclusions can be drawn. In doing so, it needs to be noted that recent years have seen the emergence and development of ideas, concepts, and practices useful in social analysis (Ulnicane et al., 2021). One such idea that has assumed a prominent place in the management and administration of a country is good governance. For Nanda (2006: 269), good governance, which is always associated with how the affairs of a country are managed, has assumed the "status of mantra for donor agencies as well as donor countries." As Gisselquist (2012) points out, "proponents argue, good governance should be at the center of development policy: donors should not only provide positive support for governance reforms in aid-recipient countries, but also should incentivize better governance by taking into account the quality of governance in decisions about the distribution of foreign assistance." Many in the donor community, including bilateral, and multilateral financial institutions such as the International Monetary Fund (IMF) and World Bank insist on giving aid and loans based on the conditions that promote good governance measures and initiatives, even though it is difficult to agree upon a single acceptable and universal model for good governance (Beshi & Kaur, 2020). Given the breadth of the idea of good governance, it is necessary to clarify the context of the concept in this chapter.

A review of the literature shows the absence of shared understandings and an objective standard for determining good governance. There are different views and perspectives regarding what constitutes good governance and various writers and organizations have adopted meanings and definitions that serve their purpose. For example, Chien and Lin (2020) underscored the fact that good governance covers the process of selecting, monitoring, and replacing governments, the capability of effectively formulating and implementing sound policies, and the respect of citizens and the country for the institutions that manage their economic and social interactions. Along those lines, the IMF (2020) sees governance as a broad concept covering all aspects of how a country is governed, including its economic policies, regulatory framework, and adherence to the rule of law. Particularly, the good governance theory from the perspective of the IMF (2020) focuses and places greater emphasis on two main areas: (i) the management of public resources through reforms covering public sector institutions; and (ii) the development and maintenance of a transparent and stable economic and regulatory environment conducive to private sector activities. The Commission on Global Governance in its report, *Our Global Neighborhood* (1995: 2–3) defined governance as the "sum of the many ways individuals and institutions, public and private, manage their common affairs. It is a continuing process through which conflicting or diverse interests may be accommodated and cooperative action may be taken. It includes formal institutions and regimes empowered to enforce compliance, as well as informal arrangements that people and institutions either have agreed to or perceive to be in their interest." Additionally, Keping (2018) is of the view that governance means exercising authority to maintain order and meet the needs of the public within a certain range. The purpose of governance is to guide, steer and regulate citizens' activities through the power of different systems and relations to maximize the public interest. According to Chien and Lin (2020), the World Bank's Worldwide Governance Indicators project captures six dimensions of governance: perceptions of voice and accountability, political stability and absence of violence, government effectiveness, regulatory quality, rule of law, and control of corruption.

Despite the lack of consensus and precise definition employed to explain the concept, this chapter notes that there is still some broad agreement that good governance entails some key characteristics and attributes. At the core of good governance, which is followed in this chapter, is the idea of accountability, efficiency, and effectiveness of public institutions, openness and transparency, control of corruption, participation, trustworthy leadership, the rule of law, and responsiveness to the needs of citizens (Abdou, 2021; Bhargava, 2015; Nanda, 2006; van Doeveren, 2011). For example, not only is accountability conceptualized as the extent to which government is answerable for its decisions and actions to the public (Mansoor, 2021), but also, it involves the duty of public officials to report and inform the populace on governmental activities, with a corresponding right of the public to impose sanctions on their behavior and outcomes (Asamoah, 2022). Zumofen et al. (2022) note that although accountability is classified into several types, it can be divided into two broad categories: internal and external. Internal accountability involves public officials reporting to those who supervise their work at all organizational levels. This means hierarchical accountability, based on the presumption that governmental organizations are arranged hierarchically and that they are politically responsible. In contrast, external accountability involves public servants and organizations being answerable to the relevant authorities outside their organizations. In this case, accountability for the officials and/or the organization's actions and level of performance is often diagonal. It involves pressure on governments by civil society and media actors, especially via the provision of information or through concrete demands for accountability (Zumofen et al., 2022).

While accountability deals with how the government uses resources, takes important policy decisions and communicates the same with citizens, transparency on the other hand, is termed as the clarity and accessibility of information provided by the government while keeping the public's interest in consideration. It is aimed at creating confidence among the public regarding the government's decision-making process (Mansoor, 2021). Also, the rule of law, as a key element of good governance, is critical to provide society with "predictability—which, in addition to formal laws, requires regulations and administrative provisions that are clear, known in advance, and uniformly and effectively enforced. And participation by users of services, government employees, other relevant stakeholders, and citizens at large, are necessary to design effective government programmes, supply the government with reliable information, and provide it with a reality check" (McFerson, 2010: 338). Furthermore, responsive government is linked to attention, interaction, and provision of efficient feedback and is measured by how well the public perceives that the government listens to them and responds to their queries (Mansoor, 2021).

Finally, trust, an important component of good governance, is defined by Rousseau et al. (1998: 395) as "a psychological state comprising the intention to accept vulnerability based upon positive expectations of the intentions or behavior of another." While there is widespread disagreement concerning how to measure political or social trust (Devine et al., 2021), Hartwig and Hoffmann (2021) indicate that trust in government is a crucial determinant of effective crisis management, and governments lacking such trust suffer a profound disadvantage. Greater trust in the government leads to more compliance with health policies (Devine et al., 2021). Asamoah (2022) reminds us of how distrust in government implies the government's failure and the inefficient manner in delivering public service. When the citizens see trust to be higher, it is assumed that the gap between the government and the people is lessened and that the level of trust remains stable over time. This view is shared by Beshi and Kaur (2020) who argue that trust in government is considered as indispensable for the effective functioning of democratic government. Trust in government is not also necessary for the fair and effective functioning of public institutions, but also for practices of good governance that come in the form of responsiveness, accountability, and transparency, which helps in developing and restoring public trust in government.

Good Governance & Public Policy in Africa

Fombad (2023) indicates that "by the late 1980s and early 1990s, a combination of bad governance and repression had led the African continent into severe economic crisis, high unemployment, poverty, famine, disease, and civil wars, all of which made change imperative." Faced with these numerous and severe challenges, the consensus that emerged in the academic literature and among the donor community, particularly the IMF and WB, was that the way out for African countries was to engage in both good economic and political governance. First, the IMF and World Bank insisted that African countries undertake economic reforms that were embodied in the neo-liberal structural adjustment policies (SAPs). The usual conditionalities that were prescribed by IMF and World Bank for African counties as part of the economic reform policies and support agreements included eliminating protectionist policies that had supported the farming sector, lowering debt, currency devaluation, privatization of services, promoting exports, and raising interest rates (Taylor, 2021). However, as noted by Fombad (2023), SAPs failed to spur development and with its emphasis on widespread cutbacks in state expenditure and subsidies, led to increased poverty, reduced social services, and widespread degradation of infrastructure. Also, with the IMF and World Bank forcing African countries to open up their economies, the penetration by Western companies led to Western governments and institutions becoming the main beneficiaries of economic activities in African countries.

In addition to the SAPs, many donors insisted on the adoption and promotion of good political governance before financially supporting African countries. These good governance policies became epitomized in political reforms, constitutionalism, respect for the rule of law, human rights, and the transition to liberal democracy that many African countries embarked on from the early 1990s. Another governance supports and initiatives from the donor community involved the emphasis on the reduction of corruption, authoritarian rule, and the promotion of transparency and accountability. For Fombad (2023: 15), a clear example and sign of the fundamental change in African governance was the collapse of the former bastions of apartheid, Namibia and South Africa, both countries that had been symbols of human tragedy.

Aside from the donor community, the African Union (AU), through initiatives and instruments—the Declaration on the Framework for an OAU (AU) Response to Unconstitutional Changes of Government (2000), the Declaration Governing the Democratic Elections in Africa (2002), the Guidelines for African Union Electoral Observations and Monitoring Missions (2002), the African Union Convention on Preventing and Combatting Corruption (2003), the African Charter on Democracy, Elections and Governance (2007), and African Peer Review Mechanism (APRM)—also developed a framework for promoting democracy and good governance amongst member states (Fombad, 2023: 18). The AU's commitment to good governance and intolerance to undemocratic means of political power has been particularly evident in its suspension of member countries (Burkina Faso [2022], Guinea [2021], Mali [2020], and Sudan [2019]), which were ruled by military leaders following the staging of coups and ousting of democratically elected leaders. As a result of the above measures, African countries can be described as having made some governance gains from the early 1990s (Mbaku, 2020). According to Fombad (2023: 22), the IIAG showed that governance in Africa between 2010–2019 improved by +1.2 from 47.6 to 48.8. While 36 countries had improved, only 17 deteriorated in this period. The IIAG also showed that between 2008 and 2017 for example, countries such as Kenya, Morocco, and Côte d'Ivoire experienced significant improvements, particularly in overall governance, with Côte d'Ivoire registering the greatest improvement in overall governance during the period 2008–2017 (Mbaku, 2020).

Despite this progress, Mbaku (2020) as well as Fombad (2023) have argued that African countries have a long way to go when it comes to good governance. Fombad (2023: 23) asserts that the minimal improvement in governance by +1.2 over the decade (2010–2019) is due largely to improvements in two categories, foundations for economic opportunity and human development. The other two categories have shown a general decline, with security and the rule of law deteriorating steadily while participation, rights, and inclusion declined at an accelerating rate. The IIAG showed in its 2020 report that the African average score for Overall Governance had declined in 2019 for the first time over the ten-year period (Mo Ibrahim Foundation, 2022). A particular area of increasing concern with good governance is the democratic backsliding that is occurring on the African continent.

Faced with growing public discontent over governments' failure to address citizens' need for jobs, health care, education, infrastructure, and security, which have fueled political discontent and instability in the region, Gyimah-Boadi (2021a) states that many West African countries have seen moves by governments and political elites aimed at authoritarian control and state capture. For example, while President Adama Barrow has managed to block a term-limit provision in the new Gambian constitution, Benin's Talon jailed opposition candidates or forced them into exile, including the first and second runners-up in the 2016 polls. Also, Mali underwent coups in August 2020 and May 2021, while Niger also had a coup in March 2021, just days ahead of the scheduled inauguration of a newly-elected President (Gyimah-Boadi, 2021a). Similar coups occurred in Guinea and Burkina Faso in September 2021 and January 2022, respectively. Furthermore, threats to democracy and good governance were evident in Ghana where, according to Gyimah-Boadi (2021a), the special prosecutor, whose office was established in 2018 as part of the government's anti-graft efforts, resigned in 2020, alleging government attempts to downplay and interfere with his report. Also, as Gyimah-Boadi (2021a) points out, manipulation of elections through voter suppression, restrictive voter-registration laws, padding of the voter roll with "ghost names," and voter intimidation have contributed to the democratic backsliding and poor governance that has become part of the political landscape of many African countries over the last decade. Moreover, ballot tampering, ballot-box stuffing, willful wrong vote tallying or results announcement, and hacking into poll results transmission systems are other forms of electoral fraud deployed in democracy-capture schemes. Additionally, some African leaders such as Macky Sall of Senegal changed election and defamation laws to constrain the opposition and the media. The new press code, signed into law in January 2021, allowed for two years in prison for defamation and three years in prison for publishing "fake news." It therefore comes as no surprise that "the Democracy Index shows that Africa, with an overall score of 4.36 in 2018 compared to a world average of 5.48, and an overall score of 4.31 for 2006–2018 as compared to a world average of 5.51, has consistently performed below the world average" (Fombad, 2023: 28).

Apart from concerns with democratic backsliding, the 2019 Corruption Barometer report by Transparency International (2019), from more than 47,000 respondents across 35 African countries, found that more than half of all citizens think corruption is getting worse in their country and that their government is doing a bad job at tackling corruption. Similarly, the 2021 Corruption Perception Index (CPI) by Transparency International showed that with the exception of a few good-performing countries (Seychelles, Cape Verde, and Botswana), there had not been a significant improvement in addressing corruption on the continent, as the average score was 33 out of 100 for African countries, with Somalia and Sudan remaining at the bottom of the global CPI (Transparency International, 2021). Also, in its 2021 report, Freedom House, according to Campbell and Quinn (2021), rated only eight countries in sub-Saharan Africa as free. Of these eight, half are small island states: Cape Verde, Mauritius, Sao Tome and Principe, and Seychelles. It is because of these that Mbaku (2020) argues that too many African countries have not yet achieved the type of governance and reforms that can prevent dictatorship, corruption, and economic decline. For Mbaku (2020), the absence of good governance in many African countries has been extremely damaging to the government's corrective intervention role, particularly in the maintenance of peace and security, as well as the promotion of economic growth and the creation of the wealth needed to confront poverty and improve human development. It is within this context that the ensuing discussions analyze the implication of the COVID-19 pandemic for good governance among African countries.

Good Governance and COVID-19 in Africa: An Analysis

The preceding discussions highlighted the significance of good governance in public policymaking. It is therefore reasonable to argue that the nature of governance in place would go a long way in determining a government's response to health-related challenges such as COVID-19. Martínez-Córdoba et al. (2021) posit that the policies implemented to solve the COVID-19 pandemic are many and varied, depending on the governments of each country, and although facing the same problem, the responses have been different, and countries with good governance fared much better in dealing with the pandemic. In fact, Bunyavejchewin and Sirichuanjun (2021) suggest that the efficacy of public policy responses to COVID-19 was related to the regime and governance type. For Baris and Pelizzo (2020), good governance matters because countries with better governance are more successful in treating diseases like COVID-19 and in reducing negative outcomes. It is because of this that according to Martínez-Córdoba et al. (2021), good governance, as embodied in effective management, and the ability to take decisive action based on scientific knowledge rather than a political opportunity, coordination, resource availability, and political accountability, contributed to the effective response to COVID-19.

Investigating the role of good governance and government effectiveness indicators in the acquisition and administration of COVID-19 vaccines at the population level, Tatar et al. (2021) found that good governance indicators, particularly, regulatory quality, voice and accountability, and government effectiveness, were the most important indicators in predicting COVID-19 vaccinations across countries. Corroborating this point, Alon et al. (2020) argued that although countries with good democratic governance such as Taiwan, South Korea, and Japan faced their own sets of challenges, it at the same time provided an opportunity to recognize the strengths of their institutions and democratic systems, and therefore the need to protect the democratic system of governance worldwide. In fact, a country like South Korea succeeded in suppressing the level of COVID-19 transmission through quick and appropriate policy responses because of its good governance structures (Kusumasari et al., 2022). For Alon et al. (2020), the relative success of countries such as Taiwan, South Korea, and Japan show that accountability to the people in democracies is key to addressing public health emergencies. In parallel, Chien and Lin (2020) found that countries such as South Korea and Austria with better governance were more likely to mitigate the spread of COVID-19 than countries with worse governance. Finally, using data obtained from the World Health Organization and the World Bank, Kusumasari et al. (2022) also found that countries such as Singapore and New Zealand that succeeded in managing the COVID-19 pandemic were the ones that possessed good indicators of good governance, namely, voice and accountability, political stability and absence of violence/terrorism, government effectiveness, regulatory quality, rule of law, and control of corruption. The findings and arguments of the above research work are a timely reminder of why the importance of good governance in helping to deal with health crises such as COVID-19 cannot be taken for granted by African countries.

In Africa, in response to COVID-19, various countries, as Dzinamarira et al. (2020) note, undertook decisive measures such as implementing airport screening and adopting mitigation efforts such as hand washing, social distancing, and stay-at-home lockdown measures. In Ghana for example, the government's response strategy sought to stop the importation of cases; contain its spread; offer adequate care for the sick; mitigate the impact of COVID-19 on social and economic life; and build domestic capacity to deepen self-reliance (Owusu-Mensah et al., 2021). Moreover, African governments, as Kavanagh et al. (2020) state, applied an assortment of non-pharmaceutical interventions including quarantines, curfews, closures of markets and schools, and restrictions on the types and number of attendees at social gatherings, with successes and challenges. Furthermore, as observed by Ossome (2021), the responses of many low- and middle-income households to COVID-19 in Africa were mediated by the state through various means including direct cash transfers, food distribution, and distribution of rural agricultural produce to urban areas, in response to the social reproduction crisis that the pandemic precipitated. Similarly, Haider et al. (2020) point out that most countries implemented some measures to support poor households and small, micro, and medium enterprises. In South Africa, a social relief and economic support package of R500 billion (about US$3 billion) was established to provide additional welfare and emergency water, sanitation, and shelter services, among other things. In Uganda, the government distributed food to vulnerable households (but only in Kampala and neighboring towns in the central region) (Haider et al., 2020). Thus, although a contemporary warm climate may have impacted the dynamics of the SARS-CoV-2 transmission in African countries, Umviligihozo et al. (2020) are of the view that early initiation of preventive measures, a faster response by timely testing of suspected cases and immediate contact tracing done by SSA countries mitigated a faster and more extensive spread of the virus in the population. These interventions demonstrate the fact that some African countries proved themselves to be capable of being transparent and accountable in the provision of services during the COVID-19 period. It is because of such decisive intervention measures that ACET (2021) asserts that African governments were able to respond with appropriate policies rapidly and effectively, and the strongest leadership and most effective COVID-19 responses have come from those that were committed to improving governance and instilling trust with citizens. As Hartwig and Hoffmann (2021) observed, countries where trust in the president was high—such as Senegal, for which the pan-African survey Afrobarometer reports levels of trust in the president 73%, and even higher ratings for state legitimacy (78%), saw high levels of compliance and praise for their COVID-19 measures.

Notwithstanding such intervention measures to stem the tide of COVID-19 in African countries, at the same time, COVID-19 exposed fundamental challenges of governance and development in a weak institutional environment and the shortcomings of weak structures and leadership at all levels of governance in several African countries (ACET, 2021). In other words, the optimism and enthusiasm expressed regarding how some African countries dealt with COVID-19 needs to be tempered because COVID also highlighted the worsening governance challenges evident in many African countries. First, according to Fombad (2023: 37), due to the COVID-19 pandemic, the traditional checks, which normally ensure that emergency powers are not abused, were unable to function properly. In the words of Fombad (2023: 37), "many autocratic regimes in Africa seized this opportunity to grab more powers for themselves, silence their critics, and undermine the rule of law, safe in the knowledge that the world was too busy fending off the ravages of the virus to take notice." Similar observations are made by Segun (2021) who noted that the enforcement of pandemic restriction measures triggered arbitrary arrests, beatings, torture, and extrajudicial killings by government forces in countries like Kenya, Nigeria, Rwanda and South Africa. Thus, although one can argue that good governance backsliding predated the pandemic, many African countries used COVID-19 as an excuse to further undermine governance and democratic gains. As showed by the IIAG in its 2020 report, the fallout from COVID-19 compounded already alarming trends in security, human rights, and the participatory environment, with measures to contain the virus used by leaders to conceal interference with election monitoring and to restrict civic space, thereby contributing to the restrictions, curtailing and decline in basic freedoms such as assembly, movement, and personal expression (Mo Ibrahim Foundation, 2022).

Also, COVID-19, as argued by Campbell and Quinn (2021), exacerbated the problem of democratic backsliding by giving leaders greater leverage, providing a further pretext for postponing elections in Somalia and Ethiopia, muzzling opposition figures in Uganda and Tanzania, and imposing restrictions on media across the continent. As APRM (2020) points out, public participation and accountability are critical components of good governance as they help to build social trust, without which the affected public may not comply with measures instituted to manage the pandemic and its impact. However, many incumbents in African countries developed several strategies including stifling the opposition and disrupting internet and social media during elections to rig elections and undermine the free and fair nature of elections. For example, Burundi, which was scheduled to hold its general elections on May 2020, warned that international observers would be placed under mandatory 14-day quarantine due to COVID-19 (APRM, 2020). ACET (2021) also indicates that COVID-19 measures that limited the size of crowded gatherings affected participation and turnout in Guinea, Mali, Benin, and Burundi. Furthermore, due to lockdowns and other social distancing measures which were imposed by almost all countries, many countries used that to insinuate that general elections could not be held.

Additionally, imposing far-reaching executive powers and restrictions on basic individual rights, ACET (2021) points out that countries like Ghana, Kenya, Guinea-Bissau, Uganda, and Senegal passed controversial laws that provided discretionary powers to the executive branch to impose various restrictions. Moreover, measures such as the suspension of the functioning of parliament or judicial proceedings, made it impossible for civil society organizations in many countries to bring lawsuits to challenge COVID-19-related laws and practices that infringe on human rights. In Ghana, often touted as a beacon of democracy on the African continent, Kumi (2022) points out that the government instituted policies such as partial lockdowns and bans on social gatherings but also introduced the Imposition of Restriction Act, 2020 (Act 1012), Imposition of Restrictions (COVID-19) Instrument, 2020 (E.I. 64) and the declaration of Public Health Emergency to contain and control the spread of COVID-19. The legislations and responses such as lockdowns and bans on social gatherings and demonstrations imposed by the Government of Ghana (GOG) were considered proportionate and justified by the government on the grounds of protecting lives and public health. Nonetheless, the application of such COVID-19 regulations constrained rights to privacy and freedoms of peaceful assembly and movements, expression, and association, which negatively affected civic space.

Finally, not only did some African governments cite COVID-19 for their inability to provide essential social services and amenities to citizens, but also, in some instances, resources and funds that were made available by the international community to help fight COVID were rather plundered by those in positions of power to meet their own selfish needs. For instance, according to Yaya et al. (2020), in Nigeria, the government failed to provide vital details for a cash transfer programme implemented to cushion household expenditure, and this raised questions and doubts about the criteria for selecting beneficiaries; many sensed political influences in the decision-making process leading to a crisis of confidence in the leaders. In Kenya, although health workers did not have enough protective equipment to protect them from COVID-19, Bwire et al. (2022) note that some funds intended to support the vulnerable poor was diverted for unintended use. Such situations were not unique to Nigeria and Kenya. In Ghana, former President, John Mahama, and his National Democratic Congress (NDC) opposition in April 2022 called for an independent forensic audit into how the monies received during the COVID-19 pandemic were used. Their call is based on the claim that not only were the funds misused and misappropriated by the ruling National Patriotic Party (NPP) government, but also that those funds were used to finance the NPP's 2020 electioneering campaign. The NDC alleged that COVID-19 funds were disbursed to Parliamentary candidates who used the monies to run their campaigns to keep the NPP in power. The economic mismanagement that the NDC alluded to seems to have been borne out by the incumbent NPP government announcing in June 2022 that it would formally engage the IMF for a support package to address its economic challenges that had come about because of COVID-19 pandemic. Faced with increasing inflation and a depreciating currency, the NPP government turned to the IMF for financial support and an economic recovery package after initially asserting that it did not need such support and assistance.

Such reports of irregularities and corruption in the management of COVID-19 funds in African countries impeded the effectiveness of those measures and undermined trust and legitimacy in government leaders and core institutions (Gyimah-Boadi, 2021b). In Ghana for example, as Asamoah (2022: 90) put it, the "trust Ghanaians have in the governance architecture has been negatively affected by the failure of governments to control the canker of corruption perpetuated by government officials." The tendency of many of the leaders in the region to engage in corrupt practices and seek their self-interests as opposed to the broader collective good has raised the issue of the commitment of some leaders to adequately deal with the public health crisis associated with COVID-19. The floundering of democracy, and corruption among others, in a context of governance, deepened the COVID-19 problems that some African countries faced, and negatively impacted their performance relative to COVID-19. This is because these governments undermined the opportunity that citizens had in participating in governmental affairs or holding governments accountable, thereby undermining the good governance agenda, which was critical to how governments responded to COVID-19 (Yaya et al., 2020).

Policy Recommendations & the Way Forward

The foregoing section noted that faced with a public- health emergency of unprecedented scale in the form of COVID-19, some African countries, as Loembé et al. (2020) note, demonstrated solidarity and collective leadership in acting quickly. As Bwire et al. (2022) point out, African countries developed multi-sectoral plans which ensured preparedness and timely, consistent, and coordinated response to COVID-19 pandemic. In fact, Talisuna et al. (2022) suggest that African countries' response to the COVID-19 pandemic was prompt and may have contributed to the lower cases and deaths in the region compared with countries in other regions. While African countries can take some comfort in the fact that some of their leaders acted promptly and well in dealing with the COVID-19 pandemic, at the same time, Talisuna et al. (2022) note that many areas, especially as it relates to good governance approaches, still require improvements. They contend that the area of good governance needs immediate attention to guide decision-making by African countries in the post-COVID-19 period. In other words, despite the laudable efforts of some countries, it became also evident, as many observers and writers with a focus on Africa have bemoaned, that poor governance on the continent was still an issue. The challenging governance environment in that many countries find themselves is illustrated by the fact that lack of transparency and accountability in political and economic decision-making processes are firmly implanted in many African countries. Gyimah-Boadi and Yakah (2012: 3) argue that government accountability and transparency in Ghana, for example, are severely inadequate. For them, "institutional checks-and-balances remain weak.... The rule of law also remains poorly entrenched, and access to justice is inadequate, especially for ordinary citizens in the rural and peri-urban areas which, partly explains the high incidence of mob justice and vigilantism."

However, as consistently argued in this paper, countries with better governance are more capable of adopting and implementing appropriate policies because they are considered more trustworthy by their people (Nabin et al., 2021). With good governance, it would be possible to engineer long-term healthcare changes to deal with various diseases and healthcare challenges (Menon-Johansson, 2005). It is lamentable that one of the biggest challenges African countries would face in their post-COVID-19 development efforts would be how to deal with governance issues. While always an area of concern, the problem with poor governance in many parts of Africa became much more visible during the COVID-19 pandemic.

The theoretical insights offered above show that poor governance, as embodied in the absence of strong institutions, political transparency, and accountability, coupled with the high incidence of corruption can combine to undermine the ability of the various levels of government from putting in place policies and programmes that would contribute to the overall socioeconomic development of their country (Arthur, 2014, 2017). Also, among the other reasons and explanations that have been adduced to explain the lack of good governance in Africa is the lack of trust and increasing corruption among those in leadership positions. Significantly, given the governance problems, many African countries find themselves lagging behind other parts of the world when it comes to measures that can facilitate the development process post-COVID-19. It is these challenges that starkly should remind African countries of the need to adopt a much-focused and concerted effort to address the governance problems as part of its efforts to accelerate its socioeconomic efforts in the post-COVID-19 period. With a growing body of literature pointing to the positive relationship between good governance and economic growth and poverty alleviation (Arthur, 2017), if African countries are to create the conditions and environment to promote development in the post-COVID-19 period, one of the first steps they must take would be to promote good governance. Limiting severe illness and death from COVID-19 means that African countries, as Loembé et al. (2020) suggest, must ensure sustained access to essential acute-care equipment and supplies in health facilities, including triage protocols, staff recruitment plans, intensive care units, oxygen, ventilators, and critical-care medications. While governments of African countries should make it a point of engaging in the promotion of social welfare and health protection programmes to provide people with resources to maintain economic productivity (Yaya et al., 2020) in the post-COVID-period, the need for also promoting good governance cannot be ignored. Since the prevalence of diseases in various societies is significantly associated with poor governance, it is important to have the necessary structures in place to create strong foundations upon which effective healthcare interventions and control of an epidemic can be implemented (Menon-Johansson, 2005). The importance of good governance is that it helps to promote and ensure the development of human capabilities of society, ensures transparency and accountability in development efforts, and allows governments to improve their effectiveness and efficiency (Wandaogo, 2022).

Furthermore, the absence of strong institutions, political transparency, and accountability, coupled with the high incidence of corruption have all combined to undermine the ability of African countries to adequately address specific challenges that came with COVID-19. As Stasavage (2020) observes, the ability of autocracies to maintain secrecy means that they can also suppress information and ignore a problem, which is unlikely to be the case in a democracy where greater transparency makes it hard to cover up a health threat like COVID-19, although the inherent decentralization of power in a democracy can lead to a slow response. Since evidence from the literature reveals that good governance practices influence citizens' attitudes and behaviours toward the government, good governance needs to be implemented to attain the maximum level of public trust in the government (Mansoor, 2021). Thus, developing good governance principles based on the rule of law, transparency, and accountability would represent an important step in the efforts to build trust in the citizens and get buy-in from them in efforts to promote development in the post-COVID period. The strategy linking transparency with accountability assumes that the greater the transparency around issues, the greater the opportunity and possibility for these governments to be held more accountable for their actions. The promotion of good governance not only helps mobilize and enhance the performance of the untapped potential of many African countries but more importantly, it could help achieve the goal of leadership transformation and utilizing African skills, and potentials for development. If governance structures and institutions are transparent, strong, well-defined, and functioning in the way society expects them to, the prospects of resources being properly managed will be enhanced (Arthur, 2014, 2017). It is in this regard that African countries that engage in good governance that involves transparency, accountability, and the existence of independent, professional, and competent institutions, have a greater chance of coming out of the post-COVID-19 situation on top.

While promoting good governance is a key strategic objective of the global development agenda, poor governance, as Bhargava (2015) indicates, has opposite characteristics and is at the heart of corruption. It is because of this that Bhargava (2015) argues that citizen and civil society engagement to demand and promote good governance can improve the overall effectiveness of good governance and anti-corruption programmes. Additionally, promoting socioeconomic development in the post-COVID-19 period calls for African countries to ensure the combating of corruption. Joseph (2013) therefore argues that addressing corruption entails the creation of a policy environment and a development strategy that offers few opportunities for state capture and rent-seeking behavior. Particularly, it is important that there is transparency regarding the various funds that were allotted to deal with the COVID-19 pandemic and accountability in terms of how the funds were disbursed. Martínez-Córdoba et al. (2021) believe that the speed and nature of post-COVID-19 economic recovery will be dependent on governance in various countries, of which African countries are no exception. Similarly, Wachira (2020) emphasizes that to enhance effective governance, states should start by addressing governance deficits and redefining and prioritizing improvement of state–society relations, as well as revitalizing the social contract. This should include abolishing impunity, corruption, and accountability deficits based on human rights principles and focusing on the most marginalized segments of the population. Munzhedzi (2021) also adds that the involvement of relevant stakeholders as well as giving them space to operate may contribute constructively to the implementation of government policies.

To Fox and Signé (2020), post-COVID-19 African economic development policy needs must be centered around both improving resiliency and accelerating transformation to realize sustained economic welfare gains. Strategies for resiliency should build on the COVID-19 experience, helping households, communities, and countries to strengthen coping measures that reduce losses thus allowing for a faster recovery, and investing to adapt to and mitigate the effects of future shocks. However, to achieve these socioeconomic goals, African countries need to have the necessary governance infrastructure in place. As Arthur (2017) points out, the UNCTAD (2014: 49) holds that promoting good governance calls for African governments to strive to maintain political stability, have and strengthen oversight bodies like the legislature and judicial apparatus, secure its independence to encourage respect for rule of law, as well as improve bureaucratic efficiency in state institutions. In the absence of good institutions, which entail the rule of law, property rights, checks and balances, opportunities of education, and economic activity for broad segments of the society, inequality will prevail, thereby undermining the development capacities of countries (Acemoglu, 2003).

Another important step toward the promotion of good governance is the building of trust in government institutions. Apart from citizens needing to have the trust that the institutions they rely on operate in a transparent and fair and impartial manner, Nabin et al. (2021) stress that compliance with government policy requires individuals to sacrifice some of their autonomy to adhere to the orders of the state, and very often compliance with public health policy can be deemed an act of faith on the part of citizens. However, to be willing to sacrifice personal freedoms (especially the freedoms of mobility and social association) as a necessary part of compliance with governmental directives, citizens must have the trust that complying with governmental directives is in their own best interests rather than solely in the interests of the governing regime. Brown (2022) argues that a high level of societal trust in government greatly assists a state's potential for adaptability and resilience. States are most likely to positively affect these types of interpersonal trust when their political leaders have demonstrated consistency, proven their character, and act for principle rather than self-interest and when they can make credible commitments and have self-enforcing institutions such that citizens do not have to personally invest in monitoring the government. Brown (2022) therefore opines that controlling corruption is a key precondition for building resilience. To respond to exogenous shocks, states need to be both willing and able to take action, yet corruption often erodes both the government's will to act, through perverting incentives, and its ability to act, through draining resources and hollowing out the state corruption has undermined resilience during the coronavirus pandemic, delaying recovery as it diverts resources from health care and weakens trust in public health institutions. This point is clarified by Asamoah (2022: 92) who argues that poor governance and the concomitant falling levels of trust offer a unique opportunity for African countries to take robust measures such as strengthening key institutions which play an essential role in ensuring trust in politicians, transparency, accountability, judicial independence, freedom of expression, and the fight against corruption.

Finally, the role of transformational and effective political leadership cannot be discounted in the efforts to promote good governance. This point is accentuated by Sackey (2021) who states that the record of African leadership as being quite poor and unimpressive, which has negatively impacted economic growth. With Africa's quest for increased and sustainable economic growth depending largely on the quality of its leaders as well as its political regimes, Sackey (2021) argues that the lack of quality leadership coupled with the absence of exceptional skills and character have hindered the achievement of the desired growth and development. In fact, there have been quite several suppositions and explanations underlying the need for effective leadership as part of a good governance agenda. For Sackey (2021), good leadership and democratic governance have an advantage over an autocratic one in the process of promoting increased and sustainable growth and investments. Tettey (2012) makes a similar argument by indicating that good leadership not only helps the institutions of the state to function appropriately, but also, helps to consolidate a culture of responsibility, rule of law, and accountability at all levels of the state structure. Equally important is the argument by Tettey (2012) to the effect that quality leadership helps to transform the lives of citizens for the better. The importance of effective leadership is very much epitomized in how some African leaders positively responded to the COVID-19 pandemic. For example, Witter (2020) points out that while Rwanda launched an effective contact tracing programme and implemented Smart Anti-Epidemic Robots to check the body temperature of travelers to and from the nation during the COVID-19 pandemic, in Senegal, innovations including trials for at-home COVID-19 diagnostic kits and the use of multifunctional robots that has allowed caregivers to treat patients without running the risk of contracting the virus themselves, were part of the measures to deal with COVID-19. The performance of leaders in Rwanda, Senegal, and South Africa who successfully responded to COVID-19 through various intervention measures could thus serve as a guide and lesson to other African leaders regarding how to operate in their quest to deal with socioeconomic and health-related issues in the post-COVID-19 period.

Conclusion

The focus of this chapter was to examine the good governance measures and the related challenges that are taking place in the efforts to promote development on the African continent. Drawing largely from the extant literature and scholarly work on good governance, the COVID-19 pandemic, as well as making use of various sources and especially examples from various African countries, the chapter highlighted how governance arrangements will be critical to the recovery of African countries in the post-COVID-19 period. It was argued in the chapter that moving forward, the ability and capacity of African countries to contend with the blows that may likely occur in the efforts to promote socioeconomic development, alleviate poverty, as well as address any future health-related challenges in the post-COVID-19 issues would be dependent on the kind of good governance structures that they have in place. Such good governance structures should entail the strengthening and improvement of institutions that will improve accountability and transparency, promote efficiency, and the rule of law as well as build the trust that citizens have in government institutions. Realizing these also calls for political leadership that is transformational, trustworthy, effective, and responsive to the needs of citizens.

References

Abdou, A. M. (2021). Good governance and COVID-19: The digital bureaucracy to response to the pandemic (Singapore as a model). *Journal of Public Affairs*, e2656. https://doi.org/10.1002/pa.2656

Acemoglu, D. (2003). Root causes: A historical approach to assessing the role of institutions in economic development. *Finance and Development*, 40(2), 27–43.

African Center for Economic Transformation (ACET). (2021). *COVID-19 and governance in Africa: Threats, opportunities, and the way forward*. https://acetforafrica.org/publications/policy-briefs-and-discussion-papers/covid-19-and-governance-in-africa-threats-opportunities-and-the-way-forward/

African Peer Review Mechanism (APRM). (2020). *Africa's governance response to COVID 19*. https://au.int/sites/default/files/documents/38893-doc-covid_19_final_english.pdf

Alon, I., Farrell, M., & Li, S. (2020). Regime type and COVID-19 response. *FIIB Business Review*, 9(3), 152–160.

Arthur, P. (2014). Governance of natural resource management in Africa: Contemporary perspectives. In K. Hanson, C. D'Alessandro-Scarpari, & F. Owusu (Eds.), *Managing Africa's natural resources: Capacities for development* (pp. 39–65). Palgrave.

Arthur, P. (2017). The African State and development initiatives: The role of good governance and the realization of the MDGs and SDGs. In K. Hanson, K. Puplampu, & T. Shaw (Eds.), *From MDGs to SDGs: Rethinking African development* (pp. 11–31). Routledge.

Asamoah, K., et al. (2022). The trust puzzle: Policy implications for promoting good governance in Africa. In R. E. Hinson (Ed.), *New public management in Africa: Contemporary issues* (pp. 67–103). Palgrave Macmillan.

Baris, O. F., & Pelizzo, R. (2020). Research note: Governance indicators explain discrepancies in COVID-19 data. *World Affairs*, 183(3), 216–234.

Beshi, T. D., & Kaur, R. (2020). Public trust in local government: Explaining the role of good governance practices. *Public Organization Review*, 20(2), 337–350.

Bhargava, V. (2015). *Engaging citizens and civil society to promote good governance and development effectiveness* (The Governance Brief, Issue 23). https://www.adb.org/sites/default/files/publication/172999/governance-brief-23-engaging-citizens-and-civil-society.pdf

Brown, F. (2022). *Governance for resilience: How can states prepare for the next crisis?* https://carnegieendowment.org/files/Brown_Governance_for_Resilience_final.pdf

Bunyavejchewin, P., & Sirichuanjun, K. (2021). How regime type and governance quality affect policy responses to COVID-19: A preliminary analysis. *Heliyon*, 7(2). https://doi.org/10.1016/j.heliyon.2021.e06349

Bwire, G., Ario, A. R., Eyu, P., et al. (2022). The COVID-19 pandemic in the African continent. *BMC Medicine, 20*(167). https://doi.org/10.1186/s12916-022-02367-4

Campbell, J., & Quinn, N. (2021). *What's happening to democracy in Africa?* https://www.cfr.org/article/whats-happening-democracy-africa. Accessed July 3, 2022.

Chien, L. C., & Lin, R. T. (2020). COVID-19 outbreak, mitigation, and governance in high prevalent countries. *Annals of Global Health, 86*(1), 119. https://doi.org/10.5334/aogh.3011

Commission on Global Governance. (1995). *Our global neighborhood.* Oxford University Press.

Delapalme, N. (2021). *Governance in Africa: Citizen dissatisfaction is growing, and COVID-19 is likely to reverse recent gains.* https://www.brookings.edu/blog/africa-in-focus/2021/02/25/governance-in-africa-citizen-dissatisfaction-is-growing-and-covid-19-is-likely-to-reverse-recent-gains/. Accessed February 8, 2023.

Devine, D., Gaskell, J., Jennings, W., & Stoker, G. (2021). Trust and the coronavirus pandemic: What are the consequences of and for trust? An early review of the literature. *Political Studies Review, 19*(2), 274–285.

Dzinamarira, T., Dzobo, M., & Chitungo, I. (2020). Covid-19: A perspective on Africa's capacity and response. *Journal of Medical Virology*, 1–8. https://doi.org/10.1002/jmv.26159

Fombad, C. (2023). The state of governance in Africa. In C. M. Fombad, A. Fiseha, & N. Steytler (Eds.), *Contemporary governance challenges in the horn of Africa* (pp. 13–56). Routledge.

Fox, L., & Signé, L. (2020). Building a better future of work for resilience and growth in post-COVID-19 Africa. *CIAT, 6*(1). https://medias.afreximbank.net/Building-a-Better-Future-of-Work-for-Resilience-and-Growth-in-Post-COVID-19-Africa.pdf

Gisselquist, R. M. (2012). *Good governance as a concept, and why this matters for development policy* (WIDER Working Paper, No. 2012/30). ISBN 978-92-9230-493-5. The United Nations University World Institute for Development Economics Research (UNU-WIDER), Helsinki. https://www.econstor.eu/bitstream/10419/81039/1/688432662.pdf

Gyimah-Boadi, E. (2021a). *Democratic backsliding in West Africa: Nature, causes, remedies.* https://www.kofiannanfoundation.org/app/uploads/2021a/11/Democratic-backsliding-in-West-Africa-Nature-causes-remedies-Nov-2021.pdf

Gyimah-Boadi, E. (2021b). *Institutional resources for overcoming Africa's COVID-19 crisis and enhancing prospects for post-pandemic reconstruction.* https://www.brookings.edu/essay/good-governance-building-trust-between-people-and-their-leaders/

Gyimah-Boadi, E., & Yakah, T. (2012). *Ghana, the limits of external democracy assistance* (WIDER Working Paper. No. 2012/40). ISBN 978-92-9230-503-1. The United Nations University World Institute for Development Economics Research (UNU-WIDER), Helsinki. https://www.econstor.eu/bitstream/10419/80887/1/715348736.pdf

Haider, N., et al. (2020). Lockdown measures in response to COVID-19 in nine sub-Saharan African countries. *BMJ Global Health, 5*, e003319. https://doi.org/10.1136/bmjgh-2020-003319

Hartwig, R., & Hoffmann, L. (2021). Challenging trust in government: COVID in Sub-Saharan Africa. *GIGA Focus Africa, 3*. https://pure.giga-hamburg.de/ws/files/25199327/web_afrika_2021_03_en.pdf

IMF. (2020). *IMF and good governance*. https://www.imf.org/en/About/Factsheets/The-IMF-and-Good-Governance

Joseph, R. (2013). *Is good governance necessary for economic progress in Africa?* https://africaplus.wordpress.com/2013/08/04/is-good-governance-necessary-for-economic-progress-in-africa/

Kavanagh, M. M., Erondu, N. A., Tomori, O., Dzau, V. J., Okiro, E. A., Maleche, A., Aniebo, I. C., Rugege, U., Holmes, C. B., & Gostin, L. O. (2020). Access to lifesaving medical resources for African countries: COVID-19 testing and response, ethics, and politics. *Lancet, 395*(10238), 1735–1738. https://doi.org/10.1016/S0140-6736(20)31093-X

Keping, Y. (2018). Governance and good governance: A new framework for political analysis. *Fudan Journal of Humanities and Social Sciences, 11*, 1–8.

Khambule, I. (2022). COVID-19 and the informal economy in a small-town in South Africa: Governance implications in the post-COVID era. *Cogent Social Sciences, 8*(1), 2078528.

Kumi, E. (2022). Pandemic democracy: The nexus of covid-19, shrinking civic space for civil society organizations and the 2020 elections in Ghana. *Democratization*. https://doi.org/10.1080/13510347.2021.2020251

Kusumasari, B., Munajat, M. E., & Fauzi, F. Z. (2022). Measuring global pandemic governance: How countries respond to COVID-19. *Journal of Management and Governance*. https://doi.org/10.1007/s10997-022-09647-4

Loembé, M. M., Tshangela, A., Salyer, S. J., et al. (2020). COVID-19 in Africa: The spread and response. *Nature Medicine, 26*, 999–1003. https://doi.org/10.1038/s41591-020-0961-x

Lu, Y., Wu, J., Peng, J., & Lu, L. (2020). The perceived impact of the COVID-19 epidemic: Evidence from a sample of 4807 SMEs in Sichuan Province China. *Environmental Hazards, 19*(4), 323–340.

Mansoor, M. (2021). Citizens' trust in government as a function of good governance and government agency's provision of quality information on social media during COVID-19. *Government Information Quarterly, 38*(4), 101597. https://doi.org/10.1016/j.giq.2021.101597

Martínez-Córdoba, P. J., Benito, B., & García-Sánchez, I. M. (2021). Efficiency in the governance of the Covid-19 pandemic: Political and territorial factors. *Global Health, 17*, 113. https://doi.org/10.1186/s12992-021-00759-4

Mbaku, J. (2020). *Deepening good governance Inclusion, democracy, and security. In Foresight Africa: Top priorities for the continent 2020–2030*. Brookings Institution. https://www.brookings.edu/wpcontent/uploads/2020/01/ForesightAfrica2020_20200110.pdf. Accessed February 8, 2023.

McFerson, H. (2010). Extractive industries and African democracy: Can the 'resource curse' be exorcised? Extractive industries and African democracy. *International Studies Perspectives, 11*(4), 335–353.

Menon-Johansson, A. S. (2005). Good governance and good health: The role of societal structures in the human immunodeficiency virus pandemic. *BMC International Health Human Rights, 5*(4). https://doi.org/10.1186/1472-698X-5-4

Mo Ibrahim Foundation. (2022). *2020 Ibrahim Index of African Governance: Key findings*. https://mo.ibrahim.foundation/news/2020/2020-ibrahim-index-african-governance-key-findings

Munzhedzi, P. H. (2021). Analysing the application of governance principles in the management of COVID-19 in South Africa: Lessons for the future. *Africa's Public Service Delivery and Performance Review, 9*(1), a490. https://doi.org/10.4102/apsdpr.v9i1.490

Nabin, M. H., Chowdhury, M. T. H., & Bhattacharya, S. (2021). It matters to be in good hands: The relationship between good governance and pandemic spread inferred from cross-country COVID 19 data. *Humanities and Social Sciences Communications, 8*(203). https://www.nature.com/articles/s41599-021-00876-w#citeas

Nanda, V. P. (2006). The "good governance" concept revisited. *The ANNALS of the American Academy of Political and Social Science, 603*(1), 269–283.

Nchanji, E. B. (2021). Immediate impacts of COVID-19 pandemic on bean value chain in selected countries in sub-Saharan Africa. *Agricultural System, 188*, 103034.

Ossome, L. (2021). The care economy and the state in Africa's Covid-19 responses. *Canadian Journal of Development Studies / Revue canadienne d'études du développement, 42*(1–2), 68–78. https://doi.org/10.1080/02255189.2020.1831448

Owusu-Mensah, I., Felitse, K., & Yeboah-Assiamah, E. (2021). How did your government perform? Assessing institutional response to the COVID-19 pandemic in Ghana. *Journal of African Political Economy and Development, 6*(1), 1–17.

Rousseau, D., Sitkin, S., Burt, R., & Camerer, C. (1998). Not so different after all: A cross discipline view of trust. *The Academy of Management Review, 23*(3), 393–404.

Sackey, F. G. (2021). Impact of African leaders' characteristics and regime transitions on economic growth in Africa: A dynamic model approach. *Social Sciences & Humanities Open, 4*(1), 100147.

Segun, M. (2021). *Human rights abuses escalate in Africa during the pandemic: Governments on the continent should co-operate fully with the International Criminal Court.* https://www.hrw.org/news/2021/01/18/human-rights-abuses-escalate-africa-during-pandemic. Accessed February 9, 2023.

Stasavage, D. (2020). Democracy, autocracy, and emergency threats: Lessons for COVID-19 from the last thousand years. *International Organization, 74*(S1), E1–E17. https://doi.org/10.1017/S0020818320000338

Taylor, M. (2021). The international financial institutions. In P. Haslam, J. Schafer, & P. Beaudet (Eds.), *Introduction to international development: Approaches, actors, issues and practices* (4th ed., pp. 274–304). Oxford University Press.

Talisuna, A., Iwu, C., Okeibunor, J., et al. (2022). Assessment of COVID-19 pandemic responses in African countries: Thematic synthesis of WHO intra-action review reports. *British Medical Journal Open, 12*, e056896. https://doi.org/10.1136/bmjopen-2021-056896

Tatar, M., Faraji, M. R., Shoorekchali, J. M., Pagán, J. A., & Wilson, F. (2021). The role of good governance in the race for global vaccination during the COVID-19 pandemic. *Scientific Reports, 11*, 22440. https://doi.org/10.1038/s41598-021-01831-0

Tettey, W. J. (2012). Africa's leadership deficit: Exploring pathways to good governance and transformative politics. In T. Shaw, K. Hanson, & G. Kararach (Eds.), *Rethinking development challenges for public policy* (pp. 18–53). Palgrave Macmillan.

Transparency International. (2019). *Global corruption barometer: Africa 2019.* https://www.transparency.org/files/content/pages/GCB_Africa_2019_Full_report_spread.pdf

Transparency International. (2021). *CPI 2021: Highlights and insight.* https://www.transparency.org/en/news/cpi-2021-highlights-insights

Ulnicane, I., Eke, D. O., Knight, W., Ogoh, G., & Stahl, B. C. (2021). Good governance as a response to discontents? Déjà vu, or lessons for AI from other emerging technologies. *Interdisciplinary Science Reviews, 46*(1–2), 71–93.

Umviligihozo, G., Mupfumi, L., Sonela, N., Naicker, D., Obuku, E. A., Koofhethile, C., Mogashoa, T., Kapaata, A., Ombati, G., Michelo, C. M., Makobu, K., Todowede, O., & Balinda, S. N. (2020). Sub-Saharan Africa preparedness and response to the COVID-19 pandemic: A perspective of early career African scientists. *Wellcome Open Research*, 5, 163. https://doi.org/10.12688/wellcomeopenres.16070.3

UNCTAD. (2014). *Economic Development in Africa Report 2014: Catalyzing investment for transformative growth in Africa*. United Nations.

van Doeveren, V. (2011). Rethinking good governance. *Public Integrity*, 13(4), 301–318.

Wachira, G. M. (2020). COVID-19 reaffirms the importance of good governance and effective states in Africa. *ECDPM Great Insights Magazine*, 9(3). https://ecdpm.org/great-insights/navigating-eu-au-post-covid/covid-19-good-governance-africa/

Wandaogo, A.-A. (2022). Does digitalization improve government effectiveness? Evidence from developing and developed countries. *Applied Economics*, 54(33), 3840–3860. https://doi.org/10.1080/00036846.2021.2016590

Witter, A. (2020). *5 countries that took proactive action on COVID-19*. https://www.one.org/africa/blog/proactive-action-countries-covid-19-response/

Yaya, S., Otu, A., & Labonté, R. (2020). Globalization in the time of COVID-19: Repositioning Africa to meet the immediate and remote challenges. *Global Health*, 16, 51. https://doi.org/10.1186/s12992-020-00581-4

Zumofen, R., Bellarminus, G. K., & Mabillard, V. (2022). Outcomes of government digitization and effects on accountability in Benin. *Transforming Government: People, Process and Policy*, 16(3), 305–317.

PART II

Natural Resources Governance and Socio-Economic Systems

CHAPTER 4

Reimagining Natural Resources Governance in Africa: Is Digitalization the Game Changer?

Peter Arthur

INTRODUCTION

Natural resources, including extractive ones, are often expected to contribute to the economies of these countries in terms of employment generation, and growth in gross domestic product (GDP). The exploitation of resources such as minerals and hydrocarbons or fossil fuels generates easily taxable rents that can finance socioeconomic development (Stijns, 2006). Despite the potential of the natural resource sector for economic growth, the much-anticipated benefits have often not occurred in many African countries (Kumah-Abiwu, 2017). Rather, natural resources are often seen as contributing to negative economic impacts, mismanagement, widespread poverty, or even conflict. It is in this regard that the last few years has seen increases in activities by

P. Arthur (✉)
Department of Political Science, Dalhousie University, Halifax, NS, Canada
e-mail: peter.arthur@dal.ca

© The Author(s), under exclusive license to Springer Nature Switzerland AG 2023
K. P. Puplampu et al. (eds.), *Sustainable Development, Digitalization, and the Green Economy in Africa Post-COVID-19*, International Political Economy Series, https://doi.org/10.1007/978-3-031-32164-1_4

several governments, civil society, and the academic community devoted to natural resource governance and improving its impact in host countries (Geipel & Nickerson, 2021).

Meanwhile, several important developments in the last two decades in the governance and management of natural resources in Africa have centered on the adoption of various transnational initiatives such as the Extractive Industries Transparency Initiative (EITI), Kimberley Process Certification Scheme (KPCS), and Africa Mining Vision (AMV) (Grant & Wilhelm, 2022). Coupled with the aforementioned have also been the great advances made in digitalization (robotics, big data and analytics, internet of things (IoT), and artificial intelligence of services), which as Balogun et al. (2022) argue, are breaking innovation boundaries and creating intriguing solutions. Digitalization is the result of large amounts of data availability, cloud-based data using data mining, and machine-learning methods for decision-related purposes (Maroufkhani et al., 2022). It is a technology-driven change process that originated from abundant data, connectivity, and making a non-intuitional decision. Considering the new opportunities being increasingly offered by transnational governance initiatives and digitalization, an area of significant interest is on how the factors hindering effective natural resource governance and management can be overcome with the introduction of digital technologies and these transnational measures. What is the nature of the extractive resource landscape in Africa, and can various transnational governance initiatives and digitalization help overcome some of the main challenges that have undermined natural resource governance and management in Africa? This chapter therefore examines and sketches out the extent to which transnational initiatives and digitalization can help in the governance, management, and transformation of the natural resource sector in Africa.

The chapter starts in section "Natural Resources: Theoretical Discussions and Literature Review" with an in-depth review of the existing theoretical debates on the impact of natural resource discovery on countries. Special attention is paid to the debate on the role and contribution of natural resources to development, particularly in African countries. Section "Transnational Initiatives & Digitalization of Natural Resources Governance and Management in Africa" analyzes the impact of various transnational governance initiatives and digitalization on the development process in Africa. It pays attention to how new transnational governance initiatives and digitalization are helping to shape the governance of natural resource sectors in Africa. Section "Challenges & Obstacles in Natural Resource Production, Governance, and Management in Africa" analyzes and reflects on the challenges and bottlenecks of natural resource governance and management in African countries. The penultimate section offers suggestions regarding the best approaches to addressing the problems associated with the transnational initiatives and digitalization process in order to positively impact the governance and management of natural resources in Africa. The final section concludes the chapter.

Natural Resources: Theoretical Discussions and Literature Review

Kumah-Abiwu (2017) has indicated that the discovery of oil and natural gas across the continent of Africa in recent years has renewed global interests in the continent's economic significance and contributed to the belief that it would lead to improvements in socioeconomic development on the continent. According to Badeeb et al. (2017: 124), those who hold a positive perspective contend that natural resource endowments would enable developing countries to make the crucial transition from underdevelopment to industrial take-off, just as they had done for countries such as Australia, the United States, and Britain. A consensus view is that natural resources would facilitate industrial development, create markets, and encourage investment. This view is exemplified by Mwakumanya and Mwachupa (2018) who postulate that the extractive sector boosts a wealth of opportunities that the national and county governments can exploit for wealth creation and the socio economic transformation of the people. Similarly, Lederman and Maloney (2007) note that several plausible indicators of the incidence of natural resource exports seem to have a positive rather than negative effect on subsequent economic growth. Basedau and Lay (2009) also claim more strongly that governments can use resource revenue to assure peace through patronage, large-scale distribution policies, and effective repressions of insurrection.

Ovadia and Graham (2022) have, however, argued that natural resources, particularly oil, have not translated into expected developmental outcomes in most parts of the global South. In fact, in the sub-Saharan Africa (SSA) region, there is increasing evidence of negative impacts of resource wealth. Countries with abundant resources have been shown to experience less socio economic growth than those with fewer (Auty, 2001; Glyfason, 2001; Karl, 1997, 1999). Ross and Voeten

(2013) highlight the fact that rather than facilitating development and ameliorating poverty, the discovery of natural resources can contribute to high rates of poverty. Despite the resource wealth of SSA countries, the average growth rate has remained below 3% over the years and that natural resource dependence has a negative impact and a retardation in the growth of non-natural resource sectors such as agriculture, manufacturing, and services sectors (Asiamah et al., 2022). McFerson (2009) blames weak public integrity and "hyper-corruption" that restricts political and civil rights and causes excessive, discretionary regulation of economic activity. For example, in Nigeria, a country rich in oil resources, GDP per capita, in purchasing power parity (PPP) terms, remains at about the same level as in 1970, and the share of the population living on less than $1 a day has doubled to about 70% in the same period (Kolstad & Søreide, 2009). Similarly, in Ghana, Ovadia et al. (2022) have shown how the expectations of local communities where natural resources are extracted for economic growth and development have not been met, leading to increasing anger and frustration from members of the local community. Furthermore, in Ghana, while the vast majority of mineral-related investment is tied to the gold industry, indicating an overdependence on one commodity, "little of the gold-derived income trickles down to communities, even those adjacent or associated with mine sites. This suggests that gaps in conditions of state governance institutions for natural resources can inhibit sustainable economic development, even in a politically stable country" (Besada, 2021). This is corroborated by Ovadia and Graham (2022) who argue that the Sekondi-Takoradi Municipal Assembly (STMA) in Ghana is experiencing all the negative impacts of oil, strained local infrastructure, higher cost of living, forced evictions, a land rush, and various social ills, with very little benefit in terms of revenues or employment.

Kolstad and Søreide (2009) contend that corruption in the form of rent-seeking and patronage is the main reason why resource-rich countries perform badly in economic terms. Apart from individuals competing for a share of the rents rather than using their time and skills more productively, resource revenues induce patronage as governments pay off supporters to stay in power, resulting in reduced accountability and an inferior allocation of public funds. To corrupt officials, the lack of scrutiny is alluring because they are able to sell mineral or oil rights under a veil of secrecy (Kasekende et al., 2016). Hilson (2021: 81) also reasons that because of an overreliance on rents from resource extraction, resource-rich states in

SSA often divert attention away from developing industries which could yield sustained employment opportunities for the citizenry, electing rather to prioritize the collection of income from large-scale resource extraction. These states become over-reliant on these extractive rents, as oftentimes corrupt governments put their personal enrichment from these rents above the national gain. As Kumah-Abiwu (2017) points out, rentier activities tend to occur when a resource-abundant country earns large revenues to the point where lower taxes are imposed on citizens. The "Dutch disease," one of the noticeable problematic signs, occurs when economic resources shift from a competitive sector such as manufacturing, known for creating economic growth, to a newly booming sector of an economy, especially in the natural resource field (Kumah-Abiwu, 2017).

Aside from the negative economic impact, Jensen and Wantchekon (2004) indicate that the discovery of natural resources can negatively impact the prospects of democratic governance in a country. They hold that this is due to the poor management and governance of the revenues that are accrued by governments from these natural resources. Also, resource-rich countries in the developing world engage in high government consumption, as well as fail to save and invest adequately in their resource revenue. Several analysts have highlighted the fact that natural resources such as oil, diamonds, gold, and timber in countries like Nigeria, Central African Republic (CAR), Angola, and Democratic Republic of Congo (DRC) have been the basis for civil wars and conflicts (Collier & Hoeffler, 1998; Huggins, 2021; Le Billon, 2008, 2012). Collier (2007) says that the absence of good governance often leads to greed that helps turn a "resource into a curse." Sachs and Warner (2001) argue that resource wealth has the undesirable effect of exacerbating poverty because it inevitably aggravates political and social conflict: weak governance institutions are unable to prevent misuse of revenues at the same time as lack of transparency promotes unfair revenue distribution and deepens inequalities.

Furthermore, natural resources motivate and finance armed conflict, and weaken the ability of political institutions to pursue peaceful resolutions; and that society's vulnerability to armed conflict is both cause and effect of weak governance (Le Billion, 2008). Gyampo (2011) explains resource-related conflict in the former Zaire, Congo Brazzaville, Liberia, and elsewhere by arguing that resource wealth can cause or consolidate the power of authoritarian and dictatorial governance. Obi (2010) argues explicitly that resource-rich states are susceptible to conflict because they are weak, corrupt, and authoritarian. That is, poor governance creates a "resource curse." Goldman and Young (2015: 5) echo the analysis that "in the absence of good governance systems and institutions, land, pasture, forests, and other natural resources central to livelihoods are often a source of local conflict." Finally, according to Mwakumanya and Mwachupa (2018), the exclusion of communities in Kwale county in Kenya from involvement in the extractive sector has been a recipe for conflicts with citizens demanding corporate accountability among the investors in the affected areas. A lack of sufficient consultation, and community engagement, as well as differing expectations of social and economic benefits, environmental concerns, influx into mining areas, land use disputes, and economic compensation are some of the causes of social conflicts in the extractive sector. Building on the analysis of several writers, Huggins (2021: 266) points to the fact that the "erosion of natural resources, or exclusion of sections of the population from the natural resource base, exacerbates poverty and social tensions. Mounting poverty may force people to join militia as an economic survival strategy, while communal disputes over specific resources can flare into violence."

Thus, despite what various writers and researchers indicate regarding how natural resources can facilitate the development process, other analysts conclude that a plenitude of natural resources often results in negative economic impacts, or even conflict. It is because of this that utilizing and leveraging digitization, which involves the increasing penetration and pervasiveness of digital technologies, tools, and applications in the daily functioning of operations (Palumbo, 2022), as well as transnational initiatives, have recently been touted as crucial to the efficient and effective governance and management of natural resources in African countries.

Transnational Initiatives & Digitalization of Natural Resources Governance and Management in Africa

The increasing problems associated with the extractive natural resource sector in several African countries have led to a growing focus and discussion of how various measures including transnational governance initiatives and digitalization would improve and enhance their governance and management on the continent. As Rjoub et al. (2021) point out, transnational initiatives have been adopted by African governments in the natural resource sector with the aim of enhancing the level of accountability and transparency for private corporations and government when licensing, exploring, extracting, contracting, generating revenues, and allocating natural resources. These initiatives include, for instance, the EITI, KPCS, and AMV. The EITI, launched in 2002, aimed at promoting global transparency, good governance, and civil society participation and accountability within different extractive industries, particularly the oil, gas, and mining sectors (Adekele, 2017). Okada and Shinkuma (2022) state that EITI "mandates the disclosures of revenue allocation information so that the public is aware of its recipients and if resource revenue is being effectively used. This disclosure of extractive industry data is expected to contribute to a wider public debate." Under the EITI, member countries are required to make full disclosures of license allocations, license registers, contracts, beneficial ownership provisions, and state participation in the extractive industry (Adekele, 2017). Not only are roughly half of all EITI member-states drawn from Africa (Grant & Wilhelm, 2022), but also, Adekele (2017) notes that 24 African countries have implemented the EITI standard, with 18 of them being fully compliant.

Similarly, there is the KPCS, an international certification and monitoring initiative, which was created and launched in 2003 to address the problem of "blood diamonds." Although participation in the Protocol is voluntary, dos Santos (2015) argues that since almost all diamonds traded originate in the signatory States of the KPCS, the participation becomes practically mandatory for any country wishing to do business in the global market of diamonds. In this way, the price of diamonds exported from a non-member would be drastically inferior to those in the legal market of diamonds, legitimized by the KPCS. Finally, the AMV was adopted by the African Union (AU) in 2009 as an attempt to ensure that mining revenue benefits the public and is distributed equitably. It is also, according to Hilson (2020), a "potential platform to push for an overhaul of the liberalized mining codes implemented across the continent in the 1980s and 1990s." Ackah-Baidoo (2020) adds that a major objective of this extractive industries-led development manifesto is to stimulate and optimize economic linkages in the mining sector, with a view toward facilitating broad-based and inclusive local economic development. It is therefore unsurprising that the AMV has been embraced with enthusiasm by African governments because it focuses heavily on extracting more revenue from mining activities, including royalties, taxes, and permit fees, for the state (Hilson, 2020). Countries such as Malawi, Sierra Leone, and Lesotho have undertaken comprehensive reforms of their mineral sector in accordance with the AMV. In fact, Zambia has recently adopted a new mining code that aims for the broad-based development of the mining sector (Busia & Akong, 2017: 178).

Aside from these transnational governance initiatives, digitalization and many information technology initiatives have also emerged in recent years with the aim of improving natural resource production, management, and governance (Aarvik, 2017; Bansal et al., 2022). As Gosine and Warrian (2017) note, the widespread application of disruptive technologies, such as the internet of things (IoT), big data and analytics, automated vehicle technology, robotics, advanced imaging and sensing systems, wearable computing, and other intelligent systems technology are becoming commonplace within the extractive resource industry. For Ralston et al. (2018), digital technologies are strongly advocated across the natural resource sector for example, because of the opportunity it provides to efficiently address and overcome current challenges associated with the sector. Digitalization and related technologies offer an improved ability to "connect information at process, system and ecosystem levels through introduction of new and enhanced mining capabilities and services" (Ralston et al., 2018: 104). As Lazarenko et al. (2021) note, for mining companies for example, digital technologies have the potential to provide new directions for the transformational changes in the way they do business, identify new ways to manage variability and enhance productivity, and hence develop a new paradigm for growth and development. Particularly, digitalization helps to speed up work, organizational performance and management, predict the failure or maintenance of equipment, increase and maximize returns and outputs, increase productivity, efficiency and performance, contribute to environmentally sustainable mining operations, and reduce operational costs (Harris, 2021; Maroufkhani et al., 2022; Ndemo & Weiss, 2017; Ralston et al., 2018; Ranjith et al., 2017). Also, digital tools facilitate greater connectivity and autonomy of assets, with increased amounts of data collected and processed in real-time to aid in planning, optimization, and execution of operations (Ndemo & Weiss, 2017). By getting real-time information, accurate decisions can also be undertaken because of the availability of information, which in itself is generated in a faster way (Maroufkhani et al., 2022).

Many African governments are incorporating digitalization, as a more rational resource management, into their policy frameworks (Ayakwah et al., 2021). Governments in African countries such as Ghana, Mali, South Africa, Kenya, and Botswana among others, are mainstreaming digitization into their policy frameworks to improve operations in the natural resource sector. For example, the Australia-based Resolute Syama mine in Mali is a site that has become one of the first fully automated mines in the world (Signé, 2021). Lempriere (2018) indicates that the Syama mine has a fiber-optic network, ensuring that the autonomous haulage trucks and other elements are in constant contact with the control centers above ground. The use of a fiber-optic network connected to above-ground control centers, according to Signé (2021), helps to manage and monitor all activities, from the clearing of the drill point to extraction, loading, and hauling. In fact, the automation of the Syama mining operations has not only increased efficiency and reduced costs by 15%, but also, improved safety (Lempriere, 2018). Also, South Africa, according to Zhuwarara (2019), has "managed to successfully complete a proof of concept for autonomous trucking at a coal operation through collaborative efforts between an equipment manufacturer and Cisco." Through the use of IOT, the mining sector in South Africa is "helping remote monitored devices to decrease the risk of human lives, e.g. self-driving trucks, controlled excavators and bulldozers, and wearable sensors" (Klarian, 2016). As Gosine and Warrian (2017) argue, these technologies help manage and coordinate various manually operated, remotely controlled, semi-automated, and automated vehicles and machinery working simultaneously at a production site.

Moreover, through the use of integrated platforms and increased data analysis, the German Federal Ministry for Economic Cooperation and Development (2022) states that system errors can be detected and corrected more quickly before staff is harmed. The increased use of remote control of mines additionally improves safety in operations by providing a robust intelligent communication technique, and thus contributes to fewer accidents as less people are working in hazardous areas. It therefore comes as no surprise that the Kamoa-Kakula Copper Project in the Democratic Republic of Congo secured in December 2020 an equipment financing facility that is geared toward digitalization of operations in order to reduce injuries to miners and other employees. Also, remote-controlled drilling equipment, geofencing, and sensors on tailings dams are, as Harris (2021) argues, helping mining companies operate safer, more efficient, and more productive sites. Again, in the case of South Africa, Andreoni et al. (2021: 268) note that firms in the mining vehicles industry can monitor the conditions of vehicles on a real-time basis for an extended period, while the mineral-processing industry can use digitalization together with machine learning for condition monitoring and predictive maintenance. Similarly, in mineral-processing machinery, digitalization enables machinery manufacturers in partnership with engineers to provide mines with a total cost of the processing service. Systems and processes can be customized to specific mines, the wear of parts can be tracked, enabling optimal replacement, and performance can be monitored across plants (Andreoni et al., 2021: 271).

The benefits of the digitalization of activities are also evident in the oil and gas industry in Africa where it is helping to reduce costs, improve productivity, as well as streamline and facilitate the connections in the supply chains (Maroufkhani et al., 2022). The oil and gas industry is embracing a range of digital solutions, including data analytics, artificial intelligence, and IOT, to streamline operations, optimize production and enhance competitiveness. This shift toward digitalization is driven by several factors, including the need to reduce costs in a challenging economic environment, the desire to improve operational performance, and the need to ensure that the industry remains relevant in a rapidly changing world. Maroufkhani et al. (2022) point out that in the oil and gas industry, artificial intelligence and real-time analysis help to improve worker and environmental safety in the exploration process. Also, the ability of digital tools to provide accurate data and information is helping operators in the natural resource sector to come to firm conclusions on decisions that can also assist them to attain operational efficiency and greater returns on their investments (Maroufkhani et al., 2022). Automated plating systems that can be easily integrated into existing oil and gas production processes lead to error reduction, better safety, and faster turnaround time for repairs and maintenance work and results in downtime and better productivity (Power Technology, 2021). Similarly, deploying in the oil and gas industry, the IoTs basically integrates sensing, communications, and analytics capabilities, helping with the improvement of reliability, optimization of operations, and creation of new value (Slaughter & Mittal, 2015). Particularly, Slaughter and Mittal (2015) opine that the opportunity to automate thousands of wells spread across regions and monitor multiple pieces of equipment per well makes production the biggest potential oil and gas beneficiary of IoTs applications.

Ghana's Petroleum Commission and companies such as Petroleum Geo-Services (PGS) are making use of digital processes as part of their exploration, production, and drilling practices in Ghana. Digitalization is used to enhance hydrocarbon production through its ability to get real-time data from many sources, thereby helping to predict possible production deviation and inform of possible action to take. With the availability of digitalized data and information, the companies use complex vessels to gather subsurface information such as rock type, fluid types, geological structures, etc. which can inform and shape the decision of companies for reservoir modeling and drilling. In the area of drilling, companies such as Maersk Drilling, Sea Drill Noble, Tullow Ghana, and Eni Ghana stream their operations on digital display systems that allow them to view the process in real time both offshore and onshore. Digitalization has helped companies such as Tullow Ghana, Eni Ghana, Modec, and Yinson in their oil production operation through a centralized control system (CCS), which enables them to ensure that the commands given can activate the opening or closing of equipment on the field. Also, flow rates and charts can also be viewed on the digital display systems both offshore on onshore.[1]

Besides the exploration, drilling, and production benefits that have come about because of the digitalization of operations in the mining, and oil and gas sector, Zumofen et al. (2022) mention that in Africa, digitization is contributing to better governance and management of natural resources. Digital platforms provide an opportunity to create awareness of governance structures and show the flow of information that facilitates the engagement of communities effectively in conflict resolution when appropriate (Mwakumanya & Mwachupa, 2018). Aarvik (2017) points out that digitized record-keeping and electronic service delivery, which aim to enhance transparency and accountability, have played a key role in the effective management of natural resources. Since processes of resource extraction and production can create both incentives and opportunities for corrupt behavior due to the high value of many resources and the large amounts of discretionary and monopoly government power over access to, and use of, resources, a digitalized system has the potential

---

[1] This paragraph is based on information provided by a top-level official at Ghana's Petroleum Commission in February 2023.

of eliminating the potential for corruption. For example, technology-facilitated information flows and participatory mechanisms can remove the information asymmetries that may contribute to corrupt practices and illegal activities and help to ensure that oil and mining revenues are spent for public rather than private interests. Ouédraogo and Sy (2020) argue that digitalization is helping to promote transparency, accountability, and citizen participation, facilitating advocacy, and the closer interaction of government and citizens. In an environment of imperfect information, high transaction costs, and discretionary rent-seeking tasks, digitalization as they further argue, helps reduce search costs, disseminate information in a cost-effective way and reduce the moral hazard problem from monitoring public sector agents. In Botswana for example, by collecting revenue, digitalizing records, and efficiently managing the revenue and investing for development, it has demonstrated how through good governance in the resource sector can be realized to improve the lives of citizens. It is in this regard that Pedro et al. (2017) argue that a country like Botswana provides evidence of the importance of governments putting in place comprehensive, and transparent laws, building strong institutions, and setting up accountability mechanisms to ensure that policy frameworks and rules are implemented.

Finally, digitalization is employed by Ghana's Petroleum Commission, for example, to ensure that localization and succession planning policies and regulations in the gas and oil sector are adhered to. The Petroleum (Local Content and Local Participation) Regulations 2013, LI 2204, passed by the parliament of Ghana to develop local capacities and ensure local participation in the oil and gas industry (Ackah & Asaah, 2020), requires that preference be given to qualified locals instead of expatriate employees. With provisions in the law designed to increase local content, all expatriates require Ghanaian successors who would succeed the expatriate within a specified number of years of operation. Ghana's Petroleum Commission is thus employing a real-time localization system where the Commission is informed through its digitalized platform in monitoring the development of the local successors and their readiness to take up the role and responsibilities on the departure of the expatriate.[2]

---

[2] This paragraph is also based on information provided by a top-level official at Ghana's Petroleum Commission in February 2023.

Challenges & Obstacles in Natural Resource Production, Governance, and Management in Africa

The preceding discussion highlighted particularly strong arguments why transnational initiatives and digitalization are important in natural resource governance and management in Africa. African countries have not only become part of the myriad of transnational initiatives, but also, demonstrated a high degree of political desire to connect its citizen to the rest of the world through the digitalization of services (Demuyakor, 2020). Notwithstanding their contribution to natural resource governance and management, transnational initiatives have faced their fair share of challenges and have very little in the way of tangible results to show for (Grant & Wilhelm, 2022). According to Khadiagala (2015: 31), critics of the EITI for example, have pointed out that revenue transparency has neither improved resource governance nor overall development outcomes because many compliant countries have long histories of corruption, civil violence, and dictatorships. Moreover, many participating countries, as Lujala (2018: 358) has argued, are slow to fully implement it. Some countries, such as Guinea, and the DRC, took almost a decade after having officially committed to implementing the EITI Standard before becoming fully compliant members. Also, the EITI has not been a resounding success because it has not meaningful impacted on communities (Dashwood et al., 2002). EITI has fallen short in its efforts to ensure increased transparency and improved accountability among participating countries since there has been cases of corruption-related under-reporting of production volume, which decreases tax revenues that could otherwise improve citizens' welfare (Okada & Shinkuma, 2022).

Regarding the KPCS, Khadiagala (2015: 31) notes that apart from international initiatives in resource-rich countries focusing on boosting transparency in public revenues rather than expenditures, transparency reforms aimed at better resource management often target corrupt and insular countries that are less inclined to accept international pressures on governance. Finally, transnational initiatives such as the AMV have not attained their desired implementation ends. While the AMV helped usher in new legislation in parts of Africa (Hilson, 2020), Shaw (2017: 224) noticed that "key players within the mining industry and civil society organizations—both within and outside of Africa—have delivered a muted response to the initiative. Mining companies may be deterred from actively participating because the implementation of the vision could require them to invest large sums in managing projects to preserve the environmental and social integrity of the regions in which they operate over many years." Also, civil society organizations, on the other hand, may have been dissuaded from becoming involved in AMV implementation because of its emphasis on facilitating economic production without having adequately accounted for local ecological considerations (Shaw, 2017: 224).

While digitalization could lead to a wide range and considerable opportunities in the management and governance of natural resources, it goes without saying that there are several challenges and obstacles that may prevent this from coming to fruition. According to Andreoni et al. (2021: 269), their limited diffusion points to challenges for both firms, public institutions, and government. Ndemo and Weiss (2017) as well as Ndemo and Weiss (2017) point out that digitization does not happen in a vacuum. Rather it is dependent on prevailing favorable economic, organizational, political, social, and cultural development of an environment, many of which are not currently present in many African countries. Thus, despite all the good reasons to digitalize natural resource governance and management, there are widespread barriers and obstacles in Africa in the efforts to digitalize (Mitchell, 2022). First, there are institutional and human capital challenges and barriers in many African countries. One of the challenges relates to securing talent with the required education and skills to undertake various responsibilities (Gosine & Warrian, 2017). Langthaler and Bazafkan (2020) argue that while education and skills development rank among the most important tools to develop the workforce needed for the 4IR, in South Africa for instance, the challenge for training institutions, technical colleges, and universities to develop and embed appropriate skills in the new and existing workforce is a big one (Andreoni et al., 2021: 276). While there are some cases of excellent training provision in South Africa, overall, the insufficient funding in the education infrastructure, in particular, the necessary laboratories, tools, and machinery to develop industry and productive task-specific skills has been a major constraint (Andreoni et al., 2021: 276).

The problem of the lack of human capital and technical expertise, as well as limited funding in Africa, is exacerbated by the issue of inadequate and deficits in infrastructure. This lack of adequate infrastructure in the digitalization process is seen in the fact that African countries are for example, behind regarding internet access, with only a portion (34%)

of the population having access to the internet in 2018 (Schopp et al., 2019). In South Africa for example, the lack of enabling infrastructural capabilities undermines domestic firms' technology efforts, specifically their absorption of digital technologies, their integration into existing production systems, and their retrofitting (Andreoni et al., 2021: 274). Additionally, as Andreoni et al. (2021: 276) indicate, data cannot be harvested if the firms' production technologies have no sensors and, thus, connectivity. Similarly, the IoTs would not be feasible without the development of coding skills and standardization capabilities (Andreoni et al., 2021: 274). Moreover, erratic power and electricity supply, weak network signals, poor and reliable internet connectivity infrastructure, and limited broadband penetration, which are symptomatic of many African countries, remain key challenges in realizing the full benefits of digital platforms (Andreoni et al., 2021: 274; Ayakwah et al., 2021). As Mitchell (2022) points out, the deficiencies and outdated nature of infrastructure is, for example, seen in South Africa, where the country in September 2022, saw the most severe electricity blackouts or power cuts in the country's history. Load-shedding, according to Mitchell (2022) meant that most South Africans went without power for at least six hours a day. Between 1 January and 21 September 2022, South Africa witnessed 107 days of outages. Similarly, in Chad, Korovkin (2019) points out that while 52 out of every 100 inhabitants have mobile-phone subscriptions, only four percent of the population has access to electricity.

Furthermore, the digitalization and automation of operations in the natural resource sector pose the risk that many jobs will no longer be needed. Automation will have the greatest impact on low- and medium-skilled jobs—and this means that local jobs in particular will be in danger (German Federal Ministry for Economic Cooperation & Development, 2022). For example, making use of automated mining trucks and rigs implies that very few workers would be used in the production process. As Gaus and Hoxtel (2019) point out, a report by Citi and Oxford University concluded that in the next decade or two, 65% of jobs in Nigeria and 67% in South Africa are at risk of being replaced by automation, with the number in Ethiopia projected to be even higher at 85%. Similarly, the "World Economic Forum (WEF) paints a grim picture: 41 percent of work activities in South Africa, 44 percent in Ethiopia, 46 percent in Nigeria, and 52 percent in Kenya are susceptible to automation" (Gaus & Hoxtel, 2019). Moreover, Palumbo (2022) argues that although the widespread use of digital technologies and ICTs contributes to a flexibilization of work processes and practices, adding to the plasticity and flexibility of work arrangements, he writes that the literature has claimed that ICTs and digital tools contribute to fill in the hierarchical distance between employees and managers. The pervasiveness of digital technologies alters the socio-material practices in the working environment, entailing a modification of organizational behaviors and interpersonal relationships (Palumbo, 2022). That is why Lazarenko et al. (2021) are of the view that many digital transformation programs fail primarily due to insufficient attention given to the managerial aspects of the digital strategy implementation, such as a lack of necessary business skills and leadership competencies, poor cross-functional collaboration, difficulties in integrating new principles to current business models, challenges related to establishing an appropriate digital culture which includes experimentation, collaboration, employee involvement, and training.

NATURAL RESOURCE GOVERNANCE: CHARTING THE PATH FORWARD

Andrews et al. (2002) have pointed out that high commodity prices and new hydrocarbon discoveries across Africa have led the African Union (AU) and countless other international organizations, donor agencies, and non-governmental organizations (NGOs) to devote considerable attention to the possibility of natural resource–based development. Coupled with that, the increasing interest of multinationals and companies from the global North to further explore natural resources on the African continent has resulted in the continent becoming a major site for competition between various companies from across the globe (Ovadia & Graham, 2022). It has also led to an increasing interest in the various transnational initiatives that need to be put in place in order to ensure effective and efficient natural resource governance and management. However, the concerns and weaknesses with existing transnational governance initiatives had led to a focus on other new approaches that can complement them as well as help overcome the challenges.

One approach, which as noted earlier, that has recently gained prominence is the efforts to digitalize the governance and management of natural resources. Despite becoming a "cause célèbre," the digitalization of natural resource governance and management has its own sets of risks, obstacles, and barriers in Africa. Indeed, for all of its positives, gains, invaluable benefits, as well as the optimism regarding the contribution of digitalization in the governance and management of natural resources, the existing evidence and extant literature have shown that these are not without hindrances and obstacles. Particularly, Africa lags among most parts of the world in the adoption of the use of digital technologies, hence the growing quest for measures that will ensure that digitalization of natural resource governance succeeds in Africa (Ayakwah et al., 2021). Having an understanding and sense of the main challenges to the digitalization of natural resource governance represents the first and most important step in the efforts to address them. This section of the chapter, therefore, discusses and suggests the course of action that needs to be undertaken for the successful application of digital innovations in the governance and management of natural resources. The hope is that these suggestions will provide a framework and basis to realize better natural resource governance among African countries. If the right measures are put in place, there would be no reason why the applications of digital tools and other initiatives would not become a game changer for natural resource governance and management.

To ensure that natural resources are properly governed and managed, one of the first steps is through enhanced transparency and accountability, as well as combatting corruption, which can be unlocked through digital tools (Kasekende et al., 2016; Ouédraogo & Sy, 2020). As found in the research by Dobrolyubova et al. (2019), "there is statistically significant positive correlation between government digitalization and public administration performance, this relationship is stronger for government effectiveness, control of corruption, and doing business." For Collier (2010), good governance, which can include disclosing payment of royalties and concession fees, will not only avert corrupt practices by government officials but also can help strengthen the necessary institutions and capacity of various governments that have natural resources. Through increased transparency and accountability, as well as reducing the opportunities for bribes and influence in the natural resource governance process, which can be aided by the digital tools, positive influence can be yielded on the economic development of states. Additionally, it can improve trust in government officials, which is a key element in the citizens' perceived level of corruption (Rjoub et al., 2021). Dauda (2020) argues that for mining, for example, to become a true "growth pole," there is a need to fine-tune the AMV, with a view to creating adequate "space" for local participation in the industry. Only then can the

AMV foster linkages with local and regional economies, and ultimately, stimulate development across the region.

A related argument is that better functioning institutions, and modernized regulatory and legal frameworks, which can be facilitated through digital tools, can help in the governance and management of natural resources. Not only would digitalizing regulatory oversight in the sector be important, but so is the need for the creation of platforms that would efficiently disseminate and track implementation of important regulatory developments (Zhuwarara, 2019). As the report of Natural Resource Governance Institute authored by Toroskainen (2019) points out, good governance means strong, comprehensive rules; competent institutions to enforce them; independent oversight; and willingness on the part of governments to follow the rules. On this issue, countries like Ghana, Tanzania, and Uganda, for example, have the mandate to audit state-owned enterprises or sovereign wealth funds. Additionally, in Ghana for instance, the country's extensive legal and regulatory framework has contributed in no small way to the stability that has been developed in the governance of natural resources and contributed to the stability in the sector (Besada, 2021).

As Besada (2021) points out, the extensive legal basis for natural resource governance in Ghana, as well as associated policy guidelines for implementation and operationalization, provide immediate anchor conditions for the success in the country's success in the governance of the natural resource sector. For example, under the provisions of the Petroleum Revenue Management Act (PRMA) of 2011, Ghana's Public Interest and Accountability Committee (PIAC), according to Besada (2021), is designed to enhance public participation by citizen organizations in the management of resource revenues (including hydrocarbons revenues), and to serve as a platform for public debate on how petroleum revenues should be spent. Graham et al. (2020) note that despite improvements in transparency in the management of oil and gas revenues that have come about because of PIAC, there are still a severe deficit in accountability and after eight years of operation, the PIAC continues to suffer monumental challenges that undermine its effectiveness. It is in this regard that they suggest among others that not only should the PIAC have a permanent relationship with the Attorney General's Department to investigate and prosecute through a fair trail, public and private officials who may be identified in their reports for causing loss to the state, but also, that PIAC submits it budgets to a select committee in Parliament such as the Finance Committee or the Public Accounts Committee (PAC) to assess and approve, after which it would be sent to the Finance Committee for consideration before it is finally approved by parliament.

Also, in Ghana, there is the 2011 Petroleum Revenue Management Act (PRMA) (Act 815) that was passed to monitor the use of petroleum revenue in the country. The PRMA also established the Petroleum Holding Fund and Ghana Petroleum Funds, which include the Ghana Heritage Fund and the Ghana Stabilization Fund (Besada, 2021; Stephens, 2019). As pointed out by Besada (2021), the PRMA was intended to address intergenerational conflict created by the exploitation of oil and gas resources, specifically by investing natural resource revenue into safe assets for the benefit of all Ghanaians. According to Stephens (2019), while the PRMA has helped stem the wastage and misappropriation of petroleum revenue, there have been grave challenges in respect of the collection of money as well as the utilization thereof in each of the areas that it is to be disbursed to, primarily, the national oil company, Ghana National Petroleum Corporation (GNPC), the budget, the Heritage fund, and the Stabilization Fund. It is the case that the collection of the revenue has been relatively lax while, in respect of the utilization of the disbursements, political interference in the affairs of GNPC has led to an unsatisfactory utilization of its disbursements, moneys allocated from the budget for projects have sometimes been misappropriated or spread too thin minimizing their impact, yield on the Heritage Fund has been low, and the Stabilization Fund insufficiently robust. It is because of these that Stephens (2019) argues that Ghana needs to make much more judicious use of the revenue as the utilization thus far falls far short of having a transformative impact on the lives of the citizenry.

Another of the keys to the successful realization of the benefits of natural resource governance is appropriate policy support. Without the appropriate policy support, digitalization may disrupt the sector in adverse ways such as reducing employment, widening inequalities, and further exploiting already scarce resources. It is in this regard that policymakers should take prompt and comprehensive action to ensure that the digital transformation of the natural resource sector is to the collective benefit of both stakeholders and societies (Bahn et al., 2021). Moreover, for the potential benefits of digitalization to come to fruition, a nation, as Merhi (2022) argues, must have a reliable information technology (IT) infrastructure, solid policies to ICTs, high level of e-participation, online service, and human capital. As African countries move forward in their quest to digitalize governance of natural resources, it is evident from the discussions in this chapter that more needs to be done, especially in the area of investments in infrastructure. Given that a longstanding problem that many African countries face is the absence of reliable infrastructure, efforts should be particularly focused on making the internet not only reliable and affordable, but also, ensure the regular availability of electricity, which costs three times more in Africa than in comparable developing regions (Signé & Johnson, 2018: 23).

As the UN Broadband Commission has suggested, about 1.1 billion more people in Africa would need to be brought online and approximately $9 billion in investment would be required to double broadband connectivity penetration in Africa by 2021 (UN Broadband Commission for Sustainable Development, 2018: 62). If well-planned and executed, the investments in infrastructure will contribute to abundant, low-cost connectivity, which will certainly facilitate the process of digitalizing natural resource governance. This point is similar to that of Wandaogo (2022) who argues that to reap the full benefits of digitalization, especially in the natural resource sector, the governments of African countries should focus on policies that would promote technological infrastructure, including the use of ICT at all levels of the economy, the increase in the coverage of the Internet among the population, as well as achieve an easily accessible, affordable, and secure broadband. An environment with high-cost barriers to connectivity or limited electricity/energy infrastructure, which is the case with many African countries, would as argued by Zhuwarara (2019), be at a disadvantage in terms of the cost of integrating new technology. It is in this regard that she calls for an expansion of electrification grids and increase renewable energy projects that feed into their national and regional energy pools prioritization, as well as support for the even distribution and availability of internet and communication infrastructure to ensure affordability of secure and reliable connectivity anywhere in their countries. Moreover, for extractive natural resource sector such as the mining industry to take full advantage of the digitalization process, the need for a network system that is strong and resilient becomes equally critical (Zhuwarara, 2019).

It is therefore a welcome development that a growing number of African countries recognize the importance of constructing digital infrastructure. In Ghana for example, a priority area that the country is focusing on as part of its natural resource governance efforts includes, according to Besada (2021), the building of economic infrastructure to support investment (electric power supply, water access, telecommunications, and transportation), reducing clearance times at ports, and streamlining the fiscal regime to reduce challenges associated with, among other things, taxes, and interest rates. In fact, the promotion of digital infrastructure by African countries in partnership with their various development partners has become a key priority and component in their overall development strategy. For example, the main regional cooperation mechanism between China and Africa, Forum on China–Africa Cooperation (FOCAC), has highlighted the importance of digital infrastructure, as evidenced in digital infrastructure building being part of the FOCAC Johannesburg Action Plan (2016–2018) (FOCAC, 2015). Under the FOCAC Johannesburg Action Plan (2016–2018), Chinese enterprises will assist African countries to promote digitalization of radio and TV services, encourage and support the participation of competitive Chinese enterprises of information, communication, radio, and TV in building information infrastructure in Africa (FOCAC, 2015). The FOCAC Beijing Action Plan (2019–2021) again reiterated the goal of building the digital infrastructure. As part of this, the two sides will actively explore and advance cooperation in the application of new technologies including cloud computing, big data, and the mobile internet. China will support African countries in building "smart cities" and enhancing the role of ICT in safeguarding public security and fighting crime and working with the African side to uphold information security. Additionally, both sides encourage and support their companies to participate and partner in the building of ICT infrastructure of African countries, including optical fiber cable backbone networks, cross-border connectivity, international undersea cable, new-generation mobile network, and data center (FOCAC, 2018). African countries can learn from the case of the Kenyan firm BRCK, which was founded in 2013 with a mission to build the most reliable internet routers in the world. As Ndemo and Weiss (2017) note, the BRCK has developed a decentralized network of solar-powered routers for remote locations that can avail free digital content on their platform and a low-cost channel to internet use. This and comparable technological innovations can become the physical gateways that enable access to information from afar, facilitate the formation of new local and international ties, extend the reach of digitally mediated economic transactions, and provide the rails for the supply of further digital technologies.

Finally, for Rutashobya et al. (2021: 79), governments' partnership with the private sector, coupled with public policies that protect, and foster inclusion are imperatives. Most importantly, Africa must invest in education, skilling, re-purposing, re-schooling, and innovations. Choi et al. (2020) suggest that one way to skills development in Africa is to create fiscal space for investments in human capital, building human capital for a young, rapidly growing, and largely low-skilled labor force, as well as increase the productivity of informal workers and enterprises including through the creation of new formal low-skill jobs. Unsurprisingly, Bahn et al. (2021) also argue that public policies should not only foster the adoption of digital technologies in developing countries but also ensure equity of access, transparency of use, data protections, and labor protections. Policymakers should move beyond traditional, production-centric views to deliver also on social and environmental sustainability. Many digital transformation programs fail because of the insufficient attention given to the managerial aspects of the digital strategy implementation., Lazarenko et al. (2021) therefore emphasize the need to develop a conceptual digital transformation framework that would improve business' digitization processes for the mining companies by identifying the core managerial areas on which attention should be focused in order to ensure successful implementation of the digital transformation strategy.

Conclusion

The chapter highlighted the benefits that are often heralded for being natural resource-endowed have often failed to come to pass or materialize in many African countries. Critics have therefore pointed out how natural resources negatively impact resource-rich countries, and result in the emergence of the idea of a resource curse. Beyond the conflict that sometimes comes with the discovery of natural resources, many natural resource-rich countries have also seen their citizens experience poor living conditions and increased poverty. It is such negative and bleak outcomes and consequences that have necessitated new approaches to managing natural resources, of which transnational governance initiatives such as EITI, KPCS, AMV, as well as digitalization process have emerged of such new models.

At a time when the availability of natural resources seems not to facilitate development, this chapter examined how transnational initiatives and digitalization can help with natural resource governance and management. It also delved into the news discussions and reflections that have been triggered by those seeking to address some of the challenges associated with resource governance and management. The chapter argued that critical to achieving the successful governance of natural resources through transnational initiatives and digitalization is the ability to put in place measures and approaches that would address the obstacles identified. Among these measures would be the promotion of a sustainable system of transparency and accountability, and the establishment of structures and institutions that can speed up the digitalization process.

References

Aarvik, P. (2017). *Digitizing the landscape: Technology to improve integrity in natural resource management.* https://www.cmi.no/publications/6218-digitizing-the-landscape#author-details. Accessed February 19, 2023.

Ackah-Baidoo, P. (2020). Implementing local content under the Africa Mining Vision: An achievable outcome? *Canadian Journal of Development Studies/Revue Canadienne D'études Du Développement, 41*(3), 486–503.

Ackah, C. G., & Asaah, S. M. (2020). Local content law and practice: The case of Ghana. In J. Page & F. Tarp (Eds.), *Mining for change: Natural resources and industry in Africa.* Oxford Academic. https://doi.org/10.1093/oso/9780198851172.003.0007. Accessed February 19, 2023.

Adekele, F. (2017). *The extractive industries transparency initiative and Africa's mineral governance regime* (South African Institute of International Affairs, Occasional Paper 266).

Andreoni, A., Barnes, J., Black, A., & Sturgeon, T. (2021). Digitalization, industrialization and skills development: Opportunities and challenges for middle-income countries. In A. Andreoni, P. Mondliwa, S. Roberts, & F. Tregenna (Eds.), *Structural transformation in South Africa: The challenges of inclusive industrial development in a middle-income country* (pp. 261–285). Oxford University Press.

Andrews, N., Grant, A. J., Ovadia, J. S., & Sneyd, A. (2002). An evolving agenda on natural resource-based development in Africa. In N. Andrews, J. A. Grant, & J. S. Ovadia (Eds.), *Natural resource-based development in Africa: Panacea or Pandora's box?* (pp. 3–31) University of Toronto Press.

Asiamah, O., Agyei, S. K., Ahmed, B., & Agyei, E. A. (2022). Natural resource dependence and the Dutch disease: Evidence from Sub-Saharan Africa.

Resources Policy, 79, 103042. ISSN 0301-4207. https://doi.org/10.1016/j.resourpol.2022.103042

Auty, R. (2001). The political economy of resource-driven growth. *European Economic Review*, 45, 839–946.

Ayakwah, A., Damoah, I. S., & Osabutey, E. L. C. (2021). Digitalization in Africa: The case of public programs in Ghana. In J. B. Abugre, E. L. C. Osabutey, & S. P. Sigué (Eds.), *Business in Africa in the era of digital technology* (pp. 7–26). Springer.

Badeeb, R., Lean, H. H., & Clark, J. (2017). The evolution of the natural resource curse thesis: A critical literature survey. *Resources Policy*, 51(Issue C), 123–134.

Bahn, R. A., Yehya, A. A. K., & Zurayk, R. (2021). Digitalization for sustainable agri-food systems: Potential, status, and risks for the MENA region. *Sustainability*, 13, 3223. https://doi.org/10.3390/su13063223

Balogun, A.-L., Adebisi, N., Abubakar, I. R., Dano, U. L., & Tella, A. (2022). Digitalization for transformative urbanization, climate change adaptation, and sustainable farming in Africa: Trend, opportunities, and challenges. *Journal of Integrative Environmental Sciences*, 19(1), 17–37.

Bansal, S., Singh, S., & Nangia, P. (2022). Assessing the role of natural resource utilization in attaining select sustainable development goals in the era of digitalization. *Resources Policy*, 79, 103040. https://doi.org/10.1016/j.resourpol.2022.103040

Basedau, M., & Lay, J. (2009). Resource Curse or rentier peace? The ambiguous effects of oil wealth and oil dependence on violent conflict. *Journal of Peace Research*, 46(6), 757–776.

Besada, H. G. (2021). *Governance, conflict, and natural resources in Africa: Understanding the role of foreign investment actors*. McGill-Queen's University Press.

Busia, K., & Akong, C. (2017). The African mining vision: Perspectives on mineral resource development in Africa. *Journal of Sustainable Development Law and Policy*, 8(1), 145–192.

Choi, J., Dutz, M., & Usman, Z. (2020). *The future of work in Africa: Harnessing the potential of digital technologies for all*. World Bank.

Collier, P. (2007). *The bottom billion, why the poorest countries are failing and what can be done about it*. Oxford University Press.

Collier, P. (2010). *The plundered planet: Why we must—And how we can—Manage nature for global prosperity*. Oxford University Press.

Collier, P., & Hoeffler, A. (1998). On economic causes of civil war. *Oxford Economic Papers*, 50(4), 563–573.

Dashwood, H., Idemudia, U., Puplampu, B. B., & Webb, K. (2002). Ghana's adoption of the Extractive Industries Transparency Initiative (EITI): The path from data disclosure to community accountability. *The Extractive Industries and Society, 10*, 101068.

Dauda, S. (2020). Operationalising the "Africa Mining Vision": Critical reflections from Ghana. *Canadian Journal of Development Studies/Revue Canadienne D'études Du Développement, 41*(3), 504–524.

Demuyakor, J. (2020). Ghana go digital Agenda: The impact of zipline drone technology on digital emergency health delivery in Ghana. *Shanlax International Journal of Arts, Science, and Humanities, 8*(1), 242–253. Available at: https://doi.org/10.34293/sijash.v8i1.3301

Dobrolyubova, E., Klochkova, E., & Alexandrov, O. (2019). Digitalization and effective government: What is the cause and what is the effect? In D. Alexandrov, A. Boukhanovsky, A. Chugunov, Y. Kabanov, O. Koltsova, & I. Musabirov (Eds.), *Digital transformation and global society. Communications in computer and information science* (Vol. 1038). Springer. https://doi.org/10.1007/978-3-030-37858-5_5

dos Santos, E. G. (2015). The Kimberley process certification system—KPCS and diamond production changes in selected African countries and Brazil. *Geosciences/geociências, 68*(3), 279–285.

Forum on China-Africa Cooperation. (2015). *The Forum on China-Africa Cooperation Johannesburg Action Plan (2016–2018)*. http://www.focac.org/eng/zywx_1/zywj/t1327961.htm. Accessed August 29, 2022.

Forum on China-Africa Cooperation. (2018). *Forum on China-Africa Cooperation Beijing Action Plan (2019–2021)*. http://www.focac.org/eng/zywx_1/zywj/t1594297.htm. Accessed August 29, 2022.

Gaus, A., & Hoxtel, W. (2019). *Automation and the future of work in Sub-Saharan Africa*. https://www.gppi.net/media/Automation-and-the-Future-of-Work-in-Sub-Saharan-Africa.pdf. Accessed February 1, 2023.

German Federal Ministry for Economic Cooperation and Development. (2022). *Digitization in the extractive sector*. https://rue.bmz.de/rue-en/topics/digitalization-92354

Geipel, J., & Nickerson, E. (2021). Promoting mining local procurement through systems change: A Canadian NGO's efforts to improve the development impacts of the global mining industry. In N. Andrews, J. A. Grant, & J. S. Ovadia (Eds.), *Natural resource-based development in Africa: Panacea or Pandora's box?* (pp. 201–219). University of Toronto Press.

Glyfason, T. (2001). Natural resources, education and socioeconomic development. *European Economic Review, 45*(4–6), 847–859.

Goldman, L., & Young, H. (2015). Managing natural resources for livelihoods: Helping post-conflict communities survive and thrive. In H. Young & L. Goldman (Eds.), *Livelihoods, natural resources, and post-conflict peacebuilding*. Routledge.

Gosine, R., & Warrian, P. (2017). *Digitalizing extractive industries: The state-of-the-art to the art-of-the-possible* (Munk School of Global Affairs Innovation Policy Lab White Paper Series 2017-004). https://munkschool.utoronto.ca/ipl/files/2017/11/IPL-White-Paper-2017-4.pdf

Graham, E., Gyampo, R. E. V., Ackah, I., & Nathan Andrews, N. (2020). An institutional assessment of the public interest and accountability committee (PIAC) in Ghana's oil and gas sector. *Journal of Contemporary African Studies*. https://doi.org/10.1080/02589001.2020.1715929

Grant, J. A., & Wilhelm, C. (2022). A flash in the pan? Agential constructivist perspectives on local content, governance, and the large-scale mining–artisanal and small-scale mining interface in West Africa. *Resources Policy, 77*, 102592.

Gyampo, R. E. V. (2011). Saving ghana from its oil: A critical assessment of preparations so far made. *Africa Today, 57*(4), 49–69.

Harris, S. (2021). *Unearthing the future: How digital is revolutionizing the mining industry*. https://www.orange-business.com/en/blogs/unearthing-future-how-digital-revolutionizing-mining-industry

Hilson, A. E. (2021). Stakeholder salience and resource enclavity in Sub-Saharan Africa: The case of Ghana's oil. In N. Andrews, J. A. Grant, & J. S. Ovadia (Eds.), *Natural resource-based development in Africa: Panacea or Pandora's box?* (pp. 79–100). University of Toronto Press.

Hilson, G. (2020). The Africa Mining Vision: A manifesto for more inclusive extractive industry-led development? *Canadian Journal of Development Studies/Revue Canadienne D'études Du Développement, 41*(3), 417–431.

Huggins, C. (2021). Land, natural resources, and conflict in the Central African Republic. In N. Andrews, J. A. Grant, & J. S. Ovadia (Eds.), *Natural resource-based development in Africa: Panacea or Pandora's box?* (pp. 263–284). University of Toronto Press.

Jensen, N., & Wantchekon, L. (2004). Resource wealth and political regimes in Africa. *Comparative Political Studies, 37*(7), 816–841.

Karl, T. L. (1997). *The paradox of plenty: Oil booms and petro states*. University of California Press.

Karl, T. L. (1999). The perils of the petro-state: Reflections on the paradox of plenty. *Journal of International Affairs, 53*(1), 31–48.

Kasekende, E., Abuka, C., & Sarr, M. (2016). Extractive industries and corruption: Investigating the effectiveness of EITI as a scrutiny mechanism. *Resources Policy, 34*(4), 117–128.

Khadiagala, G. (2015). Global and regional mechanisms for governing the resource curse in Africa. *Politikon, 42*(1), 23–43.

Klarian. (2016). *IoT in mining—A South African perspective*. https://klarian.com/blog/iot-mining-south-african-perspective. Accessed January 25, 2023 and February 4, 2023

Kolstad, I., & Søreide, T. (2009). Corruption in natural resource management: Implications for policy makers. *Resources Policy, 34*(4), 214–226.
Korovkin, V. V. (2019, July). *National digital economy strategies: A survey of Africa* (ORF Issue Brief No. 303). Observer Research Foundation. https://www.orfonline.org/wpcontent/uploads/2019/07/ORF_Issue Brief_303_DigitalEcon-Africa.pdf. Accessed January 27, 2023.
Kumah-Abiwu, F. (2017). Democratic institutions, natural resource governance, and Ghana's oil wealth. *Social Sciences, 6*(1), 1–13. https://doi.org/10.3390/socsci6010021
Langthaler, M., & Bazafkan, H. (2020). *Digitalization, education and skills development in the global South: An assessment of the debate with a focus on Sub-Saharan Africa* (ÖFSE Briefing Paper, No. 28). Austrian Foundation for Development Research (ÖFSE), Vienna. https://www.econstor.eu/bitstream/10419/228970/1/1743471084.pdf
Lazarenko, Y., Garafonova, O., Marhasova, V., & Tkalenko, N. (2021). *Digital transformation in the mining sector: Exploring global technology trends and managerial issues.* E3S Web of Conferences 315, 04006 6th International Innovative Mining Symposium. https://www.e3s-conferences.org/articles/e3sconf/pdf/2021/91/e3sconf_iims2021_04006.pdf
Le Billon, P. (2008). Diamond wars? Conflict diamonds and geographies of resource wars. *Annals of the Association of American Geographers, 98*(2), 345–372.
Le Billon, P. (2012). *Wars of plunder: Conflicts, profits and the politics of resources.* Columbia University Press.
Lederman, D., & Maloney, W. (eds), (2007). *Natural resources: Neither curse nor destiny.* World Bank & Stanford University Press.
Lempriere, M. (2018). *Sizing up Syama: The world's first fully automated mine.* https://www.mining-technology.com/features/sizing-syama-worlds-first-fully-automated-mine/. Accessed January 25, 2023.
Lujala, P. (2018). An analysis of the Extractive Industry Transparency Initiative implementation process. *World Development, 107*, 358–381.
Maroufkhani, P., Desouza, K. C., Perrons, R. K., & Iranmanesh, M. (2022). Digital transformation in the resource and energy sectors: A systematic review. *Resources Policy, 76*, 102622. https://doi.org/10.1016/j.resourpol.2022.102622
McFerson, H. (2009). Governance and hyper-corruption in resource-rich African countries. *Third World Quarterly, 30*(8), 1529–1547.
Merhi, M. I. (2022). The effect of digital transformation on corruption: A global analysis Pacific Asia. *Journal of the Association of Information Systems, 14*(2), 42–58.

Mitchell, J. (2022). *Will Africa's poor power supply hold back its AI and automation charge?* https://www.investmentmonitor.ai/dashboards/robotics/africa-poor-power-supply-ai-automation-charge/. Accessed February 1, 2023.

Mwakumanya, M. A., & Mwachupa, J. (2018). Digital mapping as a tool for environmental and social corporate accountability in the extractive sector in Kwale County Kenya. *Journal of Sustainable Mining, 17*(3), 97–104.

Ndemo, B., & Weiss, T. (2017). Making sense of Africa's emerging digital transformation and its many futures. *Africa Journal of Management, 3*(3–4), 328–347.

Obi, C. (2010). Oil as the 'curse' of conflict in Africa: Peering through the smoke and mirrors. *Review of African Political Economy, 37*(126), 483–495.

Okada, K., & Shinkuma, T. (2022). Transparency and natural resources in sub-Saharan Africa. *Resources Policy, 76*, 102574.

Ouédraogo, R., & Sy, A. N. R. (2020). *Can digitalization help deter corruption in Africa?* https://file:///C:/Users/Owner/Downloads/null-001.2020.issue-068-en.pdf.

Ovadia, J. S., & Graham, E. (2022). The resource curse and limits of petro-development in Ghana's "oil city": How oil production has impacted Sekondi-Takoradi. In N. Andrews, J. A. Grant, & J. S. Ovadia (Eds.), *Natural resource-based development in Africa: Panacea or Pandora's box?* (pp. 59–78). University of Toronto Press.

Palumbo, R. (2022). Does digitizing involve desensitizing? Strategic insights into the side effects of workplace digitization. *Public Management Review, 24*(7), 975–1000.

Pedro, A., Ayuk, E., Bodouroglou, C., Milligan, B., Ekins, P., & Oberle, B. (2017). Towards a sustainable development license to operate for the extractive sector. *Mineral Economics, 30*, 153–165.

Power Technology. (2021). *The benefits of smarter automation in oil and gas*. https://www.power-technology.com/sponsored/the-benefits-of-smarter-automation-in-oil-and-gas/. Accessed February 3, 2023.

Ralston, J., James, C., & Hainsworth, D. (2018). Digital mining: Past, present, and future. In M. Clifford, R. K. Perrons, S. H. Ali, & T. A. Grice (Eds.), *Extracting innovations: Mining, energy and technological change in the digital age* (pp. 91–113). Taylor and Francis – CRC Press.

Ranjith, P., et al. (2017). Opportunities and challenges in deep mining: A brief review. *Engineering, 3*(4), 546–551. https://doi.org/10.1016/j.eng.2017.04.024

Rjoub, H., Ifediora, C. U., Odugbesan, J. A., Iloka, B. C., Xavier, R. J., Dantas, R. M., Mata, M. N., & Martins, J. M. (2021). Implications of governance, natural resources, and security threats on economic development: Evidence from Sub-Saharan Africa. *International Journal of Environmental Research and Public Health, 18*(12), 6236. https://doi.org/10.3390/ijerph18126236

Ross, M. L., & Voeten, E. (2013). *Oil and Unbalanced Globalization*. SSRN (1900226). https://deliverypdf.ssrn.com/delivery.php?ID=831111064100 004088111093020102096110060043028048003056002083106099098 092123023119105097043100107049008028122086080009005115082 020025003011053074007106117016027108002006024070125100078 071068075097031088092089076011010005118089076005067087083 097101013&EXT=pdf&INDEX=TRUE

Rutashobya, L. E., Chiwona-Karltun, L., Wilson, M., Ilomo, M., & Semkunde, M. (2021). Gender and rural entrepreneurship in digitizing Sub-Saharan Africa. In J. B. Abugre, E. L. C. Osabutey, & S. P. Sigué (Eds.), *Business in Africa in the era of digital technology* (pp. 63–84). Springer.

Sachs, J., & Warner, A. (2001). The curse of natural resources. *European Economic Review, 45*(4–6), 827–838.

Schopp, K., Schelenz, L., Heesen, J., & Pawelec, M. (2019). Ethical questions of digitalization in the Global South Perspectives on justice and equality. *Digitalization in the Global South, 28*(2), 11–16.

Shaw, T. (2017). Transnational initiatives towards natural resource governance in Africa post-2015. *Journal of Sustainable Development Law and Policy, 8*(1), 214–234.

Signé, L. (2021). *Digitalizing Africa's mines*. https://www.brookings.edu/blog/africa-in-focus/2021/12/03/digitalizing-africas-mines/. Accessed January 25, 2023.

Signé, L., & Johnson, C. (2018). *The potential of manufacturing and industrialization in Africa: Trends, opportunities, and strategies*. Africa Growth Initiative, Brookings Institution. https://media.africaportal.org/documents/Manufacturing-and-Industrialization-in-Africa-Signe-20180921.pdf

Slaughter, A., & Mittal, A. (2015). *Connected barrels: Transforming oil and gas strategies with the Internet of Things. The Internet of things in the oil and gas industry*. https://www2.deloitte.com/us/en/insights/focus/internet-of-things/iot-in-oil-and-gas-industry.html. Accessed February 3, 2023.

Stephens, T. K. (2019). Framework for petroleum revenue management in Ghana: Current problems and challenges. *Journal of Energy & Natural Resources Law, 37*(1), 119–143. https://doi.org/10.1080/02646811.2018.1485269

Stijns, J.-P. (2006). Natural resource abundance and human capital accumulation. *World Development, 34*(6), 1060–1083.

Toroskainen, K. (2019). *Resource governance index: From legal reform to implementation in Sub-Saharan Africa*. https://resourcegovernance.org/sites/default/files/documents/rgi-from-legal-reform-to-implementation-sub-saharan-africa.pdf

UN Broadband Commission for Sustainable Development. (2018). *The State of Broadband: Broadband catalyzing sustainable development.* https://www.itu.int/dms_pub/itu-s/opb/pol/S-POL-BROADBAND.19-2018-PDF-E.pdf. Accessed September 13, 2022.

Wandaogo, A.-A. (2022). Does digitalization improve government effectiveness? Evidence from developing and developed countries. *Applied Economics, 54*(33), 3840–3860. https://doi.org/10.1080/00036846.2021.2016590

Zhuwarara, S. (2019). *Is Africa ready for advanced mining technology?* https://www.miningreview.com/energy/africa-transformative-mining-technology/. Accessed January 26, 2023.

Zumofen, R., Bellarminus, G. K., & Mabillard, V. (2022). Outcomes of government digitization and effects on accountability in Benin. *Transforming Government: People, Process and Policy, 16*(3), 305–317.

CHAPTER 5

Assessing Extractive Natural Resources and Digitalization of Governance Initiatives in Africa: Rethinking Questions of Decline and Resilience

Kobena T. Hanson and Peter Arthur

INTRODUCTION

The extractive resource sector in Africa is a key factor in and a net contributor to growth and development. Extractive sectors like mining, as noted by Pedro et al. (2017), can be a driver for economic growth and improved welfare of citizens of the countries with the resource. The global transition toward clean energy is accentuating the need for and production

---

K. T. Hanson (✉)
Independent Development Evaluation, African Development Bank, Abidjan, Côte d'Ivoire
e-mail: k.hanson@afdb.org

P. Arthur
Department of Political Science, Dalhousie University, Halifax, NS, Canada
e-mail: peter.arthur@dal.ca

© The Author(s), under exclusive license to Springer Nature Switzerland AG 2023
K. P. Puplampu et al. (eds.), *Sustainable Development, Digitalization, and the Green Economy in Africa Post-COVID-19*, International Political Economy Series, https://doi.org/10.1007/978-3-031-32164-1_5

of vast amounts of metals, both common and rare types, compared to fossil fuels. The future demand outlook for extractives presents invaluable opportunities for countries endowed with such resources to harness their extractive wealth to advance economic development and human well-being. Unfortunately, for many resource-rich African nations, mining, oil, or gas exploitation has not resulted in broad-based economic, human, and social development. Also, of great importance is the rise of disruptive technologies and associated digitalization, which are reshaping the governance of Africa's extractives. However, the existing evidence on the role of the use of digital tools in governing and managing extractives in natural resource-rich economies in Africa is quite scanty. Accordingly, this chapter interrogates the role digitalization of governance initiatives in Africa's extractives sector. The chapter explores the threats, opportunities, and possibilities of the extractive sector by examining how digitalization of governance initiatives could underscore a decline or resilience of the extractive sector in Africa. The chapter acknowledges that digitalization has become an invaluable go-to weapon to diagnose, manage and address governance challenges facing the sector. However, meaningful transformation of Africa's extractives industry will require political will, enhanced capacity development at both the individual and institutional level, and a strong link between policymakers, regulators, and industry.

The chapter is structured as follows: section one examines the existing theoretical debates and reviews the literature on the role of natural resources in society. In section two, the digitalization of Africa's extractives sector and its impact is analyzed. Section three focuses on the challenges of digitalization processes in Africa, while the final section offers suggestions and recommendations on how the challenges can be addressed in order to realize the benefits of digitalization in the management and governance of Africa's extractive sector.

Theoretical Discussions & Literature Review

Pedro et al. (2017) have argued that the extractive sector now holds a predominant position for national economies. For Pedro et al. (2017: 163), "examples of countries such as Botswana today, and the Nordic countries and the USA in the last century, provide evidence that resource riches can act as positive drivers (and not a 'curse') for the required structural transformation towards sustainable development." More significantly they argue that the extractive sector can also make significant contributions to the achievement of many of the United Nations (UN) sustainable development goals (SDGs), especially on issues relating to poverty eradication, decent work and economic growth, clean water and sanitation, life on land, sustainable and affordable energy, climate action, industry and infrastructure, as well as peace and justice. To this end, extractives, when governed well, play a vital role in the economies of resource-rich countries (Pedro et al., 2017).

However, there are risks associated with resource dependence including commodity price volatility, lack of transparency and corruption, environmental degradation, displacement of communities, and labor rights violations, which can outweigh the economic benefits. Indeed, while extractive resource wealth can yield prosperity, it can also cause acute social inequality, deep poverty, environmental damage, and political instability (Addison & Roe, 2018). Thus, despite the potential of the natural resource sector to act as a catalyst for growth and development in mineral-rich developing countries, Pedro et al. (2017) state that there are a number of barriers and challenges that may prevent this potential from being realized. Central to the challenges, according to Pedro et al. (2017: 155), are "the unevenly distributed and finite nature of mineral deposits; the volatility of commodity prices which have exposed developing countries to external shocks triggering macro-economic instability; the difficulties of managing large and volatile inflows of foreign capital, technical complexities of large scale projects and limited national capacities; [and] the enclave nature of the industry with weak linkages to other economic sectors."

In fact, across the globe and Africa, many resource-rich nations abound who, unfortunately, have not benefitted from their vast resource wealth (Acemoglu, 1995; Sala-I-Martin & Subramanian, 2003), resulting in what scholars have termed the resource curse (Barma et al., 2012; Van der Ploeg, 2011). Many resource-rich countries, as Ovadia and Graham (2022) argue, have experienced a range of adverse economic, political, and social effects of resource extraction. Although natural resources per se do not necessarily lead to poor economic performance, in many instances, reliance on extractive industries has been found, according to Kasekende et al. (2016), to be associated with slow growth rates. To a certain extent, this dismal performance is a result of the "enclave" nature of the extractives sector, which often has few links to the local economy, especially in the global South. Further, the industry is often disruptive and negatively impacts communities, fragmenting society and destroying their immediate environs and livelihoods. Hilson (2021: 79) for example, notes that most mineral and/or oil-rich economies in sub-Saharan Africa (SSA) continue to score poorly on key socio-economic indicators: rural economic infrastructure remains dilapidated, healthcare services are in an impoverished state, access to clean water continues to be limited for the bulk of populations, and educational services are lacking. Moreover, environmental and social injustices are eminent in the natural resource sector as a result of a lack of communication and sharing of information, a lack of citizen engagement, environmental degradation, and the lack of relevant support infrastructure (Mwakumanya & Mwachupa, 2018).

In spite of the above, the resource curse is not inevitable. In the case of Africa, specifically, scholars question the validity and accuracy of the resource curse theory (Arthur, 2012; Humphreys et al., 2007; Obi, 2010). For instance, Humphreys et al. (2007) question the resource curse argument, noting that there is considerable room for human agency to correct the risks posed by the "paradox of plenty." In the case of Africa, it has been established that the resource curse paradigm hides the larger question of how institutions and their transformation affect growth (Jones, 2008). Others also insist that contextual variables at the national level must be considered in explaining why extractives are sometimes harmful to the development of a country (Basedau, 2005).

Various explanations have been given for the disappointing growth performance of resource-rich countries. Geipel and Nickerson (2021) note that one of the central reasons that natural resource host countries in sub-Saharan Africa and other developing areas have struggled to achieve meaningful economic development from their mineral natural resources is the fact that most goods and services used in extraction have been procured from abroad. It is in this vein that they shed light on the various ways people can help increase local procurement in their respective contexts as a way of moving forward on other issues in natural resource, especially mining governance. They argue that establishing linkages to domestic economies and increasing local procurement by the global mining industry, for example, can help address some of the concerns that often come about regarding natural resource management in sub-Saharan Africa and other developing regions. Another explanation is the Dutch disease model, which assumes that manufacturing is the main driver of the economy and argues that a resource boom will divert country's resources and efforts away from activities that are more conducive to long-run growth.

Another view advanced for the resource curse draws from rent-seeking models. The argument here is that resource rents are easily appropriable, and create the potential for bribes, distortions in public policies, and divert labor away from productive activities and toward seeking public favors. There are also institutional explanations offered to account for the resource curse. Like the rent-seeking models, proponents focus on the connections between resources and institutions, however, they add that the type of resource matters and also regard the form of government (and its policies) as the salient institutional feature (ACBF, 2013; Hanson et al., 2014a). Unlike the Dutch disease and rent-seeking models that seek to identify the best approaches for avoiding the resource curse, the implication of the institutional explanation is that the resource curse is not imperative, rather the nature of the resource, and the quality of institutions in a country, including their capacities and the ability to formulate and implement sound macro-economic policies, are critical in transforming the natural resource potential into a sustainable development outcome (Barma et al., 2012).

Criticisms leveled against resource curse theorists have led to a shift away from the initial debates over "greed versus grievance" causal binary (Arthur, 2012; Bavinck et al., 2014; Obi, 2010), and shifted the focus onto issues related to capacities, leadership, and governance (ACBF, 2013; Barma et al., 2012; Hanson et al., 2014b). The drive to correct the unfortunate afflictions facing the extractives sector, has led to a plethora of calls for and pledges to improve governance and management of the extractives sector at all stages of the value chain, from exploration to extraction to environmental remediation. So, at the World Summit on Sustainable Development in 2002, non-state actors and governments advanced a new vision to better govern extractive industries, leading to the establishment of the Extractive Industries Transparency Initiative (EITI), which aims to improve governance quality through an "open and accountable management of oil, gas and mineral resources" in resource-rich countries (Yanuardi et al., 2021). As Quartey and Abbey (2020: 338) note, the EITI is a "global effort to end the culture of opacity in the generation and use of extractive revenues and to ensure that resource extraction contributes to national development and poverty reduction. This framework encourages public disclosure of company payments and government receipts of extractive revenues as well as the demand for accountability in terms of how the revenues are used. The framework also requires countries publicly to disclose information on revenue management and expenditures, information on contracts and licenses as well as the establishment of a legally mandated open contracting regime." The EITI is generally considered a success story, given the large number of resource-rich nations that have committed to it and the vast support it has received from donors, NGOs, and extractive industry giants (Rustad et al., 2017).

Other well-known governance initiatives targeting governance of the extractives sector are the African Mining Vision (AMV), which was adopted by African Heads of State and Government in 2009 (ECA/AU, 2013). The AMV, as Quartey and Abbey (2020) point out, imposes an obligation on all African Union member States to align their governance arrangements and approaches to the management of their natural resources to a set of prescribed principles in line with international best practices as well as to the lessons drawn from the continent's century-old experience in mining. This focus affords a natural-resource-dependent African State the opportunity to integrate its natural resources into the rest of the national economy, and through that make a critical and sustainable paradigm shift from the enclave nature of resource extraction (Quartey & Abbey, 2020). Additionally, other initiatives to promote effective governance and management of extractive resources include the Publish What You Pay (PWYP), the Kimberley Process Certification Scheme (KPCS), the United Nations Guiding Principles on Business and Human Rights, the Dodd-Frank Act, the Global Reporting Initiative (GRI), the Model Mining Development Agreement, the Initiative for Responsible Mining Assurance, the Natural Resource Charter, and the development of indicators to measure resource governance and the wider work of the International Council on Mining and Metals (ICMM). All these initiatives recognize, in different ways, that extractives, when properly managed, can provide a means for resource-rich nations to decisively break with poverty (ECA, 2009; UN-IRP, 2020).

Amid the calls to enhance and advance governance of the extractives sector, civil society actors, notably global Witness and Oxfam America, together with the Natural Resources Governance Institute (NRGI) and industry bodies such as the International Council on Mining and Metals (ICMM), have been spearheading such efforts (Addison & Roe, 2018: 4). In response, extractive industry giants have in the past two decades increasingly sought to secure acceptance of their activities by local communities and other stakeholders, build public trust and prevent social conflict (Pike, 2012; UN-IRP, 2020; World Bank 2003). Such attempts to earn a "Social License to Operate" (SLO) are important in recognizing the need for mining companies to bear responsibility for the negative social implications of their practices, and have resulted in an explosion of soft regulation aimed at addressing the adverse outcomes of mining (Lesser et al., 2023; Pósleman & Sallan, 2019; UN-IRP, 2020). Pike (2012) adds that a full SLO must comprise both an acquisition and ongoing maintenance with the consent of the local stakeholders. The assurance of consent is vital as the criteria by which locals give their consent may change over time.

It is because of the view that natural resource mismanagement portends danger that many African countries have started adopting better governance measures that should contribute to effective management of natural resources. The calls for and adoption of better governance have coincided with the rapid uptake of digital technologies and innovations that are fundamentally changing the face of the extractives sector, both fostering greater efficiency and productivity, but more importantly transforming the entire value chain from contracting to revenue generation and environmental protection (Hanson & Puplampu, 2018; Iyer et al., 2021). Collier (2010) argues that good governance, which can include disclosing payment of royalties and concession fees, will not only avert corrupt practices by government officials but also can help strengthen the necessary institutions and capacity of various governments that have natural resources. Fearon (2005) argues moreover that oil is not an indicator of civil war risk because it provides an easy source of rebel start-up finance, but because oil-producing countries have relatively low state capabilities stemming from low per capita income and weak military and institutional structures that are incapable of effectively repressing the outbreak of armed insurrection, for which oil is a tempting prize. In a recent WEF survey on which technologies are likely to be used by mining companies in 2025, automation, Internet of Things (IoTs), artificial intelligence (AI), Big Data, drones, and cloud-based management systems were at forefront of digital technologies being utilized in the extractive industry. For countries in the global South, their embracing of digital technologies is expected to provide a fresh creative approach in their efforts to drive macro-economic transformation and sustainable development (Christensen et al., 2019). Therefore, drawing on the extant literature and examples of resource-rich African countries, the section that follows explores how digitalization of resources governance initiatives is transforming Africa's extractive resources landscape.

Digitalization of Africa's Extractives Sector

The rapid and widespread adoption of digital technologies associated with the Fourth Industrial Revolution (4IR)—common referred to as digitalization (Hanson & Tang, 2020), is one of the most important technological transformations in human history, affecting economies worldwide both positively and negatively at an unprecedented scale (Acemoglu & Restrepo, 2019; Hanson & Tang, 2020; Lee et al., 2018; Lenhard & Lehtimäki, 2022; Schwab, 2016). Defined by Evangelista et al. (2014) as the increased connectivity and networking of digital technologies to enhance communication, services, and trade between people, organizations, and things, digitalization, according to the OECD (2020), is helping to transform economic activities and even social interaction in society, particularly in the way we live and work. According to Ayakwah et al. (2021), the emergence of technological platforms of information and communications tech (ICT) has catalyzed the digital era. Gains from digitalization have made it attractive to both businesses and governments interested in maximizing the opportunities that the digitalized economy brings (Ayakwah et al., 2021). For Bahn et al. (2021), digitalization helps to transform various sectors of the economy into a source of improved economic growth, social inclusion, and environmental sustainability. Digitization is also not only bringing locations of production and sale closer together, but more importantly, driving major changes in the design of future value and supply chains (WEF, 2017). Indeed, the potential impact of digitization and disruptive innovation (e.g., AI, augmented and virtual reality, and blockchain technology, to mention a few), has far-reaching implications for governance and the law, highlighting not only the possibilities and opportunities; but also scale and scope of the emerging landscape that Africa has to confront with and actively thrive in (Hanson & Tang, 2020; Lazarenko et al., 2021). For Evangelista et al. (2014), the usage of ICT, and mostly digital empowerment, exerts major economic effects, especially on employment and the inclusion of "disadvantaged" groups in the labor market.

Additionally, digitalization has become the focus of significant discussions and analysis in the academic literature because as David (2018) states, there is the increasing evidence that it helps to reduce expenditures and operating costs as well as improve operational efficiency and maximize production, and environmental standards. Manas et al. (2020) elaborate on this by explaining that digitalization triggers digital social innovation by providing a platform to business, non-government organizations, social entrepreneurs, and government agencies to generate positive social impact by leveraging digital technologies. Digital technologies, as they argue, can co-create knowledge and solutions through collaboration among various entities that get attracted to this ecosystem to address a wide range of social needs of the disadvantaged, socially excluded, and marginalized groups. Moreover, this can happen at a scale that was unthinkable before the rise of Internet-based technologies. For David (2018), data generated from digital technologies is not only of significant use in the decision-making process in the natural resource sector, but also contributes to the effective and efficient governance and management of natural resources. The increased ICT infrastructure usage leads to innovation and productivity through an improvement in the allocation of scarce resources, and technical efficiency (Bankole & Mimbi, 2017). Not only does technology and innovation contribute and enhance the quality of the production process (Ahmad et al., 2020: 47), but also, as Mayer (2018: 6) points out, digitalization facilitates translating data into intangible assets and makes it easier and cheaper to use such data for design and production.

Rwanda's tantalum mining is an excellent example of blockchain technology being used to enhance the governance of extractives. Working with UK-based Circulor, Rwanda put in place a blockchain-based system to trace tantalum in three mines and an ore-sorting facility in 2018 (Campbell et al., 2021). The system slashed the high cost for compliance, satisfied regulators, reassured consumers, and built revenue for Rwanda. Today, its tantalum, previously classified as a "conflict mineral" under the Dodd-Frank Act of 2010 and the EU Conflict Minerals law, is now viewed as an innovative mineral traceability solution thanks to blockchain. It is invaluable because it provides traceability and transparency across the supply chain where it is really needed—conflict minerals, rare earth minerals, toxic and polluting waste, and child labor-based production (Campbell et al., 2021; Hyperledger.org, 2019).

As Lazarenko et al. (2021) point out, for mining companies, digital technologies are providing new directions for the transformational changes in the way they do business, identify new ways to manage variability and enhance productivity, and hence develop a new paradigm for growth and development. Also, digitalization not only helps to improve safety in operations, but by automating operations in the natural resource sector, business practices and processes through the use of digital technology will contribute to the improvements in organizational performance and management (Maroufkhani et al., 2022). Ranjith et al. (2017) note that digitalization through automation increases worker safety by reducing the dangers that come with mining. Additionally, automation increases and maximizes returns and outputs as well as contribute to greater productivity because of the fact that drilling time during the process of mining is not wasted. To this end, digital innovations play a significant role in the delivery of safer, more productive, and environmentally sustainable mining operations (Ralston et al., 2018: 110). This is corroborated by Maroufkhani et al. (2022) who note that in the mining sector, automation has been adopted to drive productivity and improve the safety and health of miners in dangerous manual exploration. The automation of machinery can speed up the work that would be undertaken and thereby improve performance and efficiency in the provision of services. By getting real-time information, returns can be boosted, and accurate decisions can also be undertaken because of the availability of information, which in itself is generated in a faster way (Maroufkhani et al., 2022).

Elsewhere, leveraging the Internet of things (IoT) is enabling the digital mine to "become a reality as planning, control and decision support systems are fully integrated and core physical processes are automated" (UN-IRP, 2020: 124). For example, De Beers Marine South Africa (together with Orange Business Services, a network-native digital services subsidiary of telecom giant Orange Group) built an Internet of Things (IoT) platform on board the MV Mafuta, currently the world's largest offshore diamond mining vessel, to make sure crew maintain a safe distance from heavy machinery (Campbell et al., 2021). Leveraging a combination of sensors and machinery allows miners to monitor and track operations in real time, increasing safety and efficiency.

Also, many extractive industry actors are increasingly utilizing unmanned aerial vehicles and drones for data collection, safety monitoring, and inspection of difficult-to-reach or dangerous areas (Deloitte, 2017). Kumba Iron Ore, a leading South African supplier of seaborne iron ore, uses drone technology in its operations, reducing the need for employees to do physical blast clearances. Drones are also used to conduct surveys and general observations (Campbell et al., 2021). Drones outfitted with cameras and scanners can provide data on operations and current conditions in the mine, increasing worker safety, efficiency, and up-skilling workers who manage the drone fleet. Moreover, digital technologies are dramatically improving performance in the natural resource sector in areas such as exploration, drilling, production, trading, and distribution. The use of digital technologies has been at the forefront in the gathering and delivering of information to companies in the natural resource sector that is assisting them in the decision-making process, thereby contributing to their increased capital investment returns.

Finally, in Ghana for example, institutions such as the Petroleum Commission and Ministry of Energy are employing digitalized tools in both reporting and information-sharing activities. Specifically, reporting on petroleum activities such as production figures, crude oil liftings, petroleum agreements, laws and regulations are reported and submitted through electronic platforms and subsequently uploaded online on the internet. Hence, not only is intra-organization information sharing mostly done through shared drives, but also, companies including Ghana's Petroleum Commission, have adopted the concept of virtual meetings as part of their operational activities to hold meeting and transmit information much quicker. Similarly, the offshore operational facilities virtual meetings are held on a daily basis to communicate with the onshore team. So, from a social perspective, utilization of digital technologies is helping enhance transparency. Establishing seamless communication channels is enabling "companies [such as Ghana's Petroleum Commission] to clearly transmit information about their social and environmental performance and their impact on, for example, the surrounding communities" (Palomares et al., 2022: 39). Doing so, is in turn facilitating the renewal of the social licenses, which are requisites for companies operating in the extractive sector (Palomares et al., 2022). In sum, as Stoyanova (2020) argues, digitalization is becoming a determining factor in our time. It is a tool that provides greater efficiency, speed, and individuality for different industries. It is also a prerequisite for developing new services and innovative business models.

Problems and Challenges with Digitalization Processes

While Africa has made great strides in its efforts to digitalize, it is nowhere near what pertains in the global North. Also, there is a widespread variation in terms of the digital preparedness, utilization, and needs of different African countries (Abimbola et al., 2021; Teevan & Shiferaw, 2022). It is widely acknowledged that digitalization, such as e-payments and the use of RFID, for example, play a crucial role in unlocking trade, enhancing governance, and streamlining the value chain in industries such as the extractives sector (Hanson & Puplampu, 2018; Iyer et al., 2021). Indeed, the widespread appeal for and utilization of digitalization, has mandated a "rethink or revamp of the regulatory structures ... consumer protection, labor regulation, property rights, taxation and discriminatory practices" (Hanson & Puplampu, 2018: 139), as extant regulatory frameworks no longer suffice (Ranchordás, 2015). For countries embracing digitalization, the objective among others is to leapfrog development and to provide a fresh creative approach in their efforts to drive economic transformation and sustainable development (Christensen et al., 2019). Digitalization in essence is transforming all end-to-end steps in production and business models in most sectors of the economy (WEF, 2017), the extractive industry included.

Indeed, today, the role of technological innovation as a means to strengthen institutional capacities in the extractives sector is unquestioned and rapidly being mainstreamed. Digital tools have become an invaluable go-to weapon to diagnose, manage and address governance challenges facing the sector (Lazarenko et al., 2021). Digital technologies enable a fundamental shift in vision, strategy, operating model, business skills, and capabilities in the mining industry. The adoption of integrated digital communication networks, automated mining equipment, intelligent design, and production management software systems, and advances in analytics provide the basis for the maximization of value (Lazarenko et al., 2021). That said, transforming Africa's extractives industry requires more than digitalization and strategies. There is a key need for strong links between policymakers and industry, and real support to digitalization and industrialization, such as through digital industrial hubs (Traoré et al., 2022).

As Manas et al. (2020) have observed, digitalization is not always neutral in its impact. If a digital world is capable of fetching the benefits of bringing people together globally, the footprints of digital shoppers are collected and sold to advertisers to facilitate targeted advertising. In essence, users' data thus can unknowingly be sold as digital products to the highest bidder. There is a risk even in global connection leading to overwhelming internationalization and social media impact; crowding out local content, culture, and entrepreneurship. Herein lies, according to Manas et al. (2020), the need for judicious use of technology, which can happen only at the back of effective regulation, undoubtedly a challenging balancing task. Also, digitalization, as Dianoux (2021) points out, is not a silver bullet. It takes time, effort, and expertise to unlock its profound impacts. For sectors facing financial pressure and tough choices, good data management can provide immediate insights to support revenues, charting a pathway toward a sustainable industry. However, for any digital effort to succeed, the creation of a robust digital culture is critical. Building a digital culture requires buy-in at every level, from the boardroom to the quayside, the rig, and the vessel to do things differently (Dianoux, 2021).

Discussing the barriers experienced in leveraging the digital opportunities within the fourth industrial revolution within South Africa, Mtotywa et al. (2022) found the prevailing prohibitive costs of data, low economic inclusion, poor digital culture, literacy and skills deficiency among the youth, the manual-automation job dilemma, high crime prevalence, low entrepreneurial intent as well as inadequate privacy and security within the technological and social media space, as the main challenges. Moreover, Korovkin (2019) states that digital issues have not been incorporated in the national strategizing in most leading African economies to any significant extent. It is such challenges that make Cigna (2018) skeptical of the emerging literature that focuses on the supposed benefits of digitalization, especially the claim that it can address existing inequality in society. For him, the mere existence and availability of digitalization does mean that the gap in skills and capital distribution will be necessarily closed. Although there are opportunities in the process of digitalization, there are challenges and risks galore that need to be addressed at the societal level (Manas et al., 2020). Issues such as low digital literacy skills, high internet costs, information and cybersecurity risks, and intellectual property thefts are some of the dangers associated with the digitalization process. Moreover, the lack of exposure, coupled with the insufficient access in low-income countries, because of a lack of devices, bandwidth, speed or necessary skills or because of high access cost are also part of issues that crop up from the digitalization process (Manas et al., 2020). A similar argument is made by Rutashobya et al. (2021: 79) who suggest that as more and more data become digitalized, issues such as trust, security, and privacy become increasingly more important. Also, remote rural areas, marginalized groups, the poor, women, youth, as well as non-skilled individuals may not be included in some of digitalization opportunities yet acutely suffer the mentioned challenges.

Finally, Mwakumanya and Mwachupa (2018) have indicated that the challenges encountered in the efforts to enhance community participation in decisions that impact the governance of natural resources include false information or propaganda disseminated on digital media, e.g., Twitter and Facebook. In Kenya for instance, the Kwale county citizenry has limited access to internet services as well as limited network connectivity, especially in the remote areas of the county, which hinders the effective sharing of information through digital media. Limited public awareness, inadequate knowledge of environmental injustices, and high illiteracy levels limit effective community participation in promoting social and environmental accountability. The extractive companies sometimes restrict access to some information, which when coupled with local communities' inadequate capacity to develop and manage interactive webpages and mobile phone applications, negatively impacts the content and citizen engagement on digital platforms. Furthermore, Maroufkhani et al. (2022) have highlighted the fact that in spite of the interest in the adoption of big data analytics (BDA) among the oil and gas industry for instance, a lack of business support and awareness about big data, the complexity of its applications, and the quality of the data are the most challenging issues within the industry. Additionally, they argue that costs associated with data recording, storage, analysis, and quality of the recorded data are the main challenges of using BDA in the oil and gas industry. It is in this regard that addressing these challenges that undermine the successful employment of digital technologies and their use in the governance of extractive natural resource sector become key and necessary in the efforts to achieve the benefits associated with the digitalization process.

Digitalization, Good Governance, and a Revised Extractives Landscape: The Way Forward

While digital technology has the potential to unlock developmental capacities essential to the natural resource management process, the preceding discussions highlighted some of the challenges and constraints hampering the benefits that are supposed to accompany the digitalization process. The challenges and problems identified earlier raise concerns about how they can be effectively navigated to ensure that the benefits are realized. The challenges and constraints in the use of digital tools in many African countries call for the necessary and appropriate interventions by governments, policymakers, and other stakeholders. If Africa is to attain meaningful sustainable development and meet the goals of the UNSDGs Agenda 2030 and the AU Agenda 2063, then undoubtedly strengthening of governance, institutions, laws, and regulatory policies is critical if sustainable development policies are to be effective (ACBF, 2013, Hanson et al., 2014a). The proper utilization of digitalization is central to this goal. Embracing available and future technologies is significant for the resilience and sustainability of the African extractive sector, enabling African extractives to jump from Industry 2.0 to 4.0. The good thing is that already glimpses of the development and use of new and digital technologies are everywhere. Starting with mobile money platforms, today the continent lists a plethora of such innovations in almost every sector imaginable. The continent currently is home to over 500 tech hubs, some of which have active links to the extractives sector, which in the context of the current global development agenda, is intricately linked to a large number of the 17 UNSDGs—notably "those relating to poverty eradication, decent work and economic growth, clean water and sanitation, life on land, sustainable and affordable energy, climate action, industry and infrastructure, as well as peace and justice" (UN-IRP, 2020: 6).

How the sector is governed is key to economies, development plans, and livelihood destinies of the citizens of resource-rich African nations. In this era of digitalization and disruptive innovations, the utilization of these novel tools—big data, block chain, artificial intelligence, IoT, UAV/Drones, etc.—to enhance governance is essential. For instance, as Palomares et al. (2022: 5) point out, blockchain has emerged "as a powerful tool to meet transparency and traceability goals in the context of sustainability and social impact. Blockchain [is a vital] tool for tracking minerals and metals from the extraction sites to the sale of the final good as a means of verifying that the final good complies with sustainability standards." Blockchain, in this regard, helps allay fears around the quality and transparency of existing product certification schemes, as it "enables the geo-tagging of ores with cryptographic tokens allowing the identification, trading, and management of ore as well as secure and monitored maintenance of records from the moment of extraction and throughout the lifetime of minerals and metals" (UN-IRP, 2020: 124). This capability is invaluable in the context of Africa in light of the trillions lost each year to illicit financial flows stemming from underpricing and other illegal practices.

Similarly, the widespread adoption of digitalization has the "potential to leverage the social license in diverse aspects, mainly through enhancing transparency (Palomares et al., 2022: 6)." In this context, digitalization of the extractive sector has emerged as an opportunity to process data and present it as information. However, as Wandaogo (2022) argues, to achieve these objectives and to reap the full benefits of digitalization in the governance of extractive natural resources, African government should adopt policies that would promote the use of ICT at all levels of the economy, that is, the government itself, businesses, and individuals. These policies should focus more on increasing the coverage of ICT and the Internet among the population and in all sectors of activity. This could include building and improving the technological infrastructure (Wandaogo, 2022).

A final element in the efforts to ensure effective natural resource governance is centered around the Sustainable Development License to Operate (SDLO), and the earlier Social License to Operate (SLO) which have been increasingly sought by mining companies since the 1990s to secure the acceptance of mining activities by local communities and stakeholders, build public trust and prevent social conflict (Pedro et al., 2017). As the UN-IRP (2020: 266) has indicated, the SDLO seeks to address both the "inadequacies of the existing [extractive industry] governance landscape and instruments for mining, and the need to translate the complex array of post-2015 global commitments into a manageable set of principles and requirements" for use by key stakeholders involved in extractive sector governance. The SDLO extends the SLO in several important ways. This new governance model is relevant to all actors in the extractive sector, and its implementation is a shared responsibility by "host" and "home" countries along the extractive value chain. Moreover, it sets out principles, policy options, and good practices for enhancing the extractive sector's contribution to achieving the SDGs (UN-IRP, 2020). Building on the SLO, according to Pedro et al. (2017: 154), draws "attention to the need for mining companies to bear responsibility for the negative social implications of their practices and to engage in an inclusive and meaningful ways with stakeholders." Pedro et al. (2017) further argue that governments need to put in place clear, comprehensive and transparent laws, policies and regulations, build strong institutions, train skilled professionals and set up accountability mechanisms to ensure that policy frameworks and rules are implemented.

These suggestions by Pedro et al. (2017) can be best realized with the deployment of digital tools, hence the importance of speeding up the digitalization process in the natural resource sector in African countries. As Burns (2022) states, technology through various social media platforms, video calls, mobile apps, group chats, and data portals, all offer significant opportunities to improve stakeholder engagement in the natural resource sector and also ensure good governance in the natural resource sector. Leveraging the myriad platforms, apps and portals individually and collectively, Burns (2022) highlights, has made it so much easier to connect with a wide group of people.

Conclusion

Many African countries, as pointed out in this chapter, are very dependent on extractive resources for their socioeconomic development goals and objectives. Despite its potential to facilitate the development process, the possession of extractives has not always led to improvements in the socioeconomic conditions of citizens. As a result, numerous approaches and initiatives have been developed by various stakeholders in order to address the challenges that have bedeviled the extractive sector. One bright spot that has recently been the focus of discussion and analysis has centered on the use of digital technologies to help govern and manage natural resources. Indeed, the extractive natural resource sector in Africa is undergoing a major transformation as companies adopt digital technologies to increase efficiency, reduce costs, and enhance competitiveness. The use of the digitalization spectrum is also providing valuable insights, optimizing production, and reducing the risk of downtime.

While various digitalized systems are contributing positively to the governance and management of extractives in Africa, the chapter also notes the challenges that have cropped up in the efforts to realize the goals and benefits of the digitalization process in the extractive sector. For extractive operations that embrace the ongoing digital transformation, not only will they witness an increase in productivity, but more importantly, they will scale up efficiency, effectiveness, be more environmentally sustainable, and have enhanced access to global value chains. From a human resource perspective, digitalization will enhance workers' health and safety, as well as build individual and institutional capacity. In sum, as Africa's extractive industries embrace digitalization, more mines will become more "green," productive, transparent, and more profitable—availing more resources to national governments to spend on public goods and investments for the living and countless generations yet unborn. It is in this regard that this chapter calls for concerted efforts by African nations to leverage digital technologies to enhance their extractive sector operations and value chains. However, to do so meaningfully, governments and extractive sector stakeholders need to address some of the challenges of digitalization (e.g., weak data management practices; labor upskilling; and data and cybersecurity concerns) in order to ensure that the benefits associated with the use of digital tools in the extractive sector do not fizzle out.

References

Abimbola, O., Aggad, F., & Ndzendze, B. (2021). What is Africa's digital agenda? *Policy Brief No.3*. APRI (Africa Policy Research Institute).

ACBF. (2013). *Africa capacity indicators 2013: Capacity development for natural resource management*. ACBF (African Capacity Building Foundation).

Acemoglu, D. (1995). Reward structures and the allocation of talent. *European Economic Review, 39*(1), 17–33.

Acemoglu, D., & Restrepo, P. (2019). Automation and new tasks: How technology displaces and reinstates labor. *Journal of Economic Perspectives, 33*(2), 3–30.

Addison, T., & Roe, A. (Eds.). (2018). *Extractive industries: The management of resources as a driver of sustainable development* (Online ed.). Oxford Academic. https://doi.org/10.1093/oso/9780198817369.001.0001. Accessed 14 March 2023.

Ahmad, M., Khattak, S. I., Khan, S., & Rahman, Z. U. (2020). Do aggregate domestic consumption spending & technological innovation affect industrialization in South Africa? An application of linear & non-linear ARDL models. *Journal of Applied Economics, 23*(1), 44–65.

Arthur, P. (2012). Averting the resource curse in Ghana: Assessing the options. In L. Swatuk & M. Schnurr (Eds.), *Natural resources and social conflict: Towards critical environmental security* (pp. 108–127). Palgrave Macmillan.

Ayakwah, A., Damoah, I. S., & Osabutey E. L. C. (2021). Digitalization in Africa: The case of public programs in Ghana. In J. B. Abugre, E. L. C. Osabutey, & S. P. Sigué (Eds.), *Business in Africa in the Era of Digital Technology* (pp. 7–26). Springer.

Bahn, R. A., Yehya, A. A. K., & Zurayk, R. (2021). Digitalization for Sustainable agri-food systems: Potential, Status, and risks for the MENA region. *Sustainability, 13,* 3223. https://doi.org/10.3390/su13063223

Bankole, F. & Mimbi, L. (2017). ICT infrastructure and its impact on national development: A research direction for Africa. *The African Journal of Information Systems, 9*(2). https://digitalcommons.kennesaw.edu/ajis/vol9/iss2/1

Barma, N. H., Kaiser, K., Le, T. M., & Viñuela, L. (2012). *Rents to riches: The political economy of natural resource-led development.* World Bank.

Basedau, M. (2005). *Context matters—Rethinking the resource curse in sub-Saharan Africa* (DUI Working Papers # 1). German Overseas Institute.

Bavinck, M., Pellegrini, L., & Mostert, E. (Eds.). (2014). *Conflicts over natural resources in the Global South: Conceptual approaches* (A Balkema Book). CRC Press. https://doi.org/10.1201/b16498

Burns, C. (2022). *Using technology and data to strengthen your social license to operate.* https://www.canadianminingjournal.com/featured-article/using-technology-and-data-to-strengthen-your-social-license-to-operate/. Accessed 24 March 2023.

Campbell, R., Omietanski, A., Burnell, M., & Felthun, G. (2021, April 5). African Mining 4.0: Innovative sunrise for African miners—Transformative technologies are ushering in a new era of efficiency, safety and growth. *Insight.* https://www.whitecase.com/insight-our-thinking/african-mining-40-innovative-sunrise-african-miners-0. Accessed 20 March 2023.

Christensen, C. M., Ojomo, E., & Dillon, K. (2019). *The prosperity paradox: How innovation can lift nations out of poverty.* HarperCollins.

Cigna, L. (2018). Digital inequality in theory and practice: Old and new divides in the broadband era. *Interações: Sociedade e as novas modernidades, 34,* 47–63.

Collier, P. (2010). *The plundered planet—Why we must—And how we can—Manage nature for global prosperity.* Oxford University Press.

David, R. M. (2018). Advancement in digital oil field technology: Maximizing production and improving operational efficiency through data-driven technologies. In M. Clifford, R. K. Perrons, S. H. Ali, & T. A. Grice (Eds.), *Extracting innovations: Mining, energy and technological change in the digital age* (pp. 137–143). Taylor and Francis and CRC Press.

Deloitte. (2017). *Tracking the trends 2017: The top 10 trends mining companies will face in the coming year.* https://www2.deloitte.com/content/dam/Deloitte/global/Documents/Energy-and-Resources/gx-er-tracking-the-trends-2017.pdf. Accessed 17 March 2023.

Dianoux, A. (2021). Maximizing digitalization's benefits: How the offshore sector can use data, expertise to thrive. *Sea Technology, 62*(5), 17–20.

ECA (Economic Commission on Africa). (2009). *African governance report II.* Oxford University Press.

Evangelista, R., Guerrieri, P., & Meliciani, V. (2014). The economic impact of digital technologies in Europe. *Economics of Innovation and New Technology, 23*(8), 802–824.

Fearon, J. D. (2005). Paradigm in distress? Primary commodities and civil war. *The Journal of Conflict Resolution, 49*(4), 483–507.

Geipel, J., & Nickerson, E. (2021). Promoting mining local procurement through systems change: A Canadian NGO's efforts to improve the development impacts of the global mining industry. In N. Andrews, J. A. Grant, & J. S. Ovadia (Eds.), *Natural resource-based development in Africa: Panacea or Pandora's box?* (pp. 201–219). University of Toronto Press.

Hanson, K. T., D'Alessandro, C., & Owusu, F. (Eds.). (2014a). *Managing Africa's natural resources: Capacities for development.* Palgrave Macmillan.

Hanson, K. T., Owusu, F., & D'Alessandro, C. (2014b). Toward a coordinated approach to natural resource management in Africa. In K. T. Hanson (Ed.), *Managing Africa's natural resources: Capacities for development* (pp. 1–14). Palgrave.

Hanson, K. T., & Puplampu, K. P. (2018). The internet of things and the sharing economy: Harnessing the possibilities for Africa's sustainable development goals. In K. T. Hanson, K. P. Puplampu, & T. M. Shaw (Eds.), *From MDGs to SDGs: Rethinking African development* (pp. 133–151). Routledge.

Hanson, K. T., & Tang, V. T. (2020). Perspectives on disruptive innovations and Africa's services sector. In P. Arthur et al. (Eds.), *Disruptive technologies, innovation & development in Africa.* Palgrave.

Hilson, A. E. (2021). 'Stakeholder salience and resource enclavity in Sub-Saharan Africa: The case of ghana's oil.' In N. Andrews, J. A. Grant, & J. S. Ovadia (Eds.), *Natural resource-based development in Africa: Panacea or Pandora's box?* (pp. 79–100). University of Toronto Press.

Humphreys, M., Sachs, J. D., & Stiglitz, J. E. (2007). *Escaping the resource curse.* Columbia University Press.

Hyperledger.org. (2019). *Case study: Circulor achieves first-ever-mine-to-manufacturer traceability of a conflict mineral with hyperledger fabric.* https://www.hyperledger.org/wp-content/uploads/2019/01/Hyperledger_CaseStudy_Tantalum_Print.pdf. Accessed 20 March 2023.

Iyer, N., Achieng. G., Borokini, F., & Ludger, U. (2021, June). *Automated imperialism, expansionist dreams: Exploring digital extractivism in Africa.* Pollicy.
Jones, S. (2008). Sub-Saharan Africa and the resource curse: Limitations of the cenventional wisdom, DIIS Working Paper #2008/14, Danish Institute for African Studies. Available at: https://files.ethz.ch/isn/92331/2008_14.pdf
Kasekende, E., Abuka, C., & Sarr, M. (2016). Extractive industries and corruption: Investigating the effectiveness of EITI as a scrutiny mechanism. *Resources Policy, 34*(4), 117–128.
Korovkin, V. V. (2019). National digital economy strategies: A survey of Africa. ORF Issue Brief No. 303, July 2019, Observer Research Foundation. https://www.orfonline.org/wpcontent/uploads/2019/07/ORF_IssueBrief_303_DigitalEcon-Africa.pdf. Accessed January 27, 2023.
Labhard, V., & Lehtimäki, J. (2022). *Digitalization, institutions and governance, and growth: Mechanisms and evidence* (ECB [European Central Bank] Working Paper Series, No. 2735).
Lazarenko, Y., Garafonova, O., Marhasova, V., & Tkalenko, N. (2021). *Digital transformation in the mining sector: Exploring global technology trends & managerial issues.* E3S Web of Conferences 315, 04006. VIth International Innovative Mining Symposium. https://doi.org/10.1051/e3sconf / 202131504006.
Lee, M. H., Yun, J. J. H., Pyka, A., Won, D. K., Kodama, F., Schiuma, G., Park, H. S., Jeon, J., et al. (2018). How to respond to the 4IR, or the 2nd information technology revolution? *Journal of Open Innovation: Technology, Market and Complexity, 4*(21), 1–24. https://doi.org/10.3390/joitmc4030021
Lesser, P., Poelzer, G., Gugerell, K., Tost, M., & Franks, D. (2023). Exploring scale in social license to operate: European perspectives. *Journal of Cleaner Production, 384,* 135552.
Manas, P., Upadhyay, P., & Dwivedi, Y. K. (2020). Roadmap to digitalization of an emerging economy: A viewpoint. *Transforming Government: People, Process and Policy, 14*(3), 401–415.
Maroufkhani, P., Desouza, K. C., Perrons, R. K., & Iranmanesh, M. (2022). Digital transformation in the resource and energy sectors: A systematic review. *Resources Policy, 76,* 102622. https://doi.org/10.1016/j.resourpol.2022.102622
Mayer, J. (2018). *Digitalization and industrialization: Friends or foes* (UNCTAD Research Paper No. 25). https://unctad.org/system/files/official-document/ser-rp-2018d7_en.pdf. Accessed 10 March 2023.
Mtotywa, M. M., Manqele, S. P., Seabi, M. A., Mthethwa, N., & Moitse, M. (2022). Barriers to effectively leveraging opportunities within the fourth

industrial revolution in South Africa. *African Journal of Development Studies (formerly AFFRIKA Journal of Politics, Economics and Society)*, No. si2.

Mwakumanya, M. A., & Mwachupa, J. (2018). Digital mapping as a tool for environmental and social corporate accountability in the extractive sector in Kwale County, Kenya. *Journal of Sustainable Mining, 17*(3), 97–104.

Obi, C. (2010). Oil extraction, dispossession, resistance, and conflict in Nigeria's oil-rich Niger Delta. *Canadian Journal of Development Studies, 30*(1–2), 219–236.

OECD. (2020). *Digital transformation in the age of COVID-19: Building resilience and bridging divides, digital economy outlook 2020 supplement.* OECD.

Ovadia, J. S., & Graham, E. (2022). The resource curse and limits of petro-development in Ghana's "oil city": How oil production has impacted Sekondi-Takoradi. In N. Andrews, J. Andrew Grant, & J. S. Ovadia (Eds.), *Natural resource-based development in Africa: Panacea or Pandora's box?* (pp. 59–78). University of Toronto Press.

Palomares, Z. R., García, J. G., & Rodríguez, D. P. (2022). *Digitalization in the extractive sector: A comparative analysis of the Andean region*. Carbon Trust & Inter-American Development Bank.

Pedro, A., Ayuk, E. T., Bodouroglou, C., et al. (2017). Towards a sustainable development licence to operate for the extractive sector. *Mineral Economics, 30*, 153–165. https://doi.org/10.1007/s13563-017-0108-9

Pike, R. (2012). *The relevance of social license to operate for mining companies.* Schroders Fund Advisors LLC, Member FNRA, SIPC 875 Third Avenue, New York, 10022-6225.

Pósleman, C. S., & Sallan, J. M. (2019). Social license to operate in the mining industry: The case of Peru. *Impact Assessment and Project Appraisal, 37*(6), 480–490. https://doi.org/10.1080/14615517.2019.1585142

Quartey, P., & Abbey, E. (2020). Ghana's oil governance regime: Challenges and policies. In A. Langer, U. Ukiwo, & P. Mbabazi (Eds.), *Oil wealth and development in Uganda and beyond* (pp. 331–350). Leuven University Press.

Ralston, J., James, C., & Hainsworth, D. (2018). Digital mining: Past, present, and future. In M. Clifford, R. K. Perrons, S. H. Ali, & T. A. Grice (Eds.), *Extracting innovations: Mining, energy and technological change in the digital age* (pp. 91–113). Taylor & Francis and CRC Press.

Ranchordás, S. (2015). Does sharing mean caring? Regulating innovation in the sharing economy. *Minnesota Journal of Law, Science & Technology, 16*(1), 414–475.

Ranjith, P., et al. (2017). Opportunities and challenges in deep mining: A brief review. *Engineering, 3*(4), 546–551. https://doi.org/10.1016/j.eng.2017.04.024

Rustad, S. A., Le Billon, P., & Lujala, P. (2017). Has the extractive industries transparency initiative been a success? Identifying and evaluating EITI goals. *Resources Policy, 51*, 151–162.

Rutashobya, L. E., Chiwona-Karltun, L., Wilson, M., Ilomo, M., & Semkunde, M. (2021). Gender and Rural Entrepreneurship in Digitizing Sub-Saharan Africa. In J. B. Abugre, E. L. C. Osabutey, & S. P. Sigué (Eds.), *Business in Africa in the Era of Digital Technology* (pp. 63–84). Springer.

Salai-I-Martin, X., & Subramanian, A. (2003). *Addressing the natural resource curse: An illustration from Nigeria* (Working paper 9804). NBER, Cambridge.

Schwab, K. (2016). *The fourth industrial revolution.* Crown.

Stoyanova, M. (2020). Good practices and recommendations for success in construction digitalization. *TEM Journal, 9*(1), 42–47.

Teevan, C., & Shiferaw, L. T. (2022, October). *Digital geopolitics in Africa: Moving from strategy to action* (ECDPM Briefing Note, No. 150).

Traoré, B., Yawson, F., Floyd, R., & Mittal, V. (2022, September). *Promoting innovation and digital transformation in the infrastructure technology in Africa* (Policy Brief No. 12). Accra, ACET.

UN-IRP. (2020). *Mineral resource governance in the 21st century: Gearing extractive industries towards sustainable development.* A Report by the International Resource Panel. UNEP.

Van der Ploeg, F. (2011). Natural resources: Curse or blessing? *Journal of Economic Literature, 49*(2), 366–420.

Wandaogo, A.-A. (2022). Does digitalization improve government effectiveness? Evidence from developing and developed countries. *Applied Economics, 54*(33), 3840–3860. https://doi.org/10.1080/00036846.2021.2016590

WEF. (2017, October). *Impact of the fourth industrial revolution on supply chains.* WEF. http://www3.weforum.org/docs/WEF_Impact_of_the_Fourth_Industrial_Revolution_on_Supply_Chains_.pdf. Accessed on August 18, 2022.

World Bank. (2003). *Striking a better balance: The World Bank and extractive industries.* Washington DC.

Yanuardi, Y., Vijge, M. J., & Biermann, F. (2021). Improving governance quality through global standard setting? Experiences from the extractive industries transparency initiative in Indonesia. *The Extractive Industries and Society, 8*(3), 1–9.

CHAPTER 6

Natural Resources Management, Sovereign Wealth Fund, and the Green Economy: Digitalization, Policies, and Institutions for Sustainable Development in Africa

Korbla P. Puplampu, Hosea O. Patrick, and Benjamin D. Ofori

K. P. Puplampu (✉)
Department of Sociology, Grant MacEwan University, Edmonton, AB, Canada
e-mail: puplampuk@macewan.ca

H. O. Patrick
Department of Geography, Geomatics and Environment, University of Toronto, Toronto, ON, Canada

B. D. Ofori
Institute for Environment and Sanitation Studies (IESS), University of Ghana, Accra, Ghana

© The Author(s), under exclusive license to Springer Nature Switzerland AG 2023
K. P. Puplampu et al. (eds.), *Sustainable Development, Digitalization, and the Green Economy in Africa Post-COVID-19*, International Political Economy Series, https://doi.org/10.1007/978-3-031-32164-1_6

Introduction

There is no denying that the development of any society requires the complex interaction between human and natural resources. Human resources range from essentials like the knowledge base of the society, including the human capital that can be brought to bear on institutions and institutional capacity in a wider socio-political environment. Natural resources, for example land, water, minerals, have assumed a pivotal role in the development discourse for a long time. Since Africa is endowed with natural resources, it is possible, with the appropriate human resources, to improve the development trajectory of the continent (ACBF, 2013; Barma et al., 2012; Hanson et al., 2014). Specifically, African countries have significant extractive resources, mainly oil and gas, as well as other minerals (AfDB & AU, 2009; World Bank, 2012). The Gulf of Guinea, stretching from Ghana, to Nigeria, Equatorial Guinea, and Angola has become a site of oil rigs, a situation that has also been bolstered with discoveries of oil in Uganda and Tanzania (World Bank, 2012: 16). The African continent also has significant deposits of bauxite, copper, gold, and other valuable minerals (World Bank, 2012: 15). Additionally, African countries such as South Africa, Democratic Republic of Congo and Zimbabwe are some of the leading producers of lithium, cobalt and rare earth elements that are essential in the discourse on the transition to a green economy (African Natural Resources Centre, 2021a, b).

While the wealth creation implications of natural resources for African development are huge and worth celebrating, there is also the nagging worry of how natural resources can give rise to the paradox of plenty (AfDB 2007; Auty, 1993; Karl, 1997). The idea of the "paradox of plenty" stems from the resource curse theory which summarily argues that countries with abundant presence of natural resources (especially in the global South, as in the case of African countries) have lower economic growth and worse development outcomes despite the resource availability (Badeeb et al., 2017; Manzano & Gutiérrez, 2019; Zhou, 2017). The curse therefore leads to these countries being prone to conflict and generally poor while having the landlord advantage over such valuable economic resources (Duruji & Dibia, 2017).

One institutional framework at the heart of the ongoing debate about how African countries can escape the natural resource curse is the creation of sovereign wealth funds (SWF) or rainy-day financial facilities (Amoako-Tuffour, 2016; Cieslik, 2014; Diallo et al., 2016; Malobola, 2020; Markowitz, 2020). A major issue in the literature on SWF is how to manage them as part of the development agenda, specifically the institutional and policy framework to ensure that returns from natural resources are optimized in the national development process, given the finite character of natural resources. The focus on the policy and institutional framework is therefore significant for three main reasons.

First, in less than a decade, the global community will reconvene to examine the extent to which the UN-sponsored Sustainable Development Goals (SDGs) have attained the desired milestones. While the 17 SDGs are focused on specific factors, they also constitute a call to address the complex relations among people, the planet, and prosperity (UNDP, 2015). It is also important to note that issues like natural resource management and climate change, the focus of this chapter, involve several SDGs in direct and indirect ways. For example, SDG 1 (no poverty), SDG 2 (zero hunger), SDG 8 (decent work and economic growth), SDG 9 (innovation and infrastructure), SDG 10 (reduced inequalities), SDG 13 (climate action), SDG 16 (peace, justice, and strong institutions) and SDG 17 (partnership).

Second, the prospects of the success of the SDGs are confronted with two main interrelated factors, the impact of the COVID-19 global pandemic on the global economy and the tensions and missed opportunities that continue to bedevil the transition towards the green economy, especially in a framework of sustainable development. At the same time, there are significant opportunities for African countries to employ digitalization to enhance the prospects of sustainable development in a post-COVID-19 world. One aspect of pushing the frontiers in terms of sustainable development has been the importance of technology. The focus has been on technological innovations that have the potential in addressing environmental problems. Digitalization, as a form of technological advancement, implies the creation of new patterns of production, consumption, and opportunity for economic development, based on innovative computer technologies (Mondejara et al., 2021). As Mondejar et al. (2021: 1) put it, digitalization provides "access to an integrated network of unexploited big data with potential benefits for society and the environment," thereby generating opportunities for strategically addressing challenges associated with environmental sustainability, equitability, and a healthy society. Yang et al. (2021) opined that the increased momentum of digitalization has enormously transformed the "global way of doing" in all ramifications. This implies a fusion of digital technologies into our everyday lives (Aghimien et al., 2020; Mondejar et al., 2021).

Third, several African countries have established SWFs and have some of the minerals that can aid the transition to the green economy (ANRC, 2021a; Geng et al., 2019; Olawuyi, 2021; Markowtiz, 2020). However, the literature is yet to sufficiently grasp how natural resource wealth can be harnessed, against the backdrop of digitalization, in the transition to the green economy in a post-COVID-19 world. It is therefore important to engage in a study on the extent to which African countries can respond to the opportunities and related challenges, not only in terms of SWFs, but harnessing the rare minerals as part of discussions on the green economy. This chapter analyzes SWFs, against the backdrop of natural resources management in Africa, with a specific focus on countries that are producing some of the rare minerals essential in the transition towards a green economy. The chapter pays close attention to how digitalization can facilitate natural resources management in terms of SWF and the green economy with the appropriate policies and institutions for sustainable development in Africa. The chapter is divided into three sections. Section one examines the broad literature on natural resources management in Africa and the place of SWFs in natural resources management. The second section discusses sustainable development, digitalization and surveys specific African countries endowed with the rare minerals essential to the transition towards a green economy. The final section discusses the relationship between natural resources management and the prospects of the green economy in Africa, before proceeding to a conclusion and remarks on policy directions.

Natural Resources Management and the SWF in Africa

At the global level, one instrument in the natural resources management regime is the sovereign wealth fund (SWF). The instrument can be traced to the 1950s, with the establishment of the Kuwait Investment Fund in 1953 to invest excess oil revenue. Since then, several countries, from Singapore (1981) to Norway (1990) have established SWFs as an investment vehicle. Botswana, the first African country with an SWF, launched the Pula Investment Fund in 1994 to manage revenue from the diamond market. In the aftermath of the 2008 global financial crisis, several countries became interested in the role of SWFs in national development. Thus, countries with a SWF created the International Working Group of Sovereign Wealth Funds (IWGSWF), in conjunction with organizations such as the International Monetary Fund (IMF) and the Group of Twenty Countries (G20). The IWGSWF, in 2009, endorsed the Kuwait Declaration and paved the way for the International Forum for Sovereign Wealth Funds (IFSWF).

> SWFs are special purpose investment funds or arrangements owned by the general government. Created by the government for macroeconomic purposes, SWFs hold, manage, or administer assets to achieve financial objectives, and employ a set of investment strategies which include investing in foreign financial assets. The SWFs are commonly established out of balance of payments surpluses, official foreign currency operations, the proceeds of privatizations, fiscal surpluses, and/or receipts resulting from commodity exports (IWGSWF, 2008: 27).

At the global level, countries with SWF have also signed onto the set of principles known as the Santiago Principles, 24 voluntary organizational principles to govern SWFs (IFSWF, 2016). The goal of the principles is to utilize SWF to create wealth and improve the human development of the citizens of a given country as part of the broader debate of the role of natural resources in development. The debate is significant because the African state, contrary to pronouncements on its demise under contemporary neoliberal globalization, continues to be the primary site and viable partner in national development (Hanson et al., 2014; Puplampu, 2014a). Given that national development is not an apolitical exercise, political calculations will always factor into how resources are explored and allocated in the name of national development.

The African state, its political calculations, including leadership are critical factors in the institutional framework, policy and regulatory regimes, utilization, planning, options, and choices in natural resources management (ACBF, 2013, 2019; Hanson et al., 2014). For example, policies on how to manage natural resources will require political leadership and a prominent role for non-state actors or social forces. As Puplampu (2014b) argues, political leadership sets the tone for natural resources management, providing strategic policy options and the willingness to adopt available policy choices while working with a range of non-state actors.

SWFs are one policy choice to minimize the curse and elevate the blessing in natural resources management. Three interrelated variables underpin a SWF: motive, nature, and the organizational structure. The variables which imply notions of ownership, investment strategies, as well as the purpose and objectives take a different form and significance in each country (IWGSWF, 2008, 27). While the motive is the formal or official reasons for establishing the fund, these reasons and the subsequent activities require insights into the nature and organizational structure of the fund. A SWF can be created for the purpose of intergenerational transfer, parking, and stabilization (Quantum Global, 2014; Wills et al., 2016).

The intergenerational transfer fund is designed to counteract the cyclical or finite nature of resource revenue. A properly managed intergenerational SWF aligns with sustainable development in the sense that revenue from today can be managed to be of value to present and future members of a resource-endowed society. That, of course, means intergenerational accounts are savings vehicles that need to be managed in a prudent manner with clearly defined goals, processes, and outcomes. The point is that the value of intergenerational funds will depend on the extent of savings, the currency instrument, the volume of the windfall, and a diversified portfolio (Quantum Global, 2014).

Another aspect of SWFs is the desire to save money, not only for the present but also for future use, hence the spending of resource wealth also deserves attention, especially in terms of present needs of the society. On spending in the present, the expectation is that it "is tightly managed, [because] intergenerational funds need strong, independent and transparent governance" (Wills et al., 2016: ii7). For example, Norway and Alaska have been spending their natural resource wealth in ways and that could offer lessons to African countries (Cappelen & Mjøset, 2009; Moss & Young, 2009; Olawuyi & Onifade, 2018). While Norway routes sovereign funds into general government revenue, the state of Alaska basically shares the funds directly to citizens of the state. For either system to continue, the funds would have to be properly managed and situated in a nearly apolitical policy and legal regime. A SWF requires both clarity in its nature and organizational processes when it comes to the motives of parking and stabilization.

The parking motive of the SWF is about when and where to invest and the optimum time or conditions under which to dip into or draw on these investments (Amoako-Tuffour, 2016; Venables & Wills, 2016).

Venebles and Mills (2016) identify macro and micro constrains on investment options and the spending of parking funds. The macro constrains come from the demand side, specifically public spending, and mining investment, while the micro demonstrates capacity inadequacies relative to the design and development of public investment projects. The parking dimension of SWFs, like intergenerational funds, also requires adequate monitoring and oversight.

The third motive of SWFs, stabilization of funds, is to minimize the volatility of resource revenue (Quantum Global, 2014). As the name implies, it is to shield government spending in the face of volatile resource revenue. The argument is that with high commodity prices, resource revenue will increase, and the opposite occurs with low commodity prices. The response of political leaders to either case reveals the significance of stabilization funds in public revenue, spending priorities, and options in general as was the case in Norway in the 1980s and Chile, first in 1985 and then in 2000 (Wills et al., 2016).

Many African countries have established SWFs alongside their partners in the global community (Table 6.1). Two points were worth stressing. First, apart from Botswana's Pula Fund and Ghana's Heritage Fund that were established in the mid-1990s, all the others were set up in the 2000s.

Second, as Table 6.1 shows, apart from Botswana's SWF based on diamond, the others are mainly based on revenue from oil. The SWFs in Angola, Botswana, Libya, and Nigeria have membership in the global International Forum for Sovereign Wealth Funds (IFSWF), committed to and signed the institute's Santiago Principles on the management and governance of SWFs. The SWFs in the four African countries therefore require further remarks on issues such the stated goals or objectives, source of the funds, ownership, investment, and management of assets.

The Angola SWF, Fundo Soberano de Angola (FSDEA), established in 2012, was set up as a saving fund for stabilization to support national development priorities, specifically around infrastructure and targeted sectors like agriculture, water, power generation, and transport both within and outside of the African continent (Cieślik, 2014: 116; Markowitz, 2020: 15). The fund, made up of oil revenue, seeks to protect capital, maximize returns in the long term and anchor the development of infrastructure. FSDEA, commits to good governance and signed the Santiago Principles, it is independently managed by the Banco Nacional de Angola (BNA) and the Treasury, with governance oversight from the Office of the Presidency, has investments in Portugal, with impressive

Table 6.1 Selected SWFs in Africa

Country, year	Type and Name of SWF	Assets value	Source
Angola (2012)	Fund Soberano de Angola	$2 billion	Oil
Botswana (1994)	Pula Fund	$4.33 billion	Diamond
Chad (2006)	Oil Revenue Management Plan	Unknown	Oil
Equatorial Guinea (2004)	Fund for Future Generations	$80 million	Oil
Gabon (2011; 2004)	Sovereign Fund of the Gabonese Rep	$1 billion	Oil
Ghana (1994; 2011)	Ghana Heritage Fund Ghana Stabilization Fund	$485.17 million $381.2 million	Oil
Libya (2006)	Libya Investment Authority	$67 billion	Oil
Mauritania (2006)	National Fund for Hydrocarbon Reserves	$150 million	Oil
Nigeria (2004; 2011)	Excess Crude Account Nigeria Sovereign Investment Authority	$323.7 million $1.69 billion	Oil
Uganda (2015)	Petroleum Revenue Investment Reserve	$125.87 million	Oil

Source Markowitz (2020: 13)

returns or outcomes, but was the site of charges of mismanagement and corruption (ACBF, 2013: 196; Basseti et al., 2020; Markowitz, 2020).

Botswana was the first African country to establish a SWF. The Pula Fund, a long-term investment instrument made of foreign exchange reserves, excess from the export of diamonds, and is managed and fully housed within the domain of the Bank of Botswana (IFSWF, 2008; Markowitz, 2020). The Government of Botswana owns a third of the Pula Fund and with the remaining two-thirds under the control of the Bank of Botswana, a government institution. Two issues are worth stressing. First, the "Pula Fund is opaque in terms of its rules [and there] are no withdrawal restrictions explicit to the Pula Fund" (Markowitz, 2020: 21). Second, the Pula Fund has basically served as a stabilization instrument and its management has been free of any major scandals (Markowitz, 2020: 22).

The Libya Investment Authority (LIA) currently has the largest value of assets for any SWF in Africa (Table 6.1). Created with funds coming from oil reserves, LIA's objective is to build and maintain a diversified investment portfolio and create a sustainable context to maximize oil revenue in the future (IFSWF, 2008: 39). LIA has investment properties abroad, managed by an international fund or money managers, internal local partners and with jurisdictions in several African countries. Finally, Nigeria's SWF developed in two phases (Markowtiz, 2020; Triki & Faye, 2011: 18). The first phase began in 2004 with an Excess Crude Account (ECA), located in the Nigerian Central Bank, without any legal foundation and its utilization was subject to the whims and caprices of the Office of the Presidency. Thus, in 2011, the second phase, the Nigerian Sovereign Investment Authority (NSIA) was legally constituted and charged with three separate envelopes: the Future Generations Fund (savings); the Stabilization Fund, and the National Infrastructure Investment Fund (a domestic investment facility) (IFSWF, 2020; Markowitz, 2020: 30–31). The NSIA, as a legal and independent entity, is beyond the ambit of political authorities and even the Nigeria Central Bank, though the President of the Republic leads NSIA's governing council (Markowitz, 2020: 32). With a revamped institutional framework, the NSIA has led to improvements in the utilization of resource wealth, but the ECA continues to be available or at the disposal of political elites and their operatives (Markowitz, 2020: 34–35).

Beyond the illustrations in Table 6.1, there are several other African countries, for example South Africa, on the verge of creating a SWF (Malobola, 2020). However, the country has not yet established the much-touted fund largely because of the lack of fiscal capacity and the impact of COVID-19 which required a redirection of resources (Qobo & Soko, 2022). While there is enthusiasm for the establishment of SWFs, the acid test is the performance and role of SWFs to attain their policy objectives, both stated and unstated, and their contribution to natural resources management and development in Africa. Beyond the broader implications of the SWF, the discovery of rare minerals and their significance in the transition to the green economy reinforces insights into the natural resources management regime in Africa. These insights can be gleaned by examining the relationship between digitalization and sustainable development.

Sustainable Development and Digitalization: The Green Economy and Rare Minerals

The history of sustainable development is linked to global attempts to address the relationship between human nature and environmental resources. Against the findings of the Brundtland Report, the World Commission on Environment and Development (WCED) (1987: 37) conceptualized sustainable development as the "development that meets the needs of the present without compromising the ability of future generations to meet their own needs." This conceptualization has informed the subsequent global discourse on the environment and development, beginning with the 1992 Rio Earth Summit, the 2002 Johannesburg World Summit on sustainability and pollution, and the 2012 Rio+20 Earth Summit. The 2012 Rio+20's main outcome, *The Future We Want*, has become the framework for any assessment of the global commitment to sustainable development within the context of the needs and priorities of both the global North and global South (Ishwaran, 2012). Equally significant is the United Nations General Assembly 2015 Agenda 2030 resolution on "Transforming Our World: The 2030 Agenda for Sustainable Development" (Lanshina et al., 2020). The relationship between digitalization and the green economy is about the deployment of digital smart technologies to ensure sustainable economic growth while guaranteeing the integration and attainment of sustainable development goals.

The discourse of a green economy reveals how technological advancement and digitalization can underpin sustainable development. While digital technologies and the green economy are vital for sustainable development, the global pandemic has brought to the fore the striking importance of a low-carbon green economy (Lanshina et al., 2020). The green economy implies the formation of economic activities to produce low-carbon emission, resource use efficiency, and social inclusivity with an emphasis on issues such as renewable energy sources, sustainable agriculture, energy-efficient technologies, sustainable forest management, and a circular economy (Siyobi, 2021). Digital technologies make the green sector more technically efficient and reliable, however, the increase in digitalization is accompanied by contradictory positive and negative effects on the environment (Kunkel & Matthess, 2020; Lanshina et al., 2020; Vishnevsky et al., 2021).

In the case of the former, digital technology can improve the environment through the development of environmentally friendly technologies, improve economic efficiencies and reduce the burden on natural resource consumption and the environment in general. For the latter, digitalization may increase the environmental burden in terms of energy consumption during production, use, and disposal of information and communication technology-related products. Thus, there is the need to manage and ensure environmental sustainability while recognizing the developmental potentials of technological advancement in the last two decades. These developments have necessitated thinking around the relationship between digitalization and the discourse on the green economy, since issues in the environment and socioeconomic development can no longer be considered in isolation (Litvinenko, 2018). Digitalization continues to transform economies and part of the drive towards environmental quality, sustainability, and increases in the use of carbon-free energy resources, in sum, the business environment and organizational culture (Langthaler & Bazafkan, 2020).

The literature on digitalization and environmental sustainability in developing countries, especially those in Africa, is relatively limited (Kunkel & Matthess, 2020). To Atiase et al. (2022), one underlying reason must be the nature of internet connectivity, a situation that reveals the complexities of African economies, societies, and the environment in a context of digitalization. More so, the COVID-19 pandemic also exposed the unequal distribution in digitalization as well as the rising inequality and exclusion it produces, especially in Africa (Langthaler & Bazafkan, 2020). The need to minimize the environmental impact of these digitalization drives necessitates thinking around sustainability and green economy development in Africa (Nyagadza, 2021). This calls for a favorable policy environment characterized by moderate to high digital literacy. Additionally, available resources with sufficient conditions to deepen the prospects for digitalization and a green economy would be necessary for some African countries (Swartz et al., 2021).

The problem is that while digitalization is rapidly increasing in Africa, few digital solutions have reached a critical mass of nations. The initiatives by a few African countries are consistent in terms of process, the reduction of carbon emissions, and environmental sustainability while ensuring economic prosperity using digital technologies. For instance, in 2011, Rwanda and Ethiopia adopted policies towards green economic transformations targeted at mainstreaming low-carbon development and climate adaptation into their broader economic strategy. While the former tagged its green policy program as "Green Growth and Climate Resilience," the latter adopted the "Climate-Resilient Green Economy (CRGE)" policy (Nyagadza, 2021). In 2018, the Rwandan ministry of infrastructure commissioned large-scale PV solar plants to increase environmental sustainability in the energy sector by developing ICT-enabled renewable energy integration (Kunkel & Matthess, 2020). In 2013/2014, supported by the United Nations Development Programme, Mozambique also adopted a "Green Economy Action Plan" based on inclusive growth towards middle-income status by 2030. It is pertinent to note that while policy plays a crucial role in development, Patrick (2020) argued that there is a gap between policy and reality in Africa.

The search for natural resources that can enhance cleaner production fields, from the automobile, specifically electric vehicles, to other industries have focused on reducing fossil fuel emissions through the production of lithium-ion batteries (LIB). These batteries require not only lithium and cobalt, but also manganese, nickel, aluminum, graphite, rare earth elements (REE), iron, copper as well as phosphate. Several African countries are leading producers of some of these minerals (African Natural Resources Centre (ANRC), 2021a). For example, both the Democratic Republic of Congo (DRC), and Zimbabwe have known significant deposits of lithium. In terms of cobalt, the DRC, once again, is a major site, with about 51% of global reserves and together with other countries like Madagascar, South Africa, and Morocco were producing about 70% of global production in 2019 (ANRC, 2021b: 17). There are different formats of production systems of these valuable minerals in Africa. In Zimbabwe, for instance, lithium production is at the basic level, while DRC relies on artisanal and small-scale miners in the production of lithium with Morocco as the only African country producing cobalt as a primary mineral. Thus, the production systems in several African countries are not anchored into any industrial or value-chain context, even though these commodities are subject to forces of supply and demand (ANRC, 2021b).

From the supply side, the informal artisanal and small-scale mining sector as the major source of supply for lithium and cobalt has grave implications. Cobalt operations in DRC "are a serious risk due to concerns about the use of child labor in the extraction" process, as such several "countries in the Western world are so concerned that they are considering excluding the DRC from the global supply chain by boycotting its cobalt or by developing technologies that use alternatives to cobalt, thereby excluding the DRC" (ANRC, 2021b: 20). The situation is not significantly different in the production of lithium in Zimbabwe, with South Africa as the only country that has a robust value-chain mechanism (ANRC, 2021b: 20–21b). On the demand side, China, as the largest manufacturer of electric batteries, secures more than 50% of the market share while several countries in the global North, including USA, account for the remaining market share (ANRC, 2021b: 21). The next section will address the complexities in natural resources management, digitalization, and the green economy in Africa.

Natural Resources Management and the Green Economy in Africa

Given that natural resources are finite, their role in the transition to the green economy, in a context of digitalization and sustainable development, provides several analytical pathways. One analytical thrust is the policy and institutional in the management of SWF. Apart from Botswana, the other African countries, Angola, Libya and Nigeria, which signed on to the provisions of the International Forum for Sovereign Wealth Funds (IFSWF) inspired Santiago Principles, which focus on, among other things, using natural resources to improve the human development of their citizens, continue to occupy the lower levels of the human development index (UNDP, 2022). There is therefore a significant disconnect between the direct role of natural resources worth and economic growth. A significant factor is that the existence of a SWF, per se, does not equate human development. Rather, any successful "economic strategies in fossil fuel dependent African countries will need to balance managing traditional carbon-intensive assets (and their volatility) and the transition to a low-carbon growth model" (Siyobi, 2021: 11). Otherwise, the region will only reflect the case of Nigeria, one of the largest oil-producing countries in the world, but according to World Bank estimates had 86.9 million citizens below the poverty line and a situation not different in other mineral-rich countries such as South Africa, Zimbabwe, and Angola (cited in Siyobi, 2021: 10).

The persistence of depravity suggests that most of the African governments with SWFs have not managed their natural resources wealth in a manner that will uplift their citizens and enable them to escape the natural resource curse. Clearly missing in the natural resources management regime in several African countries is a supportive policy and institutional regime. While the Botswana Pula Fund has been managed in a relatively free chaotic environment, it took the Government of Nigeria a long time to establish the Nigerian Sovereign Investment Authority (NSIA) as a legal and independent body that is authoritatively situated beyond the reach of political elites. Thus, with a sound institutional leadership, the NSIA can play a more meaningful role in the natural resources and development nexus in Nigeria. Perhaps, it is important to situate what Siyobi (2021) calls stranded assets in the debate on extractives, climate and the circular economy in the post-COVID-19 era. COVID-19 led to a significant decline in the export revenue in oil revenue-dependent countries such as Nigeria and Libya. This "demonstrates that not all countries reliant on fossil fuels will be impacted in the same way. The oil-dependent economies [were] more severely affected due to the significant oil price drop exacerbated by the COVID-19 pandemic" (Siyobi, 2021: 8). The question then is the fortunes of African countries that have some of the rare minerals that are critical to the transition to a green economy.

Put differently, the issue is whether African countries which are home to cobalt, lithium, and the other rare minerals essential to a green economy, can provide a new model to analyze the role of natural resources in development and the possibility to transcend or rethink the resource curse. Arezki and Brueckner (2021) examined the conflict resource curse which is the incidence of higher risk of conflict in a resource-rich country in terms of military expenditure. The study found that countries with large military expenditure experience minimal conflict, probably to keep the peace, but at the expense of economic growth and deepening democracy. Although the study focused on North African and Middle Eastern countries, the conflict and human development via resources will have resonance in the case of several African countries, particularly the DRC.

DRC presents a useful exemplar in the discourse of digitalization and green economy adoption and development in Africa at two levels. In one context, the country can sequestrate carbon as well as the massive deforestation in the country estimated at 0.27% per year with policies such as the Reduced Emissions from Deforestation and Forest Degradation (REDD+) (Calvão & Archer, 2021; Samndong & Vatn, 2018). Any quest for environmental governance with the aim to protect the DRC forest and serve as carbon storage would be essential towards the drive for a green economy. At a second level, the mining sector with the discovery of cobalt and increases in digitalization has huge implications for the green economy. To ensure the curtailment of the environmental degradation necessitated by these mining activities and to ensure environmental restoration and sustainability, policies such as the Clean Cobalt Framework and the digital-based certification technologies program were enacted to ensure a drive towards a green economy and environmental sustainability (Sovacool, 2019).

The dilemma or persistent problem in that mining in the digital age in DRC is not problem-free (Benkenstein, 2022; Siyobi, 2021; Smith, 2022). To Benkenstein (2022), a key part of the discussion on the green economy in the age of COVID-19 is the need to re-evaluate and re-imagine existing systems of thought in how human beings relate to nature, in a broad sense. For Africa, Benkenstein (2022: 8–9) identifies not only opportunities in the relations among power, new forms of technology, such as digitalization, resource demand, and productive, but also significant risks. For instance, while DRC has green minerals such as cobalt and lithium, the infrastructural deficit in terms of limited processing capacity and governance failures in state and society relations will limit outcomes. The local based artisanal workers are locked in a struggle with private big companies for their survival in an environment of state capture and failure (Smith, 2022).

While digitalization and its smart devices are supposed to increase and advance green technologies and support the green economy, the role of these technologies with respect to rare minerals has created a sustainability dilemma (Adams, 2017). This is because with lithium, cobalt, and the REE as critical components of the push towards a green economy, there are significant questions for African countries, especially from a regional perspective to consider. The argument is a forceful one:

> Africa relies on imports from manufacturers of Li-Co consumer products in other continents and if that is to continue into the EV era, Africa will not only continue to import the vehicles themselves, but also the components to fuel EV, like the LIB [lithium-ion battery].... Due to the requirement to reduce greenhouse gases (GHG) in the environment, fossil fuels are gradually being exited and green energy substitutes, partly driven by the availability of LIB, are being developed as alternatives for the future (ANRC, 2021b: 21–22).

As Kelley et al. (2021) observed, increasing technological advancement propels demand for the non-fuel mineral resources vital for the low-carbon economy. The increasing demand for rare mineral would impact the environmental, social impact of extraction, and ultimately sustainability (McLellan et al., 2014). That is why the ANRC (2021a) identifies supply and demand opportunities and challenges in harnessing the rare earth element (REE) value chain as contributory factors to socioeconomic development in Africa and the global low-carbon transition in terms of the green economy. As stated earlier, from the supply side, the mining operations continue to occur in a policy vacuum and without any consideration of the social and environmental conflicts (Ali, 2014). From a comparative perspective, environmental compliant mining jurisdictions such as China, Malaysia, and Australia established that socio-environmental issues, such as the implications of earth processing in health (in terms of radioactive and non-radioactive contaminations), are important concerns in the rare minerals mining industry (Ali, 2014). Hence, a sustainability concern can impact the present needs and future wants. In this sense, there is an interplay between mining on the environment and human society.

With a focus on sustainability thinking and digitalization, Litvinenko (2020) stressed the importance of the digital economy in the mining sector with the shift from fossil fuel given the projected increases in energy consumption. McLellan et al. (2014) argued that while sustainability concerns in terms of the environmental impact of production and distribution of rare earth elements (extraction, processing, use, waste disposal, and recycling) are important, the implementations are relatively least developed. The underlining problem is that despite the different legislative structures in the world, the African situation is compounded by the underfunding of the information and computing infrastructure and that poses a significant challenge and undermines the development of the global mineral market (Litvinenko, 2020). In any case, the onset of the green economy, rare minerals, and digitalization can be seen as a positive contribution to sustainable development.

Considering the high dependence of modern societies and the environment on technologies, it becomes imperative to assess contemporary technological development given past and present developments as well as future needs. Digitalization and sustainability combine to shape the economy and society towards transformation for sustainable development (Castro et al., 2021). In this sense, the synergy among society, economy, and environment is important. With digitalization leading to continuous advancement and transformation in societal information absorption capabilities and connectedness, there is a real possibility of a more informed and empowered society (Castro et al., 2021). These breakthroughs in computerized tools will lead to innovative high-tech concepts and digital skills in transforming conventional work approaches, from artificial intelligence to machine learning and eventually bridging geographical gaps, uniting systems and functions by making way for collaboratively work across space (Bhutani & Paliwal, 2015; Bloomberg, 2018; Jovanović et al., 2018). At stake is the impact of digital technologies on accessing, sharing, and harnessing "information in a very cost-effective, speedy and user-friendly manner" (Bhutani & Paliwal, 2015: 12). In this sense, there would be macro and micro societal adaptation, dependence, and integration of digital technologies into everyday life through transforming information access from physically collected information and knowledge into computer-readable languages. For the mining sector, robotics and sensor technology would constitute forms in the work process (Litvinenko, 2020).

While these technological changes are rapid, changes (both positive and negative) for the society in terms of development and the interactions/synergies between the people, environment, and economy are significant (Castro et al., 2021; Jovanović et al., 2018; Vishnevsky et al., 2021).

The idea is thus to carry out actions that will manage present needs while simultaneously providing human well-being and biodiversity benefits without compromising the ability of future generations to meet their own needs. Sustainability via digitalization would be key in the UN SDGs (Balogun et al., 2020; Castro et al., 2021; Jacob, 2018). However, digitalization without considerations of social, human, and environmental implications would spell doom in the long run (Balogun et al., 2020; Fernández-Portill et al., 2019). Karki and Thapa (2021) argued that while digitalization concerns itself with the production, consumption, and disposal of information and technology for the advancement of human and the environment, sustainable development goals, sustainability, on the other hand, see development as complex, interrelated, and interdependent. In this sense, digitalization must consider social and environmental factors and economic value to stay useful. While digitalization would impact the attainment of SDGs in many ways, the literature is yet to address policy gaps and opportunities in terms of the green economy

(Castro et al., 2021; Kostoska & Kocarev, 2019; Vinuesa et al., 2020; Wu et al., 2018).

Digitalization in a context to protect biodiversity, optimize green energy production, can provide access to an integrated network of unexploited big data with potential benefits for society and the environment (Mondejar et al., 2021). This is especially important in view of enhanced ICT leading to a low-carbon future, a greener and more efficient environment (Balogun et al., 2020; Jacob, 2018). Fernández-Portillo et al. (2019) argued that the impact of digitalization on SDGs can enhance resource efficiency, transparency, and access to environmental, social, and governance performance, enhance decision-making and performance prediction as well as enabling circular economy among others.

However, the implications of digitalization for SDGs are uneven across geographical spaces, creating a need for monitoring and evaluation in terms of impacts (Brennen & Kreiss, 2016). Bobylev et al. (2018) study on the Pan-Eurasian Experiment (PEEX) program and indicators for monitoring of implementation and digitalization of Sustainable Development Goals (SDG) in Russia argued that the PEEX program provides a platform for coordinating socioeconomic research between the natural sciences, anthropology, and other human activities. Balogun et al. (2020) also examined how digitalization fosters climate-friendly urban environment and social development in Africa, Asia, Australia, Europe, North America, and South America. The central point in all these studies is the influence of digitalization in realizing a sustainable green economy. The viability of a green economy can only be achieved by the growth in the digital capabilities of the society which, in turn, is influenced by the presence of technologies and the overall political, economic, and social health of the society.

Policy Directions and Conclusion

This chapter examined natural resources management in the context of digitalization and the green economy in Africa. From the natural resources management angle, the focus was on sovereign wealth funds. While several countries have established these funds, the specific interest is the extent to which such funds would enable the respective countries to escape the natural resource curse and turn resource endowments into a blessing. Equally important in this study is the context of digitalization, sustainable development, and the transition to the green economy.

The natural resource regime, like any other system involving access to resources, is fraught with conflicts, political adventurism, and persistent power struggle. Therefore, the entrenched power sites are locked in conflict with other social forces in the control of and benefits from mineral resources. Such struggles are even likely to magnify with the increasing importance of REE in the context of weak, captured, or non-existent state policies and institutions in the drive towards sustainable development, digitalization, and the green economy.

The study focused on how the interaction between internal and external in terms of structural and substantive factors would affect the transition to a green economy. The same range of factors at play in natural resource as a curse are also at play in the production of the minerals towards the green economy. Indeed, while many African countries have a proven track record in the announcement and establishment of worthwhile development policies and institutions, policy and institutional effectives have been problematic. If African countries want to utilize natural resources in a sustainable manner based on digitalization and the green economy, the following suggestions, though not, novel, are worth stressing.

First, the goals and objectives of natural resources in the development agenda must be clearly defined, and institutions properly funded with viable policies that can address both short-term and long-term development needs. There is a persistent problem when politicians with a short-term mindset interact with policy bureaucrats, who as professionals tend to think in the long-term, even though because of the broader weak state institutions, are easily captured by political leaders. Thus, the need for effective oversight of all state institutions, from the executive, to legislative, judiciary, and autonomous state agencies should not all be on paper, but also when it comes to their activities.

Second, there is a legitimate case for the role of non-state actors, as part of the broader civil society to assert themselves, in line with the democratic governance when it comes to the natural resource wealth and the development agenda. At stake is how to advance democratic governance and holding governments to account for the sustainable management of natural resources. It is clear that "established democracies will not insist on democratic credentials in [mineral-rich African countries that offer [their] multinational oil companies an interrupted flow of [rare earth elements]. That realization suggests that changes or attempts at sustaining democratic and economic governance will have to begin from internal social forces" (Puplampu, 2014b: 176). Clearly, there is a need to minimize politics in the operations of natural resource management institutions, but rather accentuate the values of democratic governance, elements that are sorely lacking in most natural resource-rich African countries.

Finally, the prospects of African countries to better manage the resource income from lithium in the context of digitalization and the green economy calls for the need to rethink the role of regional aspects of the value-chain considerations in digitalization and natural resources management (ANRC, 2021a, b). Given the competitive and unpredictable nature of the demand and supply forces at play in the transition to the green economy, African countries have to be mindful of issues in the entire value chain, from mining to processing, marketing, and consumption of outcomes like batteries for electric vehicles. The South African energy company, the Megamillion Energy Company, for example, must explore how to synergize with suppliers either within the sub-regional Southern Africa Development Community (SADC) or similar regional entities on the continent (ANRC, 2021b: 18).

A continent-wide approach under the African Continental Free Trade Agreement (AfCFTA) would more likely lead to an ideal situation in which African countries can become leaders in the green economy and related benefits from green industrialization (Benkenstein, 2022: 9). This is also the context for specific continental initiatives such as the African Minerals Development Centre (AMDC) that can liaise with regional economic communities to influence and advise policymakers in terms of the investment and regulatory environment that can maximize the value chain in the mining section (ANRC, 2021a: 18). These possibilities reinforce the argument that African political leaders must be mindful of an old African adage that "charity begins at home." This calls for the need to have capable internal policies and institutions that can interact with external forces, and abandon any grandiose view that having natural resources, per se, will lead to a green economy that is anchored by sustainable development.

References

Adams, W. M. (2017). Sleeping with the enemy? Biodiversity conservation, corporations and the green economy. *Journal of Political Ecology*, 20, 243–257.

African Capacity Building Foundation (ACBF). (2013). *The Africa capacity indicators 2013—Capacity development in natural resources management*. African Capacity Building Foundation.
African Capacity Building Foundation (ACBF). (2019). *Africa capacity report 2019—Fostering transformative leadership for Africa's development*. African Capacity Building Foundation.
African Development Bank (AfDB). (2007). *African development report 2007—Natural resources for sustainable development in Africa*. Oxford University Press.
African Development Bank (AfDB) and African Union (AU). (2009). *Oil and Gas in Africa*. Oxford University Press.
African Natural Resources Centre (ANRC). (2021a). *Rare earth elements (REE). Value chain analysis for mineral based industrialization in Africa*. African Development Bank. Abidjan, Côte d'Ivoire.
African Natural Resources Centre (ANRC). (2021b). *Lithium—Cobalt value chain analysis for mineral based industrialization in Africa*. African Development Bank. Abidjan, Côte d'Ivoire.
Aghimien, D., Aigbavboa, C., Oke, A., & Aghimien, L. (2020). Latent institutional environment factors influencing construction digitalization in South Africa. *International Journal of Construction Education and Research, 18*(2), 142–158.
Ali, S. H. (2014). Social and environmental impact of the rare earth industries. *Resources, 3*(1), 123–134.
Amoako-Tuffour, J. (2016). Should countries invest resource revenues abroad when demands for public infrastructure are pressing at home? The dilemma of sovereign wealth funds in Sub-Saharan Africa. *Journal of African Economies, 25*(2), ii41–ii58. https://doi.org/10.1093/jae/ejw015
Arezki, R., & Brueckner, M. (2021). *Between a rock and a hard place: A new perspective on the resource curse* (Working Paper Series N° 351). African Development Bank, Abidjan, Côte d'Ivoire.
Atiase, V. Y., Agbanyo, S., Ameh, J. K., Sambian, R. M., & Ganza, P. (2022). Creating value for whom? Digitization and governance practices of nontraditional export firms in Africa. *Strategic Change, 31*(1), 31–44.
Auty, R. (1993). *Sustaining development in mineral economies: The resource curse thesis*. Routledge.
Badeeb, R. A., Lean, H. H., & Clark, J. (2017). The evolution of the natural resource curse thesis: A critical literature survey. *Resources Policy, 51*, 123–134.
Balogun, A. L., Marks, D., Sharma, R., Shekhar, H., Balmes, C., Maheng, D., Arshad, A., & Salehi, P. (2020). Assessing the potentials of digitalization as a tool for climate change adaptation and sustainable development in urban centres. *Sustainable Cities and Society, 53*, 101888.

Barma, N. H., Kaiser, K., Le, T. M., & Viñuela, L. (2012). *Rents to riches: The political economy of natural resource-led development*. World Bank.

Basseti, V., Landau, K., & Glandorf, J. (2020). A master class in corruption: The Luanda Leaks across the natural resource value chain, https://www.brookings.edu/blog/up-front/2020/07/23/a-master-class-in-corruption-the-luandaleaks-across-the-natural-resource-value-chain/

Benkenstein, A. (2022). *Transitions and resilience: Natural resource governance trends in Africa*. South African Institute of International Affairs (Policy Insights, No. 134). (www.saiia.org.za)

Bhutani, S., & Paliwal, Y. (2015). Digitalization: A step towards sustainable development. *OIDA International Journal of Sustainable Development, 8*(12), 11–24.

Bloomberg, J. (2018, August 28). Digitization, digitalization, and digital transformation: confuse them at your peril. *Forbes*. p. 2019.

Bobylev, S. N., Chereshnya, O. Y., Kulmala, M., Lappalainen, H. K., Petäjä, T., Solov'eva, S. V., Tikunov, V. S., & Tynkkynen, V. P. (2018). Indicators for digitalization of sustainable development goals in PEEX program. *Geography, Environment, Sustainability, 11*(1), 145–156.

Brennen, J. S., & Kreiss, D. (2016). Digitalization. In R. T. Craig (Ed.), *The international encyclopedia of communication theory and philosophy* (pp. 1–11). Wiley. https://doi.org/10.1002/9781118766804.wbiect111

Calvão, F., & Archer, M. (2021). Digital extraction: Blockchain traceability in mineral supply chains. *Political Geography, 87*, 102381. https://doi.org/10.1016/j.polgeo.2021.102381

Cappelen, A., & L. Mjøset, L. (2009). *Can Norway be a role model for natural resource abundant countries?* United nations University-world institute for development economics research, Research Paper No. 2009/23.

Castro, D. R. G., Fernández, M. C. G., & Colsa, Á. U. (2021). Unleashing the convergence amid digitalization and sustainability towards pursuing the Sustainable Development Goals (SDGs): A holistic review. *Journal of Cleaner Production*. https://doi.org/10.1016/j.jclepro.2020.122204

Cieslik, E. (2014, December). African sovereign wealth funds: Facts and figures. *Gospodarka Narodowa*. https://doi.org/10.33119/GN/100892

Diallo, B., Tchana, F. T., & Zeufack, A. G. (2016). *Sovereign wealth funds and long-term investments in Sub-Saharan Africa* (Policy Research Working Paper 7903). World Bank Group (Macroeconomics and Fiscal Management Global Practice Group and Africa Region Office of the Chief Economist).

Duruji, M., & Dibia, O. (2017). Crude oil, resource curse and the splintering of Nigeria into national pieces. *Covenant Journal of Business and Social Sciences, 8*(2). https://doi.org/10.20370/cjbss.v8i2.697

European Union (EU). (2019). *Sustainable development in the European Union—Monitoring report on progress towards the SDGs in an EU Context.* https://doi.org/10.2785/44964

Fernández-Portillo, A., Almodóvar-González, M., Coca-Perez, J. L., & Jiménez-Naranjo, H. V. (2019). Is sustainable economic development possible thanks to the deployment of ICT? *Sustainability, 11*(22), 6307.

Geng, Y., Sarkis, J., & Bleischwitz, R. (2019). How to globalize the circular economy. *Nature, 565*(7738), 153–155.

Hanson, K. T., D'Alessandro, C., & Owusu, F. (Eds.). (2014). *Managing Africa's natural resources: Capacities for development.* Palgrave Macmillan.

Industrial Policy Action Plan. (2018). Economic sectors, employment and infrastructure development cluster 2018/19–2020/21. *Political Geography, 87*, p.102381. https://www.gov.za/sites/default/files/gcis_document/201805/industrial-policy-actionplan.pdfchains

International Forum for Sovereign Wealth Funds (IFSWF). (2016). *Implementing the Santiago principles: 12 case studies—From demonstrating commitment to creating value.* International Forum for Sovereign Wealth Funds.

International Forum for Sovereign Wealth Fund. (IFSWF). (2020). *The rise of a bipolar world Sovereign wealth fund views on the global macro outlook.* International Forum for Sovereign Wealth Fund.

International Working Group for Sovereign Wealth Fund (IWGSWF). (2008). *Sovereign wealth funds—general accepted of principles and practices "santiago principles".* International Working Group for Sovereign Wealth Funds.

Ishwaran, N. (2012). After Rio+20: Translating words in action. *Environmental Development, 4*, 184–185. https://doi.org/10.1016/j.envdev.2012.09.006

Jacob, P. (2018). Information and communication technology in shaping urban low carbon development pathways. *Current Opinion in Environmental Sustainability, 30*, 133–137.

Jovanović, M., Dlačić, J., & Okanović, M. (2018). Digitalization and society's sustainable development–Measures and implications. *Zbornik Radova Ekonomskog Fakulteta u Rijeci: Časopis Za Ekonomsku Teoriju i Praksu, 36*(2), 905–928.

Karki, Y., & Thapa, D. (2021). Exploring the link between digitalization and sustainable development: research agendas. In *Responsible AI and analytics for an ethical and inclusive digitized society: 20th IFIP WG 6.11 conference on e-business, e-services and e-society, I3E 2021, Galway, Ireland, September 1–3, 2021, Proceedings 20* (pp. 330–341). Springer International Publishing.

Karl, T. (1997). *The paradox of plenty: Oil booms and petro-states.* University of California Press.

Kelley, K. D., Huston, D. L., & Peter, J. M. (2021). Toward an effective global green economy: The critical minerals mapping initiative (CMMI). *SGA News, 8*, 1–5.

Kostoska, O., & Kocarev, L. (2019). A novel ICT framework for sustainable development goals. *Sustainability, 11*(7), 1961.

Kunkel, S., & Matthess, M. (2020). Digital transformation and environmental sustainability in industry: Putting expectations in Asian and African policies into perspective. *Environmental Science & Policy, 112*, 318–329.

Langthaler, M., & Bazafkan, H. (2020). *Digitalization, education and skills development in the global South: An assessment of the debate with a focus on Sub-Saharan Africa* (No. 28). ÖFSE Briefing Paper.

Lanshina, T. A., Barinova, V. A., Kondratyev, A. D., & Romantsov, M. V. (2020). Sustainable development and digitalization: The unusual COVID-19 crisis requires original solutions. *Bulletin of International Organizations, 15*(4), 91–114.

Litvinenko, V. (Ed.). (2018). *Innovation-based development of the mineral resources sector: Challenges and prospects*. CRC Press. https://doi.org/10.1201/9780429022388

Litvinenko, V. S. (2020). Digital economy as a factor in the technological development of the mineral sector. *Natural Resources Research, 29*(3), 1521–1541.

Malobola, B. (2020, February 19). SA to establish a sovereign wealth fund, but what is it? *SABC News*. https://www.sabcnews.com/sabcnews/what-is-a-sovereign-wealth-fund/. Accessed 18 September 2022.

Manzano, O., & Gutiérrez, J. D. (2019). The subnational resource curse: Theory and evidence. *The Extractive Industries and Society, 6*(2), 261–266.

Markowitz, C. (2020). *Sovereign wealth funds in Africa: Taking stock and looking forward*, South African Institute of International Affairs (Occasional Paper, No. 304).

McLellan, B. C., Corder, G. D., Golev, A., & Ali, S. H. (2014). Sustainability of the rare earths industry. *Procedia Environmental Sciences, 20*, 280–287.

Mondejar, M. E., Avtar, R., Diaz, H. L. B., Dubey, R. K., Esteban, J., Gómez-Morales, A., Hallam, B., Mbungu, N. T., Okolo, C. C., Prasad, K. A., & She, Q. (2021). Digitalization to achieve sustainable development goals: Steps towards a Smart Green Planet. *Science of the Total Environment, 794*, 148539.

Moss, T., & Young, L. (2009). *Saving ghana from its oil: The case for direct cash distribution, center for global development*, Working Paper 186, Center for Global Development.

Nyagadza, B. (2021). Fostering green economies in Africa through green marketing strategies for environmental sustainability: An overview. *Journal of Environmental Media, 2*(1), 17–22.

Olawuyi, D. S. (2021). Can MENA extractive industries support the global energy transition? Current opportunities and future directions. *The Extractive Industries and Society, 8*(2), 100685.

Olawuyi, D. S., & Onifade T. T. (2018). Promoting functional distributive justice in the Nigerian sovereign wealth fund system: Lessons from Alaska and Norway. In C. Eboe-Osuji, & E. Emeseh (Eds.), *Nigerian Yearbook of International Law 2017*. Springer, Cham. https://doi.org/10.1007/978-3-319-71476-9_14

Patrick, H. O. (2020). Climate change, water security, and conflict potentials in South Africa: Assessing conflict and coping strategies in rural South Africa. *Handbook of climate change management: Research, leadership, transformation* (pp. 1–18).

Puplampu, K. P. (2014a). The shifting boundaries of the African state in agricultural institutions and policies in an era of globalization. In E. Shizha & A. A. Abdi (Eds.), *Indigenous discourses on knowledge and development in Africa* (pp. 215–227). Routledge.

Puplampu, K. P. (2014b). The capacity question, leadership and strategic choices: Environmental sustainability and natural resources management in Africa. In K. T. Hanson, C. D'Alessandro, & F. Owusu (Eds.), *Managing Africa's natural resources: Capacities for development* (pp. 162–184). Palgrave Macmillan.

Qobo, M., & Soko, M. (2022). The rise of sovereign wealth funds in the global economy: Can South Africa establish a sovereign wealth fund? *Politikon, 49*(2), 195–210. https://doi.org/10.1080/02589346.2022.2076511

Quantum Global. (2014). *Sovereign wealth funds as a driver of African development*. Quantum Global Research Lab.

Samndong, R. A., & Vatn, A. (2018). Competing tenures: Implications for REDD+ in the Democratic Republic of Congo. *Forests, 9*(11), 662.

Siyobi, B. (2021). *Stranded assets: The nexus between extractives, climate, & the circular economy within the African extractives sector*. South African Institute of International Affairs (Policy Insights, No. 112) (www.saiia.org.za)

Smith, J. H. (2022). *The eyes of the world: Mining the digital age in the eastern DR Congo*. University of Chicago Press.

Sovacool, B. K. (2019). The precarious political economy of cobalt: Balancing prosperity, poverty, and brutality in artisanal and industrial mining in the Democratic Republic of the Congo. *The Extractive Industries and Society, 6*(3), 915–939.

Swartz, A., LeFevre, A. E., Perera, S., Kinney, M. V., & George, A. S. (2021). Multiple pathways to scaling up and sustainability: An exploration of digital health solutions in South Africa. *Globalization and Health, 17*(1), 1–13.

Triki, T., & Faye, I. (2011). *Africa's quest for development: Can sovereign wealth funds help?* Working Paper Series N° 142, African Development Bank.

United Nations Development Program (UNDP). (2015). *Sustainable development goals*. United Nations Development Program.

United Nations Development Programme (UNDP). (2022). *Uncertain times, unsettled lives—Shaping our future in a transforming world*. United Nations Development Programme.

Venables, A.J., & Wills, S. E. (2016). Resource funds: Stabilising, parking, and inter-generational transfer. *Journal of African Economies*, 25, AERC Supplement 2, ii20–ii40. https://doi.org/10.1093/jae/ejw016

Vinuesa, R., Azizpour, H., Leite, I., Balaam, M., Dignum, V., Domisch, S., Felländer, A., Langhans, S. D., Tegmark, M., & Fuso Nerini, F. (2020). The role of artificial intelligence in achieving the sustainable development goals. *Nature Communications*, 11(1), 233.

Vishnevsky, V. P., Harkushenko, O. M., Zanizdra, M. Y., & Kniaziev, S. I. (2021). Digital and green economy: Common grounds and contradictions. *Sci. in Nov*, 17(3), 14–27.

Wills, S. E., Senbet, L. W., & Simbanegavi, W. (2016). Sovereign wealth funds and natural resource management in Africa. *Journal of African Economies*, 25, AERC Supplement 2, ii3–ii19. https://doi.org/10.1093/jae/ejw018

World Bank. (2012). *Africa's pulse: An analysis of issues shaping Africa's economic future*. Washington D.C: The World Bank (Office of the Chief Economist for the Africa Region), October, Vol. 6.

World Commission on Environment and Development. (WCED). (1987). *Our common future*. Oxford University Press.

Wu, J., Guo, S., Huang, H., Liu, W., & Xiang, Y. (2018). Information and communications technologies for sustainable development goals: State-of-the-art, needs and perspectives. *IEEE Communications Surveys & Tutorials*, 20(3), 2389–2406.

Yang, L., Wang, X., Kim, S. H., Baek, S. W., Majeed, M. T., & Andlib, Z. (2021). *Digitalization and CO_2 Emissions in brics: What role does education play in the green economy?*

Zhou, T. M. (2017). Poverty, natural resources "curse" and underdevelopment in Africa. In M. Mawere (Ed). *Underdevelopment, development and the future of Africa* (pp. 279–346). Langaa Research & Publishing CIG.

PART III

The Green Economy, Digitalization and The Race To 2030

CHAPTER 7

Fostering Africa's Digital Trade in Services and Green Economy Post-COVID-19

Kobena T. Hanson, Vanessa T. Tang, and Katie M. Mutula

INTRODUCTION

The COVID-19 pandemic, which triggered a global economic crisis, and contracted drastically a number of African economies in 2020, clearly highlighted the vulnerability of many African nations' economies. Governments had to take decisive actions to mitigate the negative impacts of the pandemic on their respective economies. Despite African countries pursuing various economic policies, many are currently grappling with the effects of COVID-19, which plunged the region into its first recession in over 25 years, with activity contracting by nearly 5.0% on a per capita basis (Zeufack et al., 2021).

K. T. Hanson (✉)
Independent Development Evaluation (IDEV), African Development Bank Group (AfDB), Abidjan, Côte d'Ivoire
e-mail: k.hanson@afdb.org

V. T. Tang · K. M. Mutula
School of Accounting, Economics and Finance, University of KwaZulu Natal, Durban, South Africa

© The Author(s), under exclusive license to Springer Nature Switzerland AG 2023
K. P. Puplampu et al. (eds.), *Sustainable Development, Digitalization, and the Green Economy in Africa Post-COVID-19*, International Political Economy Series, https://doi.org/10.1007/978-3-031-32164-1_7

The COVID-19 pandemic and the associated lockdowns took a heavy toll on Africa's labor markets. Unemployment surged, and labor force participation plunged. During the emergency and recovery phases, job losses were more concentrated in lower-wage industries and among women and youth (ILO, 2020). For example, the ILO's Rapid Labor Force Surveys on the impact of COVID-19 revealed that among surveyed people, the unemployment rate increased by 50% in Egypt, 33% in Tunisia, and 23% in Morocco, further drawing attention to the labor market's structural weaknesses. Elsewhere on the continent, the impact of COVID-19 was equally harsh, causing untold disruption of lives and economies. In particular, micro, small, and medium-sized enterprises (MSMEs) were disproportionately impacted by the crisis, given their inability to absorb the associated shocks. Aside from the pandemic exposing the continent's structural vulnerabilities to economic shocks, it appears that the inability to handle disrupted linkages with the global economy is really what hit vulnerable economies the hardest (ACET, 2022; Zeufack et al., 2021).

COVID-19 brought to the fore many issues identified earlier by research regarding how digitization and allied disruptive technologies potentially transform work and development (Arthur et al., 2020, 2022). In the process, it laid bare several important social issues and lessons for development theory and practitioners (Arthur et al., 2022). COVID-19 clearly revealed some critical prerequisites for development, for example, the standard of governance and institutional capacities (Arthur et al., 2020), while highlighting the potential for technology to aggravate inequities where the public policy does not promote corrective measures (ACET, 2022). Across the global North, countries increased public spending to offset the hardship of the pandemic as businesses, industry, and everyday life ground to a halt. Contrastingly, emerging and developing economies and least developed countries in the global South had few possibilities to increase public spending, regardless of the gravity of setbacks suffered by their economies (UNIDO, 2021).

A key revelation, regardless, was that the crisis offered an opportunity to 'build back better' and transition to a greener economy as calls for green economic policies grew louder across the region. For many countries, COVID-19 was a wake-up call to reflect on their relationship with the environment. Unprecedented national lockdowns, travel restrictions, and the closing of national borders led to improvements in environmental quality. According to the EEA (2020a), drastic reductions in traffic—road, rail, sea, and air—resulted in steep improvements in air quality and noise levels, with the concentration of nitrogen dioxide (NO_2). The pandemic also had the immediate effect of encouraging people to choose more active modes of travel. The reduction in human activity allowed habitats to recover and species to occupy new spaces and niches (EEA, 2020b). COVID-19 further heightened the need for digital work and learning spaces linked by the internet and virtual platforms as these increasingly became the mainstay for businesses, educational institutions, and families (Arthur et al., 2020; Zeufack et al., 2021). Limited mobility, triggered by the widespread lockdowns, border closures, and travel restrictions, led to a steep uptake in digital technologies, the use of big data, satellite imagery, and geospatial data to circumvent the inability to get onto the ground.

The COVID-19 pandemic had a dramatic impact on the services sector (much like all other sectors), disrupting the activities of many businesses especially that of micro, small and medium-sized enterprises (MSMEs). During the COVID crisis, MSMEs faced numerous challenges including a loss of purchasing power, restrictions on working hours, shortages of production inputs, cancelation of orders, cash flow problems, and supply chain disruptions (Priyono et al., 2020). To respond to disruptive changes and to survive, many MSMEs worldwide, and across Africa, leveraged digital technology to upgrade and transform their businesses. For many MSMEs, digitalization did not only enable them to weather unplanned challenges, but it helped them be more competitive and stable. Digital enablement, therefore, was not just a means of survival, it made MSMEs more efficient, which in turn empowered them to expand their operations and earnings. Digital technologies thus became a useful response mechanism to disruptive changes. Nonetheless, it is worth noting that digital technologies also led to new players entering the market and disruptions in the position of established firms in various industries (Hasenpusch & Baumann, 2017).

Services have become the indispensable backbone of economies around the world. They generate more than two-thirds of the economic output and play an increasingly important role in international trade. Digital trade has also become an important driver in the growth of services. Africa's digital economy is important for sustainable growth and development and digital trade in services is growing dramatically. Fostering digital trade in services is promising, recognizing that this trade has helped cushion the COVID-19 pandemic's blow to services trade. Africa's digital trade in services can thus play a significant role in accelerating countries economic recovery and realizing a green economy.

Following the introduction, the chapter discusses the green economy, stressing its contested nature and appeal. Next, we look at how digitalization is impacting the services sector and resultant growth in digital trade in services. Thereafter, the chapter outlines country-and region-specific examples that demonstrate the acknowledgment and acceptance by governments of the essence of digitalization to issues of servicification. The chapter also highlights how digitalization is aiding MSMEs and others to strategically participate in global value chains (GVCs). The chapter concludes that if Africa seeks to leverage digitalization, then the continent will need to advance its own variety of 'servicification' (Hanson & Tang, 2020) in which entities such as MSMEs leverage digital technologies to its innovations and related services. More importantly, digitalization at the national level needs to be anchored by continent-wide initiatives such as the African Union's Digital Transformation Strategy for Africa.

GREEN ECONOMY APPROACHES

The concept of a 'green economy' was officially coined at the Rio + 20 conference and is perceived as a pathway to sustainability by international organizations such as the World Bank (2012) and the United Nations Environment Programme (UNEP, 2011). The concept focuses on the relationship and interdependence between the economy and the ecosystem providing a basis for operationalizing the concept of sustainability. It is thus a broad-ranging policy agenda and a tool to support the achievement of sustainable development, with an emphasis on aligning economic goals to social and environmental ones. Two related concepts occasionally used interchangeably with the green economy are the circular economy[1] and the bio-economy[2]—making them popular narratives in macro-level sustainability discussions in policy, scientific research, and business.

Most definitions of green economy frame it as a tool for achieving UNSDGs (Daniek, 2020). That said, an often-cited definition of a green economy is that by UNEP (2011), which defines the green economy as one that results in 'increased human well-being and social equity while reducing environmental risks and ecological shortages.' The core elements of a green economy are low-carbon development, resource efficiency, improved human well-being, and social inclusion (UNEP, 2011). An inclusive green economy reduces, reuses, and recycles goods; and invests in renewable energy and public goods that promote communal use. This economic model recognizes natural capital as a key economic asset and seeks to drastically reduce waste and limit the resources and energy that go into consumption and production (EEA, 2013). In a green economy, growth in employment and income are generally driven by public and private investment into economic activities, infrastructure, and assets that allow reduced carbon emissions and pollution, enhanced energy and resource efficiency, and prevention of the loss of biodiversity and ecosystem services (Daniek, 2020; EEA, 2013; Loiseau et al., 2016). Thus, a green economy is resource efficient and socially inclusive.

As Sabirin et al. (2022) note, green economy-based economic development hinges on five principles, notably an ability to: (a) create prosperity for all mankind; (b) foster equality, both in one generation period and with the next generation; (c) maintain, restore, and invest in various activities based on natural resources; (d) support sustainable levels of consumption and production; and, (e) be supported by strong, integrated, and accountable institutions. Green economic policies and laws are vital to transitioning into economic sectors that ultimately build a resilient economy (EEA, 2013). These policies and laws may

---

[1] A circular economy supports the transformation and development of industry and infrastructure towards sustainable consumption and production (SCP). The European Commission in 2015 adopted a "Circular Economy Action Plan" as one its major policy initiatives. UNEP also recognizes the circular economy as one of the key components of an inclusive green economy (UNEP, 2015a).

[2] While responding to concerns about resource scarcity, primarily centers on biological resources, such as those from agriculture, forestry and fisheries. It emphasizes a transition towards an optimal and sustainable use of renewable biological resources, as materials and bio-energy.

include ending fossil fuel subsidies, enforcing the polluter pays principle, supporting green jobs, and including green conditionalities in fiscal recovery policies.

Although the notion of green economy does not replace sustainable development, it helps to shift focus on the economy, investment, capital and infrastructure, employment and skills, and positive social and environmental outcomes. Green economy approaches are intricately linked with SDG 13, Climate Action, with a central focus on quality of life. Proponents of green economy see it as an effective conduit via which African countries can achieve sustainable growth; tackle poverty, create employment, and improve the overall well-being of the population; preserve the natural capital and ecosystem services that support and sustain the lives and livelihoods of people; and, an improvement in the overall performance of key sectors in the economy (Ali et al., 2021; Ofori-Amoah, 2020; UNEP 2015b). Naysayers, on the other hand, view the green economy as idealistic, projecting a notion of limitless growth, based on unachievable requirements such as being able to price the environment (Borel-Saladin & Turok, 2013). Others submit that it overemphasizes economic aspects of growth at the expense of social aspects and is just a novel way of maintaining neoliberal capitalism (Buseth, 2017). It is therefore unsurprising that the concept of green economy has gained huge traction and garnered a lot of attention both with the development and governmental circles but also with the sphere of academia.

The above notwithstanding, the green economy is a contested concept with a lot of proponents and critics (Ofori-Amoah, 2020). While advocates for a green economy tout it as an effective avenue via which Africa can achieve sustainable growth, tackle poverty, create employment, and improve the well-being of the continent's populace; critics charge, as stated earlier, the concept of green economy is oversimplified. For Africa, existing country policies, strategies, and plans have direct links with green economy. For instance, South Africa is well noted for its incorporation of green economy strategies into its national agendas (Musango et al., 2021). Ghana has similarly enacted policies and developed strategies and plans such as renewable energy policies, low-carbon development strategies (LCDs), the national climate change policies, forest and wildlife policies, and the forest investment program (FIP) among others that have a direct bearing on green economy transformation (Ali et al., 2021; Ofori-Amoah, 2020). Again, Burkina Faso, Ghana, Kenya, Mauritius, South Africa, and Uganda, have already developed their national Sustainable

Consumption and Production (SCP) programmes and national green economy strategies. Further, almost all African countries are signatories to international agreements such as the Kyoto Protocol and the Paris Agreement in response to green economy development.

SERVICES SECTOR AND DIGITAL TRADE IN THE WAKE OF AFRICA'S TRANSITION TO A GREEN ECONOMY

Globally, one sector that has seen an exponential transformation, in part due to the boom in digitalization, has been trade in services (Hanson & Tang, 2020). As a result of this growth in 'servicification,' it is estimated that well over 50% of global traded services are already digitized (Castro & McQuinn, 2015; Manyika et al., 2016). As Hanson and Tang (2020) note, the growth in digitalization is reinforcing a trend of servicification whereby there is an increase in the use, produce, and sale of services (see also Lanz & Maurer, 2015; Tang, 2018). Nonetheless, not much is known about trade in services in Africa and its prospective impact on sustainable development. The continent's potential to engage in trade in services, remains for the most part undocumented. While Africa's export potential in traditional services, such as tourism, is clearly recognized, the incipient dynamism in exports of nontraditional services is yet to receive the same attention (Dihel & Goswani, 2016: xvii). A challenge to exploring Africa's trade in services is the paucity of time series data and discrepancies between official statistics and firm-level data, which make analysis of services trade misleading (Dihel & Goswani, 2016).

The 2017 UNCTAD information economy report, however, acknowledges that the 'world is on the cusp of a new digital era. With dramatically reduced costs of collecting, storing and processing data, and greatly enhanced computing power, digitalization is transforming economic activities around the world. It is expected to affect value chains, skill requirements, production and trade.' Further the report stresses that the digital economy will help MSMEs in the developing world to connect and access international markets more easily. Indeed, for MSMEs, digitalization has made it easier for such businesses to integrate into GVCs for several reasons (World Bank/WTO, 2019). First, by reducing export costs, access to digital tools is aiding and empowering smaller firms to absorb more easily the larger fixed costs associated with the activity in foreign markets. Second, digitalization minimizes the need for intermediaries, helping MSMEs to reach consumers through online platforms, and add significant time-benefits. Yet, evidence also suggests that digitalization can buttress polarization between countries and firms due to specific constraints: lack of infrastructure, weak and/or expensive internet access; and stricter requirements to trade with larger firms, in terms of technology and data sharing (López González, 2019; World Bank/WTO, 2019).

The high fixed costs associated with the lack of economies of scale often inhibit the participation of MSMEs in global markets, which is more severe in developing countries (World Bank/WTO, 2019). However, the rise of global production networks and the digitalization of the economy is availing new opportunities to MSMEs (Ganne & Lundquist, 2019). Although participation in GVCs is dominated by large firms, the specialization in a few stages of the production chain offers growth perspectives for MSMEs. Promoting the integration of MSMEs into GVCs provides opportunities for job creation, an increase in national productivity, and reduced inequality (Ganne & Lundquist, 2019). It is thus anticipated that across Africa there is a rapid growth in services (Zeufack et al., 2021). Technologies are creating new opportunities while simultaneously boosting the productivity of existing ones. The dynamic possibilities inherent in the leapfrogging potential in digitalization (Hanson, 2023; Manyika et al., 2016; WEF 2019) are creating a new kind of twenty-first-century development process in Africa. During and post-COVID-19, digital infrastructure and digitally enabled services and applications were invaluable businesses, irrespective of size, to cope with uncertainty, and ensure business continuity in times of social distancing (Zeufack et al., 2021: 74). Digital solutions to manage supply and logistics chains proved invaluable in the face of the initial disruptions of GVCs. Also, e-commerce platforms greatly enabled MSMEs to access requisite inputs and distribution networks for their products and services; while online fintech platforms eased mobile payments (Zeufack et al., 2021: 74).

At this juncture, it is worth noting that there is 'no widely accepted standard definition for digitalization and the digital economy' (Reis et al., 2020; UNCTAD, 2017). We take the view of the digital economy in a broader sense that is somewhat similar to the WTO description of 'electronic commerce' which encompasses the 'production, distribution, marketing, sale or delivery of goods and services by electronic means' (WTO, 1998). Our conceptualization of digitalization follows Gobble (2018) who sees it as the 'use of digital technology, and digitized information, to create and harvest value in new ways.' It is worth noting that although not stated explicitly, e-commerce effectively includes an array of digital services. Akin to Gobble (2018), the G20 ministerial meetings of 2016 (Hangzhou) and 2017 (Dusseldorf) also recognize that 'the digital economy is an increasingly important driver of global inclusive economic growth and plays a significant role in accelerating economic development, enhancing the productivity of existing industries, cultivating new markets and industries and achieving inclusive sustainable growth and development' (G20, 2017).

The extant literature is replete with evidence of how digitalization is facilitating innovation and collaborations, reducing the barriers posed by geographical distance (Miroudot & Cadestin, 2017). Studies from sub-Sahara Africa (ACET, 2022; Arthur et al., 2022), Indonesia (Sabirin et al., 2022), and elsewhere (Barrutiabengoa et al., 2022) submit that challenges for macro-economic recovery post-COVID-19 are intricately tied to the technological advances of digitalization, as the pandemic deepened and accelerated digital transformation (Fu, 2020; OECD, 2019) and restrictions on mobility triggered a surge in digital service delivery (Lanz & Maurer, 2015; Tang, 2018; UNCTAD, 2022a). The COVID-19 pandemic, thus, clearly accelerated the use of digital technologies in the service industry (Priyono et al., 2020) and transformed trade in services including digital trade. According to recent UNCTAD statistics on digital trade, global exports of digital services grew from around $3.1 trillion in 2018 to $3.8 trillion in 2021 as illustrated in Fig. 7.1. This growth also helped to cushion the contraction in exports of other services during the COVID-19 period as evidenced in Fig. 7.2. It should be noted that while the COVID-19 crisis disrupted trade in other services such as transport and travel, digital services however remained resilient, increasing as a share of total services exports.

In Africa, the trend in digital services exports fared differently as illustrated in Fig. 7.3. By comparison, Northern Africa experienced the highest growth of any region while their less digitalized sub-Saharan counterparts saw the largest contraction from 2019 to 2020 (−10%). The various contractions in impacts on exports during the pandemic indicate relative weaknesses in African countries digitalization levels. Overall, however, Africa's digital trade in services hold promise evidenced by their exports of digital services rebounding strongly in 2021.

As poignantly noted by UNCTAD (2022a: 7), irrespective of which regional area, digitalization has altered the way services are supplied, which is having a transformative impact upon how services trade is framed within the multilateral trading system. For example, the use of digital

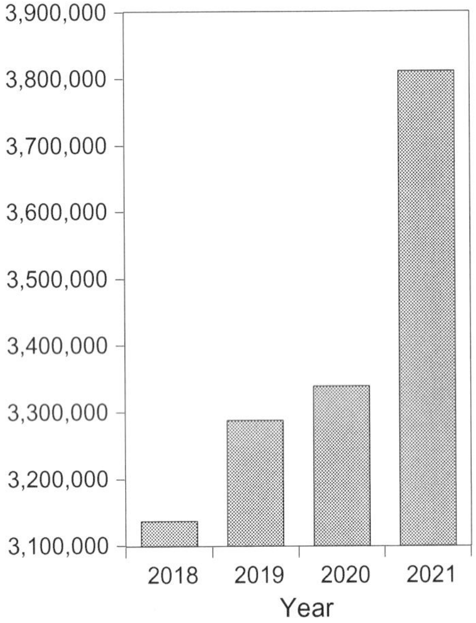

Fig. 7.1 World Digital Services Exports, 2018–2021 (US Dollars Millions) (*Source* Authors' compilation based on UNCTAD handbook of statistics data [UNCTAD, 2023])

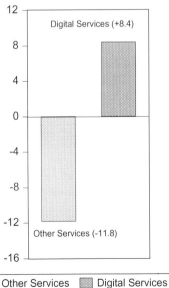

Fig. 7.2 Contributions to the total change in world services exports, 2019–2021 (percentage points) (*Source* Authors' compilation based on UNCTAD handbook of statistics data [UNCTAD, 2023])

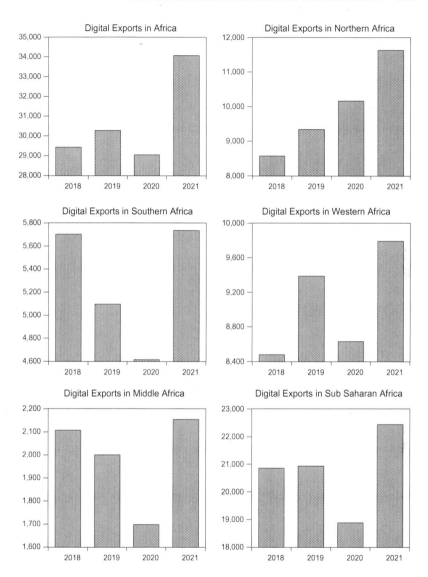

Fig. 7.3 Africa's Digital Services Exports, 2018–2021 (US Dollars Millions) (*Source* Authors' compilation based on UNCTAD handbook of statistics data [UNCTAD, 2023])

platforms has greatly helped make cross-border marketing and transactions more efficient and cost-effective than before, resulting in significant increases in the flow of cross-border supply (UNCTAD, 2022a: 7). Similarly, streaming technologies have made it feasible for services to switch from physical to digital delivery, resulting in a shift from the presence of natural persons or consumption abroad to cross-border supply. Further, services provided by subsidiaries in services consumer countries, or through commercial presence, can now be supplied by digital means, resulting in a shift to cross-border supply (UNCTAD, 2022a: 7).

Digitalization, Servicification, and the African Reality

Digital trade and digitally enabled transactions of trade in goods and services have been increasing globally post the COVID pandemic, and Africa is no exception. Across the continent, a cohort of pioneering businesses is already creating a vibrant market for e-commerce. They have developed innovative solutions to Africa's challenges around payment, identity, and delivery addresses. Africa has seen some of the fastest-growing penetrations of mobile subscribers in recent years, as the region continues to undergo a digital transformation. In 2017, mobile penetration in Africa was estimated at 44%, compared to an average internet penetration of 20% (Abdulhamid, 2020). The cause for the low internet penetration rate is largely affordability or cost factor (Hanson & Tang, 2020). This unaffordability of internet access may be due to 'telecommunications markets entry, such as high license prices or arbitrary license attribution process, translating into monopoly or oligopoly positions that are unfavorable to tariff reductions' (Cariolle, 2021: 14).

Even so, the COVID-19 pandemic has accelerated the digitization of African economies as evidenced in Fig. 7.4. It is concerning, however, that only just above half of the world population and just above one-third of Africa's population can access the internet. By the end of 2020, only 29% of the sub-Saharan African population was connected to the internet. And by the end of 2020, 495 million people in sub-Saharan Africa had a mobile subscription, approximately 46% of the population. This number is projected to increase to 615 million by 2025 (GSMA, 2021). The development of a mobile technology ecosystem is rapidly evolving, becoming more integral to digital trade, not only for MSMEs (which are dominant in Africa) but also for larger enterprises. Besides, the greater demand for 'just-in-time' services—where smaller online sales and purchases are more common, faster, and reliable than larger advanced orders—can also help MSMEs engage in digital trade and enhance their contributions to the economy (Ganne & Lundquist, 2019).

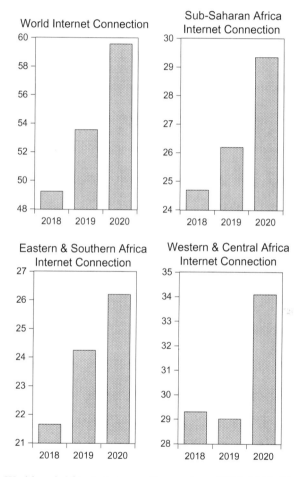

Fig. 7.4 World and Africa's Internet Connection, 2018–2020 (Percentage of Population) (*Source* Authors' compilation based on the World Bank, World Development indicators data [WDI, 2023])

While Africa doubled its services exports from 2005 to 2019, reaching $124 billion in 2019 (UNCTAD, 2022b), there are some disparities in the share of services in total exports across countries. Only eight countries export more services than goods: Cape Verde, Central African Republic, Comoros, Ethiopia, the Gambia, Mauritius, Sao Tome and Principe, and Seychelles (UNCTAD, 2022b: 72–73). For Africa's digitization to succeed, diversification is crucial. Economic diversification and structural change are key drivers of an African country's growth and development (Atta-Mensah et al., 2019; Brautigam & Diolle, 2019; Tang et al., 2019). However, successful diversification and structural transformation, like in the case of Mauritius, require commitment from political leaders, strong political leadership and institutions, and trust between the public and private sectors (Brautigam & Diolle, 2019).

The reality is that many African economies need better governance and remain commodity dependent in production and exports. As African countries strive to realize a green economy, there is a need for more knowledge on the relationship between export diversification and the green economy. Using the score obtained by the top African countries on the Global Green Economy Index (GGEI)[3] and their export diversification status as measured by the export concentration index,[4] we thus investigate the possible link between these two variables. We uncover no strong association between export diversification and the green economy. As illustrated in Fig. 7.5, there is, however, a moderate negative association between these variables. This implies that as an African country's concentration decreases (more diversified), they tend to progress more towards a green economy (GGEI increases). Additionally, it is worth noting that the estimated correlation coefficient is $R = -0.41$ which supports our statement that a moderate negative correlation exists.

---

[3] 18 underlying indicators define the Global Green Economy Index™ (GGEI), each contained within one of the four main dimensions of Climate Change & Social Equity, Sector Decarbonization, Markets & ESG Investment, and Environmental Health. Each dimension is equally weighted (25% each) in calculating the total score. Each indicator is also equally weighted within the four main dimensions. Our sample is limited to twenty-two top African leaders progressing towards a green economy (those with a GGEI score above 0.40—the highest GGEI score was 0.78 in 2022).

[4] The UNCTAD export concentration index shows to which degree exports of individual economies are concentrated on a few products. Due to the lack of export concentration data for 2022, we therefore use the 2021 export concentration index data.

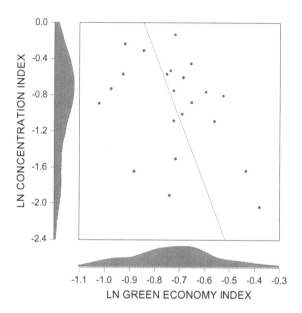

Fig. 7.5 Relationship Between Africa's Export Diversification and the Green Economy (*Source* Authors' compilation of the concentration index is based on UNCTAD handbook of statistics data [UNCTAD, 2023]. The Global Green Economy index is based on Dual Citizen LLC data [Dual Citizen LLC, 2023])

Nonetheless, as noted earlier, the COVID-19 crisis triggered some long-term structural transformations in the economies of African states. For example, the rapid uptake and surge in digitalization and associated boom in servicification is, according to ACET (2022: 8) engendering 'Growth with DEPTH'—'Diversification, Export competitiveness, Productivity increases, and Technological upgrading—all to improve Human well-being through better jobs and livelihoods.' Today, Africa leads in mobile money deployments globally. As of 2020, there were '171 live services supporting 562 million registered accounts in the region. 161 million accounts were active on a monthly basis. Their collective transaction value for the year was $495 billion' (Mobile World Live/UK-DIT, 2022).

Country-and Region-Specific Cases of the Value of Digitalization to Issues of Servicification

Against the aforementioned background, some of the specific developments strengthening trade stemming from the ongoing widespread acceptance of digitalization on the continent include inter alia:

- In Kenya, to facilitate cross-border trade, the government in 2014 launched a digitization and automation of trade transaction systems (the National Electronic Single Window System), to address challenges and bottlenecks to the processing of import and export cargo documentation. The new system, both interfaces with government agencies issuing documents such as export and import permits, licenses, and certificates (Tralac, 2022), and is linked to banks and mobile payment options, via the Kenya Revenue Authority's online taxation system and the government's e-Citizen platform, to provide comprehensive platform.
- In West Africa, Senegal has experienced strong growth in services exports driven mostly by the exports of ICT services (OECD/WTO, 2017: 124). Furthermore, Senegalese exporters have benefitted from 'liberalized' policies that facilitated services exports such as the lowering of tariffs on the imports of computers and the provision of reliable and competitively priced telecom infrastructure, and the establishment of an independent telecom regulator (OECD/WTO, 2017: 125).
- The Economic Community of West African States (ECOWAS) region and its largest member Nigeria are at varying degrees of gradually engaging in cross-border paperless trade as well as the trading through an electronic single window (Odularu, 2019). These actions will enhance trade in facilitating and expediting the exchange of trade-related data and documents electronically.
- In sub-Saharan Africa (SSA), South Africa and Mauritius lead the region and African continent on the 2022 UN-e-Government Development Index (EGDI), scoring the highest regarding the scope and quality of online services, the status of telecommunication infrastructure and existing human capacity. Unlike many SSA countries where 5G technologies have yet to be explored, both South Africa and Mauritius, have introduced 5G technologies. In the case of Mauritius, with the vision of the government to transform the country

into a Cyber Island, digital literacy initiatives include the compulsory digital literacy program for all high school leavers. Thus, giving attention to building or upgrading skills. And, in the launch of the Digital Mauritius Strategic Plan 2030, the emphasis remains on 'building capacity' while transforming the island into a high-income, sustainable, innovative, and inclusive economy. Furthermore, with the creation of the Board of Investment in 2001 (now the Economic Development Board), this initiative has indeed facilitated trade and foreign direct investment in the Information Communication Technology (ICT) sector.

Conclusion

This chapter has explored the complex dynamics of how digitalization is impacting the services sector and the resultant growth in digital trade in services. The chapter also highlighted how the drive to move Africa in a greener direction is aiding the adoption of digitalization, and positively impacting trade in services. In doing so, the chapter teased-out some country-specific examples to demonstrate the acknowledgment and acceptance by governments of digitalization, trade in services, and their ability to enhance inclusive growth and foster the achievement of Agenda 2063 and the Sustainable Development Goals.

In spite of the strides being made, there are wide disparities in the share of services in total exports across countries, with only eight nations exporting more services than goods (UNCTAD, 2022b). So, if Africa seeks to truly leverage digitalization, then countries will need to advance their own varieties of 'servicification' (Hanson & Tang, 2020) whereby MSMEs apply fit-for-purpose technologies to innovations and related services. One critical aspect of deepening the service sector and MSMEs is to ensure that digitalization needs at the national level are in sync with the African Union's Digital Transformation Strategy for Africa and the related links to existing initiatives and frameworks: Policy and Regulatory Initiative for Digital Africa (PRIDA); Program for Infrastructure Development in Africa (PIDA); African Continental Free-Trade Area (AfCFTA); Single African Air Transport Market (SAATM); and, Free Movement of Persons (FMP), all of which aim to support the development of a digital single market (DSM) for Africa. The African Continental Free-Trade Agreement's (AfCFTA) trade liberalization vision, combined with a touch of capacity development (individual, institutional, and enabling environment), plus appropriate leadership, are needed to transcend the challenges associated with consolidating trade liberalization processes across the continent.

As with all policy-induced or state-led interventions, the requisite actions outlined above, will need to be well-organized to ensure ownership and buy-in by key stakeholders, thereby minimizing or eliminating risks of unintended outcomes and political disputes. Similarly, all transformational green policy initiatives must be made integral parts of broader developmental initiatives aimed at reducing poverty and combating geospatial and social fragmentation (Scholz & Fink, 2022: 45; UNCTAD, 2022b). Also, to accelerate the digitization of African economies, in particular, the access to internet, barriers to telecommunications markets entry and internet tariffs should be reduced. And, to further facilitate trade, red tape, corruption and inefficiencies that impede cross-border trade should be addressed.

REFERENCES

Abdulhamid, N. A. (2020). M-pesa: A Kenyan solution to global financial exclusion? In P. Arthur, et al. (Eds.), *Disruptive technologies, innovation & development in Africa*. Palgrave.

ACET. (2022) *Transforming and building resilient economies in Africa: Resetting priorities for the policy agenda in the post-COVID-19 era*. ACET.

Ali, E. B., Anufriev, V. P., & Amfo, B. (2021). Green economy implementation in Ghana as a road map for a sustainable development drive: A review. *Scientific African, 12*, 1–17.

Arthur, P., Hanson, K. T., & Puplampu, K. P. (2020). (Eds.), *Disruptive technologies, innovation & development in Africa*. Palgrave.

Arthur, P., Hanson, K. T., & Puplampu, K. P. (2022). Revenue mobilization, taxation and the digital economy in post-COVID-19 Africa. *Journal of African Political Economy & Development, 7*(1), 1–12.

Atta-Mensah, J., Tang, V. T., & Shaw, T. M. (2019). Towards economic transformation: The way forward for Africa. In V. T. Tang, T. M. Shaw, & M. G. Holden (Eds.), *From development and sustainable growth of Mauritius* (pp. 239–251). Palgrave MacMillan.

Barrutiabengoa, J. M., Espinosa, L. A., Mas, P. & Urgulu, Y. (2022, May 26). How do digitalization and decarbonization efforts interact? In *Economics of Climate Change.* https://www.bbvaresearch.com/wpcontent/uploads/ 2022/05/How-do-digitalization-and-decarbonization-efforts-interact_2T22. pdf. Accessed on 15 October 2022.

Borel-Saladin, J. M., & Turok, I. N. (2013). The green economy: Incremental change or transformation? *Environmental Policy and Governance, 23,* 209–220.

Brautigam, D., & Diolle, T. (2019). Coalitions, capitalists and credibility: Overcoming the crisis of confidence at independence in Mauritius. In V. T. Tang, T. M. Shaw, & M. G. Holden (Eds.), *From Development and sustainable growth of Mauritius* (pp. 17–67). Palgrave MacMillan.

Buseth, J. T. (2017). The green economy in Tanzania: From global discourses to institutionalization. *Geoforum, 86,* 42–52.

Cariolle, J. (2021). International connectivity and the digital divide in sub Saharan Africa. *Information Economics and Policy, 55,* 1–20.

Castro, D., & McQuinn, A. (2015). *Cross-border data flows enable growth in all industries.* Information Technology and Innovation Foundation.

Daniek, K. (2020). Green economy indicators as a method of monitoring development in the economic, social and environmental dimensions. *Social Inequalities and Economic Growth, 62*(2/2020), 150–173. https://doi.org/10.15584/nsawg.2020.2.10

Dihel, N., & Goswani, A. G. (Eds.). (2016). *The unexplored potential of trade in services in Africa.* World Bank.

Dual Citizen LLC. (2023). *Global green economy index 2022.* https://dualcitizeninc.com/global-green-economy-index/. Accessed 10 March 2023.

EEA. (2020a). *Air pollution goes down as Europe takes hard measures to combat coronavirus.* https://www.eea.europa.eu/highlights/air-pollution-goes-down-as. Accessed 10 August 2022.

EEA. (2020b). *COVID-19 and the environment: Explore what we know.* European Environment Agency. https://www.eea.europa.eu/post-corona-planet/explore/#covid-19-and---. Accessed 10 August 2022.

EEA. (2013). *Towards a green economy in Europe. EU environmental policy targets and objectives 2010–2050* (EEA Report, No. 8).

Fu, X. (2020). Digital transformation of global value chains and sustainable post-pandemic recovery. *Transnational Corporations, 27*(2), 157–166.

Ganne, E., & Lundquist, K. (2019). The digital economy, GVCs and SMEs. In WTO—*Global value chain development report 2019* (Chapter 6). https://www.wto.org/english/res_e/booksp_e/gvc_dev_report_2019_e_ch6.pdf. Accessed 20 March 2023.

Gobble, M. (2018). Digitalization, digitization, and innovation. *Research-Technology Management, 61*(4), 56–59.

GSMA. (2021). *State of mobile internet connectivity 2021.* https://www.gsma.com/r/somic. Accessed 25 March 2023.

G20. (2017). *G20 digital ministerial declaration. Shaping digitalization for an interconnected World.* http://unctad.org/meetings/en/Contribution/dtl_eWeek2017c02-G20_en.pdf. Accessed 25 March 2023.

Hanson, K. T. (2023). Technological leapfrogging and innovation: Re-imagining evaluation approaches and practices in Africa. In G. Onyango (Ed.), *Public policy and technological transformations in Africa: Nurturing policy entrepreneurship, policy tools & citizen participation.* Palgrave.

Hanson, K. T., & Tang, V. T. (2020). Perspectives on disruptive innovations and Africa's services sector. In P. Arthur, et al. (Eds.), *Disruptive technologies, innovation & development in Africa.* Palgrave.

Hasenpusch, T. C. A., & Baumann, S. (2017). Strategic media venturing: Corporate venture capital approached of time incumbents. *International Journal of Media Management, 19,* 77–100.

ILO. (2020). *World employment and social outlook trends.* ILO. https://www.ilo.org/wcmsp5/groups/public/---dgreports/---dcomm/---publ/documents/publication/wcms_734455.pdf. Accessed 15 November 2022.

Lanz, R., & Maurer, A. (2015). *Services and global value chains—Some evidence on servicification of manufacturing and services networks* (WTO Working Paper ERSD 3). WTO.

Loiseau, E., Saikku, L., Antikainen, R., Droste, N., Hansjürgens, B., et al. (2016). Green economy and related concepts: An overview. *Journal of Cleaner Production, 139,* 361–371.

López González, J. (2019). *Fostering participation in digital trade for ASEAN MSMEs* (OECD Trade Policy Papers, No. 230). OECD Publishing.

Manyika, J., Lund, S., Bughin, J., Woetzel, J., Stamenov, K., & Dhingra, D. (2016). *Digital globalization: The new era of global flows.* McKinsey Global Institute.

Miroudot, S., & Cadestin, C. (2017). *Services in global value chains: From inputs to value-creating activities* (OECD Trade Policy Papers, No. 197). OECD.

Mobile World Live/UK-DIT. (2022). *Towards a flourishing digital economy for all—A spotlight on Africa* (Whitepaper). https://www.mobileworldlive.com/wp-content/uploads/2022/02/MWL-DIT-whitepaper-Towards-a-flourishing-digital-economy-for-all-%E2%80%93-a-spotlight-on-Africa.pdf. Accessed on 25 February 2023.

Musango, J. K., Brent, A. C., & Bassi, A. M. (2021). Modelling the transition towards a green economy in South Africa. *Technological Forecasting and Social Change, 87,* 257–273.

Odularu, G. (2019). The changing landscape of trade facilitation and regional development issues in West Africa. In G. Odularu & P. Alege (Eds.), *From trade facilitation capacity needs policy directions for national and regional development in West Africa* (pp. 1–24). Palgrave MacMillan.

OECD. (2019). *An introduction to online platforms and their roles in the digital transformation.* OECD.

OECD/WTO. (2017). *Aid for trade at a glance 2017: Promoting trade, inclusiveness and connectivity for sustainable development.* WTO, Geneva/OECD Publishing Paris.

Ofori-Amoah, B. (2020). Disruptive technologies, and sustainable energy generation and storage as forms of green economy. In P. Arthur, et al. (Eds.), *Disruptive technologies, innovation & development in Africa.* Palgrave.

Priyono, A., Moin, A., & Putri, V. (2020). Identifying digital transformation paths in the business model of SMEs during the COVID-19 pandemic. *Journal of Open Innovation Technology, Market and Complexity,* 6(4), 1–22.

Reis, J., Amorim, M., Melão, N., Cohen, Y. & Rodrigues, M. (2020). Digitalization: A literature review and research agenda. In Z. Anisic, B. Lalic, D. Gracanin (Eds.), *Proceedings on 25th International Joint Conference on Industrial Engineering and Operations Management—IJCIEOM. IJCIEOM 2019.* Lecture Notes on Multidisciplinary Industrial Engineering. Springer, Cham. https://doi.org/10.1007/978-3-030-43616-2_47

Sabirin, A., Budi, A. A., Adhiyaksa, F. D., Aurelya, B. P., Ridwan, S., Lesmana, J. R., & Alifta, F. D. (2022). Green economy as a law for the economic recovery post-COVID-19 amidst the increasing cross-border e-commerce in Indonesia. In 3rd International Conference on Law Reform (3rd INCLAR), *KnE Social Sciences,* pp. 25–42. https://doi.org/10.18502/kss.v7i15.12072

Scholz, W., & Fink, M. (2022). *Green jobs in cities: Challenges and opportunities in African and Asian intermediary cities* (GDI Discussion Paper 7/2022). https://doi.org/10.23661/dp7.2022

Tang, V. T. (2018). Does the sophistication of exports matter in sustaining growth in middle-income African countries? In K. T. Hanson, K. P. Puplampu, & T. M. Shaw (Eds.), *From millennium development goals to sustainable development goals: Rethinking African development* (pp. 113–132). Routledge.

Tang, V. T., Holden, M. G., & Shaw, T. M. (2019). The making of a developmental African State. In V. T. Tang, T. M. Shaw, & M. G. Holden (Eds.), *From development and sustainable growth of Mauritius* (pp. 1–15). Palgrave Macmillan.

Tralac. (2022, December 22). *Digital trade developments in Kenya: Perspective under AfCFTA.* Online Blog. https://www.tralac.org/blog/article/15850-digital-trade-developments-in-kenya-perspective-under-afcfta.html. Accessed 25 March 2023.

UNCTAD. (2017). *Information economy report 2017. Digitalization, trade and development.* https://unctad.org/system/files/official-document/ier2017_en.pdf. Accessed 24 March 2023.

UNCTAD. (2022a, May). *The evolving landscape of digital trade in services*. https://unctad.org/system/files/official-document/c1mem4d26_en.pdf. Accessed 20 February 2023.

UNCTAD. (2022b). *Economic development in Africa report 2022b*. UNCTAD.

UNCTAD. (2023). *UNCTAD handbook of statistics database*. http://stats.unctad.org/Handbook/TableViewer/tableView.aspx. Accessed 10 March 2023.

UNEP. (2011). *Towards a green economy: Pathways to sustainable development and poverty eradication—A synthesis for policy makers*. https://www.unep.org/greeneconomy

UNEP. (2015a). *Uncovering pathways towards an inclusive green economy: A summary for leaders*. UNEP.

UNEP. (2015b). *Building inclusive green economies in Africa experience and lessons learned: 2010–2015*. UNEP.

UNIDO. (2021). *The impact of the pandemic on industries. A conceptual map and key processes* (Inclusive and Sustainable Industrial Development Working Paper 17/2021). UNIDO. https://downloads.unido.org/ot/25/40/25407524/WP_17_2021.pdf

WEF. (2019, September 4–6). *World economic forum on Africa—'Shaping inclusive growth and shared futures in the fourth industrial revolution*. WEF. http://www3.weforum.org/docs/WEF_AF19_Report.pdf

World Bank. (2012). *Inclusive green growth: The pathway to sustainable development*. World Bank.

World Bank. (2023). *World Development Indicators (WDI) 2023*. [Online]. http://databank.worldbank.org/source/world-development-indicators. Accessed 30 March 2023.

World Bank/WTO. (2019). *Global value chain development report 2019: Technological innovation, supply chain trade, and workers in a globalized world* (English). World Bank Group.

World Trade Organization (WTO). (1998). *Work programme on electronic commerce—Adopted by the General Council on 25 September 1998, WT/L274, 30 September 1998*.

Zeufack, A. G., Calderon, C., Kambou, G., Kubota, M., Korman, V., Canales, C. C., & Aviomoh, H. E. (2021, April). *COVID-19 and the future of work in Africa: Emerging trends in digital technology adoption* (Africa's Pulse, No. 23). World Bank.

CHAPTER 8

Green Economic Policies in Africa

Abbi M. Kedir, Fama Gueye, Adama Kane, and Mahamadi Gaba

INTRODUCTION

There is intensified discussion of the importance of building green growth among academics, national policymakers, and international organizations to ensure sustainable economic development. A decade ago, the African Development Bank (AfDB) projected that every African country will be on a green growth development pathway by 2022 (AfDB, 2013). Currently, the Bank puts "Light up and Power Africa" as one of its top 5 priorities and allocates resources to climate adaptation and the increased use of renewable energy. Contemporary outstanding challenges for Africa to pursue green growth development path are still binding

---

A. M. Kedir (✉)
Sheffield University Management School, University of Sheffield, Sheffield, UK
e-mail: a.m.kedir@sheffield.ac.uk

F. Gueye
The Public Policy Institute, Cheikh Anta Diop University, Dakar, Senegal

A. Kane · M. Gaba
Cheikh Anta Diop University, Dakar, Senegal

© The Author(s), under exclusive license to Springer Nature Switzerland AG 2023
K. P. Puplampu et al. (eds.), *Sustainable Development, Digitalization, and the Green Economy in Africa Post-COVID-19*, International Political Economy Series, https://doi.org/10.1007/978-3-031-32164-1_8

even if the continent has the lowest emissions compared to other global regions. These challenges include poor and outdated infrastructure, weak institutions with an acute lack of effective initiatives for the desired environmental stewardship, unclear incentive structures to encourage economic agents, specifically firms or polluting companies, to respect their environmental and social responsibilities (ESR), and a clear lack of strategy to produce the required skilled manpower that will spearhead innovation in renewable energy or net zero transition.

Rather, there is strong evidence of detrimental effects of climate change, deforestation, biodiversity loss, and reliance on fossil fuels accompanied by lower living standards, rising poverty, and food insecurity in the African subregion (Gregory et al., 2005; Kedir, 1994; World Bank, 2022). For instance, 9 out of 10 most vulnerable countries to the impacts of climate change are in Africa (AfDB, 2022). The continent has a long way to go to be a serious partner among other regions that are currently attempting to make renewables their long-term choice of source of energy. Realistically, there is a lot to be done to manage land resources, water bodies, forests and to effectively enforce environmental regulations to manage pollution by firms. However, there are also encouraging measures already underway in countries such as Ethiopia (hydroelectric power using its huge water resources); Kenya (geothermal); and Tunisia, Egypt, Mozambique, and Morocco (solar and wind). Other countries in Africa, notably South Africa and Ghana, are also developing initiatives to promote greener and clean energy. If it can be taken as a serious step towards green economy, the adoption of the 2008 Libreville Declaration by about 30 African countries demonstrates at least a political commitment (Kedir, 2014, 2018).

Research indicates that green growth theory does not have strong empirical support because there is no evidence showing absolute decoupling from resource use in our drive for economic growth (Hickel & Kallis, 2019). Green growth has short-term costs with long-term gains in tackling poverty, even if there is resistance to it and limited commitments to green industrialization (UNECA, 2016). Some believe that the green growth dream is not feasible and argue that the West exploits Africa's lack of expertise in green growth to switch climate aid to emission reductions and ring fence sources of finance for development (Rogers, 2010). Aid commentators contend that major donors might use the need to adopt green growth strategies as aid conditionality. Some point to the oversimplified contexts within which green growth is discussed and emphasize the importance of innovation as a precondition for green growth (Herman, 2021).

Green growth is not merely the management of natural resources, it also seeks to change the way we think about our environment and development. Green growth is one of the most challenging issues of our time, and its intergenerational implications for global development are increasingly receiving the attention of major development actors, policymakers, and research centres. It is widely agreed that green growth is necessary, efficient, and affordable and the World Bank called for mainstreaming green growth principles a decade ago. We should note that even if Africa is not a major contributor to global climate chaos and irresponsible energy use, it might jeopardize its green economy dream by the increasingly intensive use of chemical fertilizers, which are major sources of greenhouse gases (GHGs) (UNEP, 2022). Evidently, there are issues related to the institutional and human capacities in Africa to negotiate and deal with complex issues of climate change, design, and implementation of sustainable development projects and raising funds for a better future. Other issues include coordination with national development strategies, biofuels, fertilizers, food security, renewable energy sources, financing options, institutions, and sequencing of Africa's priorities. There are outstanding challenges of policy coherence across Africa particularly in water, energy, and food sectors (Curran et al., 2018).

However, are African governments working towards developing enforceable green economic policies in vital economic sectors such as agriculture, manufacturing, transport, and energy? This is the fundamental question we attempt to answer in this chapter. In the context of recurrent climate change-induced catastrophes such as droughts, floods, and biodiversity loss, there are no better alternative initiatives than urgent and sustained reduction of carbon dioxide emissions and pollution to save our planet and guarantee a sustainable economic development for our own present existence and for generations to come. In a green economy, employment and income growth are driven by investments into economic activities and infrastructure development that allow lower industrial pollution and carbon dioxide emissions. In effect, there is an emphasis on improving efficiency in energy use, prevention of the loss of biodiversity, and ecosystem services. This chapter is organized as follows. Section 8.2 provides a general introduction to green policies in Africa with a contextual focus on economic and energy policies. This is followed by a detailed discussion of the challenges the continent is facing in implementing green economic policies in Sect. 8.3. The last section examines the prospects of green economic policies in Africa, drawing on the case of Senegal.

Green Policies in Africa

The COVID-19 pandemic was an unprecedented period for humanity. It disrupted habits, transformed the way things are done and above all it raised questions about the existence of humanity. As the world recovers from the pandemic, the prospect of rethinking a new economic trajectory along renewable lines is attracting the interest of many people around the world. Even if the crisis was painful, it is nevertheless an opportunity to look back at the way society has functioned for decades. Indeed, since the 1750 Industrial Revolution, the world has gradually been built around a system of capital accumulation and energy production sources relied on oil, coal, and natural gas.

The environmental consequences of the exploitation of these resources have been disastrous for humanity. The world is getting warmer and natural disasters and extreme weather events are multiplying over the years. For instance, life-threatening droughts, flooding, loss of biodiversity, cyclones, and hurricanes are happening at increasing frequency. In 2023, Tropical Cyclone Freddy caused floods, and mudslides which led to the loss of life and substantial property damages. Recent images by the United States of America National Aeronautical and Space Administration (NASA) show the famine threats caused by the most severe drought in 70 years of record keeping (NASA, 2022). On the agricultural side, it is a significant loss of productivity in the sector, particularly in the southern countries (Barrios et al., 2004; FAO, 2018; Kedir, 1994; World Bank, 2022). The question is the ability of humanity to survive if an unprecedented environmental crisis occurs on the same level as COVID-19. A positive answer is difficult to foresee. This is why it is becoming urgent for the authorities to rethink new policies that not only improve the standard of living of the populations, but also respect the environment. This chapter will therefore state the various green environmental policies and discuss the difficulties of implementation and the prospects in the post-COVID-19 world. The working methodology adopted consists in looking at policies from a sectoral approach and the relevant sectors in the framework of green decision-making are as follows: energy, transport, agriculture, and forestry.

Green Energy Policies

The energy sector is certainly the most sensitive sector in environmental policy making. Indeed, this sector involves important economic and environmental stakes. Fossil energies have long been a boon to exporting countries and other large exporting companies. Nowadays, the environmental stakes are becoming so high that it is urgent for countries to think about alternative green energy sources such as solar, wind, or bioenergy. Some countries such as Morocco have made impressive progress particularly in solar energy (EU, 2019). Countries are trying to work towards carbon mitigation, energy efficiency, and sustainable development. A simplified framework can illustrate the pressure points in greenhouse gas (GHG) emissions and what parameters should be kept under control for sustainable energy development. GHG can be decomposed as follows;

$$GHG = [Q/P] \times [Y/Q] \times [GHG/Y] \times P;$$

where Q/P captures the quality of life(Q) per capita (i.e. P being population); Y is consumption, hence Y/Q represents material consumption per unit of quality of life; G/Y is GHG emissions per unit of consumption, and P is population (Mahong et al., 2014). GHG needs to be reduced to enhance the quality of life while reduction in Y/Q can be achieved via dematerialization of our lives by changing our preferences, behaviour, and social values. Technological advances in the sphere of decarbonization can be channelled to tackle major environmental challenges and contribute to lowering GHG/Y. The management and control of P is of paramount importance especially where environmental degradation and per capita emissions are very high (Kedir, 1994; Mahong et al., 2014; UNDESA, 2021; Yahaya et al., 2020).

Some encouraging local policies initiatives are emerging as climate change and energy efficiency continue to grab our attention. For example, in 2007, the Ghanaian parliament passed a bill to ban the sale of incandescent light bulbs at the expense of compact fluorescent light bulbs (CFLs). One of the goals of this measure was to reduce electricity consumption especially for domestic uses (Gyamfi et al., 2017; Würtenberger et al., 2011). Another energy-saving strategy is the "Promoting of Appliance Energy Efficiency and Transformation of the Refrigerating Appliances Market in Ghana" program. This program aimed to encourage households to trade in their old refrigerators for a voucher that will allow them to purchase a new, more energy-efficient refrigerator (Gyamfi et al.,

2017; Würtenberger et al., 2011). On the renewable energy front, Ghana has implemented the Ghana Energy Development and Access Project (GEDAP), which aims to promote access to electricity through off-grid renewable energy.

Mauritius has made considerable progress in green initiatives. The Mauritius Ille Durable (MID) concept was developed by the government to change the economic and social environment based on the 5Es (Economy, Employment, Environment, Energy, and Education). Specifically, in the field of energy, the long-term energy strategy (2009–2025) has facilitated the development of the grid code which aims to reduce the country's vulnerability to fossil fuel imports and ensures affordable energy for consumers. In addition, the strategy allows for the collection of taxes on petroleum products and coal, and the funds injected into the initial budget plan mobilized for the strategy (AfDB & OECD, 2013).

To address the negative effects of the COVID-19 pandemic, the South African government has initiated a long-term response plan. This includes policies on energy security and the green economy. For example, in energy, The Integrated Resource Plan (IRP) calls for the addition of 14 GW of wind power and 6 GW of solar power to existing capacity by 2030 (Department of Energy, 2020). In addition, the plan calls for an additional 2 GW of renewable energy. On the field of wind energy, some countries have also made an effort by integrating this energy source in their energy mix strategy. These are mainly countries like Egypt, Morocco, Tunisia, and South Africa (Mas'ud et al., 2017). In Morocco, the government adopted a renewable energy policy, Law 13–09, in 2011. This law plans to act in synergy with the national energy policy, and seeks to develop, adapt the renewable energy sector to future technological developments and encourage private initiatives (IRENA, 2013). Kenya has also made many efforts in recent years to transition to renewable energy. To this end, it has taken many initiatives to promote green energy such as: geothermal, hydro, biomass, biofuel, biogas, solar energy, and wind energy (Kenyan Ministry of Energy, 2018). Kenya is the leading African country in renewable energy as 73% of its energy capacity comes from renewable energy (Ashraf & Seters, 2022).

Green Economy Policies

In terms of green economy interventions, governments are planning to retrofit public and private buildings to improve energy and water efficiency. Other interventions include supporting small-scale farmers through public–private partnerships and improving energy efficiency. Like cities such as Sheffield, Copenhagen, or Amsterdam, the Government of Rwanda wants to make Kigali a green and futuristic city through the Green City Kigali program, a plan that includes the construction of environmentally friendly housing, climate-friendly infrastructure, and the expansion of the climate-friendly public transport system (Ashraf & Seters, 2022). Program construction is scheduled to begin in 2023. The Developing Rwandan Secondary Cities as Model Green Cities with Green Economic Opportunities project goes beyond Kigali to include secondary cities in the country. Certainly, the objective of this project is to support Rwanda's economic transformation through urbanization and green growth, focusing on the development of its secondary cities (GGGI, 2015).

Transport and Agriculture

Behrens et al. (2016) present a comprehensive overview of transport systems in Africa, covering a wide range of key issues such as reforms, regulation of urban transport systems, barriers to urban transport planning, and improving public transport service. Falchetta et al. (2021) shed a useful light on accessibility to transit and urban commuting in Africa. The authors use the General Transit Feed Specification (GTFS) data to produce comparative metrics of accessibility, network, and service quality of paratransit in seven major cities such as Abidjan, Accra, Addis Ababa, Freetown, Harare, Kampala, and Nairobi. On the transport front, many countries across the continent have adopted strategies to renew their vehicle fleet. For example, in Ghana, a Bus Rapid Transit (BRT) initiative is underway through the Ghana Urban Transport Project (Asimeng, 2021). This policy aims to facilitate daily transport for the populations of Ghana's two major cities, Accra and Kumasi, at an affordable cost and above all to reduce greenhouse gas emissions along the BRT pilot project corridors (Okoye et al., 2010). This initiative has also been developed in Senegal through the Regional Express Train project linking Dakar, the capital, and its suburbs. Klopp and Cavoli (2019) highlighted the significant importance of minibuses in Africa by studying the specific cases of Maputo and Nairobi. They suggest a careful data collection effort to bring these vital conduits of paratransit into structured and inclusive transport planning across cities in the continent.

In the field of agriculture, Mali is resolutely turning towards climate-smart agriculture given the strategic importance of the sector to the country's economy (FAO, 2017). Indeed, the government of Mali has established climate-smart agriculture as a pillar of its adaptation and mitigation strategy in the fight against the effects of climate change (MEADD, 2016). There are several initiatives across Africa that encourage adoption of climate-smart agriculture. For instance, in West Africa, the Consultative Group on International Agricultural Research (CGIAR) established a research programme on Climate Change, Agriculture and Food Security (CCAFS) since 2011 to develop Climate-Smart Villages (CSV) in Burkina Faso, Ghana, Mali, Niger and Senegal (Ouédraogo et al., 2018). This and other similar initiatives aim to increase agricultural productivity and income in a sustainable and equitable manner, strengthen adaptation and resilience to climate variability and change, and control and reduce greenhouse gas emissions wherever possible and appropriate at the regional level (CCAFS, 2016). When we evaluate the uptake of climate-smart agricultural innovations, it is important to acknowledge the barriers which emanate from a complex interaction of socioeconomic, institutional, infrastructural, biophysical, and political factors almost in all countries in Africa.

THE CHALLENGES OF PURSUING GREEN ECONOMIC POLICIES IN AFRICA

The African continent still faces challenges of persistent poverty and low human development. Food security is one of the most pressing needs of the African population. In sub-Saharan Africa, 33 to 35% of the population is malnourished, especially in rural areas (Joubert & Van Niekerk, 2016). According to Lal and Stewart (2019) soil fertility loss exacerbate the problems of food insecurity by accelerating the ongoing environmental degradation. Research over the last 30 years showed that soil fertility is decreasing due to environmental degradation, which is caused by poor soil and water management, inappropriate fertilizer use, decline in the use and length of fallow periods, overgrazing and logging, and population pressures that push farmers to less favourable lands (ELD Initiative and UNEP, 2015; Kedir, 1994). Employment creation continues to be a major challenge for sustainable development in Africa, especially in terms of green jobs.

Even with the high rates of economic growth in Africa since 2000, employment creation has been limited, especially among the youth and women. Sub-Saharan Africa averaged about 5% of GDP growth since 2000 with the whole continent growing slightly lower than 5% (Coleman, 2020). This positive story is encouraging but it is well known that the growth of the continent is not inclusive. This reveals a weak correlation between economic growth and employment creation in Africa. Studies have pointed to the fact that economic growth in the last decades has been led by capital-intensive enclave sectors,[1] with a low employment elasticity of output growth. A key question, therefore, is how the transition to a green economy can improve prospects for economic development, support the structural transformation of the economy to achieve more productivity and value addition, and address distributional impacts. This has led us to consider three different key sectors: energy, agriculture, and infrastructure and transport, which are very important in policies of Green economy in Africa.

- Energy sector challenges in Africa:

Current energy production, by country, is unable to meet the energy demand of virtually all African countries. The development and industrial growth of a country is, to some extent, related to the amount of energy at its disposal (Kihombo et al., 2021). Electricity is an important necessity for any country that is really interested in industrial growth. Nerini et al. (2016), reported that more than 1.3 billion people of the world's population still do not have access to adequate electricity. IEA (2019) notes that 530 million will remain without electricity in 2030 under current policies, and 90% of people globally without electricity will be located in Africa. According to the 2019 Global Renewable Energy Status Report, in 2017 the population of people without access to electricity fell below 1 billion. About 61% are from sub-Saharan Africa and 35% from Asia. Meanwhile,

---

[1] A useful notion to describe an enclave sector is to focus on foreign capital in Africa which is often extractive as most investments by multinational enterprises target the rich resource of the continent without meaningful job creation in host economies.

countries like China, Germany, India, Brazil, the United States, etc., have diversified into other forms of renewable and sustainable energy to meet their energy needs (Brodny, 2021).

For this reason, one of the main goals of the United Nations Sustainable Energy for All is to make access to electricity universal by 2030 (UNG, 2015). Therefore, African countries need to urgently address this issue and make a conscious decision that will benefit the entire population that depends on them and in line with the UN 2030 target. Owusu and Asumadu-Sarkodie (2016) reported that the detrimental effect of carbon dioxide emissions, in the long term, can lead to irreversible damage to the Earth and as we know, this consequently leads to global warming. Energy production and consumption, among other factors, have been reported to be the main causes of carbon dioxide emissions globally (Owusu & Asumadu-Sarkodie, 2016). Obtaining reliable, affordable, and clean energy would play a crucial role in achieving the seventh Sustainable Development Goal (SDG-7) by the year 2030 (Owusu & Asumadu-Sarkodie, 2016).

Another important reason for renewable energy is the fact that most developing countries, especially in Africa, do not have access to electricity. Take, for example, Nigeria which continues to suffer constantly from inadequate energy supply, load shedding, and blackouts for several decades. According to Ogundari and Otuyemi (2021), only about 40% of the entire country's total Nigeria population is connected to the national power grid. Olatomiwa et al. (2015), reported that 60% of the Nigerian population who are not connected to the national grid, therefore, they must depend on other means of electricity, for example, firewood/biomass consumption and self-powered production (diesel/petrol generator). This scenario is common to several African countries. Growing global energy needs, coupled with increasing population, have led to the continued use of fossil fuel-based energy sources, which is now considered problematic, due to various challenges (gas emissions to greenhouse effect, depletion of fossil resources) fuel reserves and other environmental concerns) (Owusu & Asumadu-Sarkodie, 2016). Responding to the Sub-Saharan Africa's growing energy needs is critical to supporting the economic development of the region, reduce poverty, and build community resilience to climate change.

- Challenges in Agriculture

Most of Africa's poor live in rural areas and depend on agriculture for their survival. (Schoch & Lakner, 2020). Dependence is both direct in food and cash crop cultivation, and indirect in working on farms or through trade in agricultural inputs and produce (Cleaver & Donovan, 2013). Unfortunately, in most countries in sub-Saharan Africa, agriculture has grown much more slowly than population, and farm incomes have stagnated in real terms or fallen.

The main problems remain weak economic and agricultural policy and insufficient public investment in infrastructure, rural education, agricultural services such as extension and research, and rural health (Fonta et al., 2018). Poor policy and weak public investment have led to a lack of private investment in agriculture, agricultural input supply, and processing. Domestic markets were lost to imports and export markets were therefore moved to countries in Asia, the Middle East, and Latin America. Moreover, Africans are facing three core issues of great importance for the future of agriculture: the demographic, the economic, and the environmental challenges. Sub-Saharan Africa is, in fact, the only subcontinent that continues to have a consistently high population growth rate with many poor people (Schoch & Lakner, 2020).

The West and Central Africa sub-regions have the highest overall fertility rate; with a clear pattern of higher fertility rates in poorer countries with a large share of rural population (Tesfa et al., 2023). Apart from the demographic challenge, also note the economic challenge. How to initiate a process of sustainable economic growth, made necessary by the rapid increase in population, with an uncompetitive agricultural base, all in a highly competitive economic environment at the global level. The problems include the difficulty of controlling the exploitation of indigenous resources and the reconstitution of forest resources; soil erosion and the fragility of planned landscapes following deforestation; water management in the context of climate change. Environmental challenges are also present, especially with the impact of climate change in the region which has consequences on agriculture. In addition, Africans face other challenges, whether political or social, which slow down the functioning of the agricultural sector.

- Challenges in transport and the infrastructure for greening policies

Greening the transport sector is a priority in some green economy strategies for many African countries. For example, Ethiopia has made low-carbon transport and infrastructure a key intervention in its Climate Resilient Green Economy/Growth and Transformation Plan II. According to the Word Bank Transport and ICT Global Practice report (2015), Africa is faced with three urgent transport concerns: the continent has the highest road mortality rate in the world, it has an unprecedented urbanization rate, and it has the highest transport costs in the world. Indeed, the situation of road safety in Africa slows its competitiveness and its development. Although the continent has the lowest road network density and very low percentage of vehicles in the world, the road mortality rate in Africa is the highest in the world.

At the same time, the urbanization rate of Africa is unprecedented, almost 5% on average over the past two decades. The number of new city dwellers should increase sharply by more than 300 million between 2000 and 2030. By 2050, 60% of Africans will live in urban areas, against a world average of 51%. For this time, Africa remains fragmented, mainly due to the lack of transport infrastructure and ineffective transport services (African Transport Policy Program; 2015). The situation is worse for landlocked countries, where transport prices contribute to 15 to 20% of import costs—three to four times more than in developed countries. The reduction in transport costs could result in a 25% increase in exchanges (World Bank, 2015).

On the infrastructure side, there is a huge deficit and that remains a major obstacle to Africa realizing its full economic growth potential. Studies, such as that of the African Infrastructure Consortium (ICA) (2020), have shown that poor road, rail, and port infrastructure increases the cost of goods traded between African countries by 30–40%. The poor state of infrastructure in sub-Saharan Africa (i.e., electricity, water, roads, and information and communication technologies), is detrimental to future economic growth. Increased economic activity, increased efficiency, and increased competitiveness are hampered by infrastructure in transport, communication, inadequate water, and electricity. The world is eager to do business with Africa, but struggles to access African markets, especially inland, due to poor infrastructure. Physical infrastructure or social infrastructure has a direct impact on the quality of life. Without this infrastructure, Africa will not achieve the levels of growth expected or required. Important discoveries of raw materials, such as oil and gas in East and South-East Africa, as well as the enormous demand in particular from Asia for agricultural and natural resources, including minerals such as that iron ore, platinum, coal, and copper drive infrastructure needs. The lack of infrastructure is a serious obstacle to growth and development, and results in a low level of intra-African trade and with other regions.

The Prospects of Green Economic Policies in Africa: The Case of Senegal

Africa has long suffered from the undesirable impacts of climate change such as rising sea levels, drought, floods, high temperatures, and a decrease of rainfall. However, the effects of climate change as well as Africa's economic and social vulnerability have been exacerbated by the COVID-19 pandemic. In fact, adaptive capacities, available resources to tackle climate change have been restricted (Pan-Africa, 2021). Researchers argue that, using recovery efforts, this pandemic may be an opportunity to restart a more ecologically friendly economic development (Rumea & Islam, 2020). However, various obstacles hamper the success of green economic policies and strategies in Africa and thus hinder the desired green growth. The low energy supply, which explains the low level of industrialization, and the defective transport infrastructure, which imposes high additional costs on industries, thus reducing their competitiveness, are examples of obstacles and challenges. These difficulties are exacerbated by factors such as poverty, insecure employment, food insecurity, rapid population growth, and lack of access to water (Omilola, 2014).

But presently, the green recovery action plan, which runs from 2021 to 2027, and initiated by the African Union, combined with various local actions such as in Senegal, could help accelerate the necessary transformations in Africa. In fact, this plan is based on strategic sectors for Africa such as agriculture, energy transition, land management, oceans, among others (AU, 2021). And fortunately, these same sectors already constitute the areas for the implementation of the environmental commitments signed at the international level through the Nationally Determined Contribution (NDC).[2] Like other countries, Senegal, in its NDC, has also committed to low-carbon development that will ensure the resilience of communities, cities, and the economy. Senegal's contribution will focus on the implementation of agricultural and forestry projects to mitigate carbon emissions, strengthening renewable energy and energy efficiency in industries and transportation for an efficient energy transition. For the case of Senegal, some initiatives or prospects for a green economy are presented in the following boxes.

Box 8.1: Less taxes for more solar

In recent years, Senegal, like other West African Economic and Monetary Union (WAEMU) countries, has utilized several advantages such as customs tax, value-added tax, community solidarity levy for the import of energy materials. Since 1998, Senegal set up the Commission for the Regulation of the Electricity Sector (CRSE) and a Rural Electrification Agency (ASER) to liberalize renewable energies for a better development of green energies in the framework of the fight against climate change. These measures are accompanied by energy development policies such as fiscal instruments, with an adequate legislative framework from 1992 to 2000 for materials related to renewable energies including an exemption from customs duty and other taxes. In fact, solar panels are exempt from customs duties, but they are subject to other import taxes. The other accessory materials, essential to the installation, such as cables, batteries, inverters, etc., are taxed at 20% of customs duties. Income tax reductions are also granted to investors to encourage them to switch from fossil fuels to renewable energy (Sarr, n.d.).

In Senegal, the road transport sector is the main source of air pollution. Therefore, Senegal is committed to reducing the negative externalities of transport through the development of more environmentally friendly mass transport systems, such as the Bus Rapid Transit (BRT) project and the Regional Express Train (TER). The implementation of the Bus Rapid Transit (BRT) project will be effective from 2023. One of the most significant impacts of the BRT project will be to contribute to the improvement

---

[2] Nationally Determined Contributions are non-binding national plans highlighting climate actions, policies and measures that governments aim to implement in response to climate change and as a contribution to achieving the global targets set in the Paris Agreement.

of air quality in Dakar as well as preventing the release of 446,480 tons of CO_2 by 2035 (CETUD, 2019). The operating phase of the TER will save nearly 8440 tCO_2 per year, or 337600t of carbon dioxide over a 40-year life span, because of the use of the train as a means of transportation instead of vehicles. It is planned to match these avoided emissions with traction energy from renewable energy sources needed to operate the TER. It is also planned to instal mini solar power plants for the operation of the stations, central station, ticketing, surveillance system, telecommunications, and lighting (BAD, n.d.).

Oil Discovery in Senegal

Following major discoveries of oil and gas deposits in Senegal, the launch of oil production and exploration is planned from 2023. Senegal's gas resources are estimated at 1120 billion m3 for 4 fields[3] and 1030 million barrels on 4 deposits for the oil that is being exploited, in total, revenues of 700 billion CFA francs per year are expected (Bendhaou, 2021). In the use of revenues, there is a ban on any early transfer of resources. Indeed, investments should remain consistent with the development objectives set out in the Senegalese Emerging Plan. Investments will therefore be directed towards essential areas such as education, health, infrastructure, and agriculture in order to strengthen and develop human capital, improve living conditions and structurally transform the economy (Bendhaou, 2021).

Box 8.2: Carbon tax: project of Senegalese carbon taxation

As Senegal, like other African countries, seeks to recover from the crisis caused by the pandemic, one can argue that it is an ideal time for Africa to begin its sustainable transformation. Senegal was already on this path long before the arrival of COVID-19. To continue with its low-carbon development plan, which is an "Emerging Senegal", and to align it with the market mechanism proposed by Article 6 of the Paris Agreement, Senegal has committed to introducing carbon pricing by 2025. In the first phase of the study, recommendations were made on the most appropriate types of instruments in the context of Senegal, a developing country.

---

[3] One of the deposits is co-managed with Mauritania.

Energy, forestry, agriculture, and waste are considered the most appropriate sectors for a carbon tax in Senegal (CIACA, 2018). Phase 2 of the study was launched in 2020, it is ongoing and will be based on international experiences with carbon taxes. Indeed, green taxation, an innovative strategy of environmental policy, would make it possible to change the behaviour of economic actors in favour of the environment and to mobilize additional resources to finance the ecological transition (Republic of Senegal, 2019). Other policies for an ecological transition finance are also being implemented in Senegal. These include (i) Automobile pollution (based on the age of vehicles) which could generate more than 5 billion FCFA per year. It is planned in Senegal to extend this fiscal policy as in the case of plastic pollution; (ii) the eco-tax or eco-contribution on Electrical and Electronic Equipment which considers the producer's responsibility for the end-of-life management of its equipment; and (iii) Green bonds could also allow Senegal to raise significant private capital to finance the transition to the green economy.

Box 8.3: Cement factory in Senegal using biomass for energy

The company has set up a large-scale Jatropha plantation project which aims at replacing 35% of its coal consumption by Jatropha fruits, thus reducing SOCOCIM's[4] CO_2 emissions by 623,000 tons over the first 7 years, and 68 706 tons of CO_2 per year (PDD, 2019; vivre un development durable, 2012). This SOCOCIM project targets a plantation of 11,000 ha of Jatropha, on 'marginal' lands of between 300 and 600 hectares. This project will allow the local populations, who are mainly farmers, to find work and thus earn additional income. The scope of this project covers sectors such as energy, waste management & disposal, and agriculture.

Box 8.4: Positive developments emanating from COVID-19: digitization and e-commerce

During the coronavirus pandemic, several Senegalese companies turned to online sales, which had begun to take off since 2014, to maintain their business. More and more Senegalese are using the internet to make

---

[4] Signifie «Société Commerciale du Ciment—Cement Trading Company». SOCOCIM is a cement manufacturing facility located in Rufisque, 30 km West of Dakar, Senegal.

purchases or access services. To facilitate this adaptation and to better fight the spread of the corona virus, the government has accelerated the implementation of necessary e-commerce reforms. An e-commerce platform has been created by the Minister of Commerce to provide easy access to the websites of small and medium-sized enterprises (SMEs) producing needed goods. These measures have contributed to the digital transition of the country, resulting in an optimized delivery of goods (UNCTAD, 2020). With e-commerce, the customer will no longer need to travel to the store by car, which is supposed to be a less CO_2 emitting alternative (Carbone4, 2021). It should also be noted that e-commerce also provides employment opportunities for young Senegalese. For example, in one year, the startups of Africa Internet Holding such as Kaymu, Jovago, Carmudi, Hellofood, Jumia, and Lamudi have recruited more than 100 young Senegalese in various sectors: marketing, logistics, sales, communication, etc. These observations suggest that e-commerce could very quickly become one of the country's economic forces, playing a major role in the labour market (Leral, 2015).

Conclusion

Green economy has attracted a lot of attention. This chapter discussed the current state of green economic policies in Africa as well as the challenges that policy makers are confronted with and the potential opportunities the continent can exploit for sustainable transformation of African economies. Given the technology development in advanced economies in the sphere of renewable energy and net zero transition, the continent can benefit from existing innovations and leapfrog the transition to renewables. However, there are huge challenges ranging from lack of finance, poor infrastructure, and the difficulty surrounding the discovery of oil which might be a stranded asset when the rest of the world seeks to pull away from fossil fuels. Despite the desirability of the lofty ambitions of green policies, the practical difficulties are binding, and the continent has a long way to go before embedding green economy principles in the development visions of member states. There is a lot of promise from rich countries to support those who suffer from climate change disproportionately through green finance mechanisms but so far commitments and actual disbursements from so donors are woefully low. Therefore, the adoption of green economic policies is less likely to be aligned across global regions with Africa being one of the continents deserving urgent attention in climate change.

REFERENCES

African Development Bank—AfDB. (2013). *African development report 2012: Towards green growth in Africa*. Green Growth team, AfDB.
African Development Bank—AfDB. (2022). *Supporting climate resilience and a just energy transition in Africa*. African Economic Outlook.
AfDB and OECD. (2013). *Enabling green growth in Africa*. Report from the workshop held in Lusaka, Zambia on 15–16 January 2013.
Aliyu, A., Ramli, A. T., & Saleh, M. A. (2013). Nigeria electricity crisis: Power generation capacity expansion and environmental ramifications, Energy. *A green economy in the context of sustainable development and poverty eradication: What are the implications for Africa?* United Nations Economic Commission for Africa, 2012. Ethiopia's Climate Resilient Green Economy, WB 2012.
Ashraf & Seters. (2022). *Green transition in Africa: implications for Sweden and the EU* (Discussion paper no. 320). Ecdpm making policies work.
African Union Commission. (2021). *African Union green recovery action plan 2021–2027*. Addis Ababa.
Asimeng, E. (2021). Bus rapid transit implementation with the inclusion of incumbent paratransit operators in African cities: Lessons from Accra. *Urban Planning and Transport Research*, 9(1), 534–548.
BAD. (n.d.). *Résumé de l'étude environnementale et sociale stratégique (EESS)*. Projet train express régional de Dakar (TER) Sénégal.
Barrios, S., Ouattara, B., & Strobl, E. (2004). *The impact of climatic change on agricultural production: Is it different for Africa?* Institute for Prospective Technological Studies, Joint Research Centre, European Commission.
Behrens, R., McCormick, D., & Mfinanga, D. (2016). *Paratransit in African Cities operations, regulation and reform*. Routledge.
Bendhaou, F. (2021). *Sénégal/hydrocarbures: Quatre points fondamentaux pour une gestion optimale des revenus*. https://www.aa.com.tr/fr/afrique/s%C3%A9n%C3%A9gal-hydrocarbures-quatre-points-fondamentaux-pour-une-gestion-optimale-des-revenus/2453671. Consulted on May 15, 2022.
Brodny, J., Tutak, M., & Bindzar, P. (2021). Assessing the level of renewable energy development in the European union member states. *Energies*, 14(13), 3765. https://doi.org/10.3390/en14133765
Carbone4. (2021). *Le e-commerce est-il vraiment un élément clé de la décarbonation du transport de marchandises?* https://www.carbone4.com/decryptage-e-commerce-decarbonation-transport. Consulted on May 9, 2022.

CCAFS. (2016). *A climate-smart agriculture alliance and framework for West Africa*. CCAFS Outcome Case. CGIAR Research Program on Climate Change, Agriculture and Food Security (CCAFS).

CETUD. (2019). *Le Sénégal économisera 446 480 tonnes de CO_2 entre 2020–2035 grâce au projet BRT*. https://www.cetud.sn/index.php/medias/news/actualites/257-le-senegal-economisera-446-480-tonnes-de-co2-entre-2020-2035-grace-au-projet-brt. Consulted on May 15, 2022.

CIACA. (2018). *Élaboration d'une étude d'opportunité sur la mise en place d'un instrument de tarification carbone au Sénégal dans le cadre de l'initiative*. Instruments de Collaboration pour une Action Climatique Ambitieuses (CI-ACA). Troisième rapport. AEE.

Cleaver, K., & Donovan, W. (2013). *Agriculture, poverty, and policy reform in Sub-Saharan Africa Deveze 2010 "Challenges for African Agriculture"*.

Coleman, C. (2020). *Africa is the last frontier for global growth, project syndicate*. https://www.project-syndicate.org/commentary/africa-growth-potential-reforms-by-colin-coleman-2020-02. Accessed March 26, 2023.

Curran, P., Dougill, A., Pardoe, J., & Vincent, K. (2018). *Policy coherence for sustainable development in sub-Saharan Africa Policy Brief*. London School of Economics.

Department of Energy. (2020). *Integrated resource plan 2019*. South African Government.

ELD Initiative & UNEP. (2015). *The economics of land degradation in Africa: Benefits of action outweigh the costs*.

EU. (2019). *Moroccan solar power plant hailed as 'shining example' for Europe*. https://www.theparliamentmagazine.eu/news/article/moroccan-solar-power-plant-hailed-as-shining-example-for-europe. Accessed on March 30, 2023.

FAO. (2017). *Country fact sheet on food and agriculture policy trends*. Food and Agriculture Organisation of the United Nations.

FAO. (2018). Impacts of climate change on farming systems and livelihoods in the Near East North Africa: Regional initiative on small-scale family farming for the near East and North Africa.

Falchetta, G., Noussan, M., & Hammad, A. (2021). Comparing paratransit in seven major African cities: An accessibility and network analysis. *Journal of Transport Geography, 94*, 103131.

GGGI. (2015). *Developing Rwandan secondary cities as model green cities with green economic opportunities*. Report 2: Green City Framework and Guidelines. 19F Jeongdong Bldg. 21–15 Jeongdong-gil Jung-gu Seoul 100–784 Republic of Korea.

Fonta, W., Kedir, A., Bossa, A., Greenough, K., Sylla, M., & Ayuk, E. (2018). A Ricardian valuation of the impact of climate change on Nigerian Cocoa production: Insight for adaptation policy. *International Journal of Climate*

Change, Strategies and Management. https://doi.org/10.1108/IJCCSM-05-2016-0074

Gregory, P. J., Ingram, J. S., & Brklacich, M. (2005). Climate change and food security. *Philosophical Transactions of the Royal Society B: Biological Sciences, 29*;360(1463), 2139–48. https://doi.org/10.1098/rstb.2005.1745. PMID: 16433099; PMCID: PMC1569578.

Gyamfi, S., Diawuo, F. A., Kumi, E.N., Modjinou, M., & Sika, F. (2017). The energy efficiency situation in Ghana. *Renewable and Sustainable Energy Reviews*. https://doi.org/10.1016/j.rser.2017.05.007

Herman, K. S. (2021). Green growth and innovation in the Global South: A systematic literature review. *Innovation and Development*. https://doi.org/10.1080/2157930X.2021.1909821

Hickel, J., & Kallis, G. (2019). Is green growth possible? *New Political Economy*. https://doi.org/10.1080/13563467.2019.1598964

ICA. (2020). *Catalysing Africa's infrastructure development: Infrastructure financing trends in Africa 2019–2020*. African Infrastructure Consortium.

IEA (International Energy Agency). (2019). *Africa Energy Outlook (2019)*. IEA.

IRENA. (2013). *IRENA case study*. Morocco wind Atlas. www.irena.org

Joubert, S., & Van Niekerk, J. (2016). Large-scale solar water heating in South Africa: Status, barriers and recommendations. *Renewable Energy, 97*, 809–822.

Kedir, A. (1994). *Environment, population and agricultural development in Ethiopia*. Paper published in the 4th Proceedings of the Ethiopian Economic Association, Addis Ababa, Ethiopia.

Kedir, A. (2014). Debating critical issues of green growth and energy in Africa: Thinking beyond our lifetimes. In K. T. Hanson, C. D'Alessandro, & F. Owusu (Eds.), *Managing Africa's natural resources: Capacities for development* (pp. 185–205). Palgrave Macmillan.

Kedir, A. (2018). *Environment and climate change in Africa in an era of sustainable development goals*. In K. T. Hanson, K. P. Puplampu, & T. M. Shaw (eds.), *From millennium development goals to sustainable development goals: Rethinking African development* (pp. 152–166). Routledge.

Kenyan Ministry of Energy. (2018, October). *National energy policy*. https://kplc.co.ke/img/full/BL4PdOqKtxFT_National%20Energy%20Policy%20October%20%202018.pdf

Kihombo, S., Ahmed, Z., Chen, S., Adebayo, T., & Kirikkaleli, D. (2021). Linking financial development, economic growth, and ecological footprint: What is the role of technological innovation? *Environmental Science and Pollution Research, 28*, 61235–61245.

Klopp, J., & Cavoli, C. (2019). Mapping minibuses in Maputo and Nairobi: Engaging paratransit in transportation planning in African cities. *Transport Reviews, 39*(5), 657–676.

Lal, R., & Stewart, B. A. (Eds.). (2019). *Soil degradation and restoration in Africa* (1st ed.). CRC Press. https://doi.org/10.1201/b22321

Leral. (2015). *Sénégal: E-commerce, une révolution créatrice d'emplois.* https://www.leral.net/Senegal-E-commerce-une-revolution-creatrice-d-emplois_a141622.html. Consulted on May, 9, 2022.

Mahong, L., Henry, M., & Haifeng, H. (2014). *Renewable energy in China: Towards a green economy* (Vol. 1). Enrich Professional Publishing.

Mas'ud, A., Wirba, A., Ardila-Rey, J. A., Albarracín, R., Muhammad-Sukki, F., Jaramillo Duque, Á., Bani, N., & Munir, A. (2017). Wind power potentials in Cameroon and Nigeria: Lessons from South Africa. *Energies, 10*(4), 443.https://doi.org/10.3390/en10040443

MEADD (Ministère de l'Environnement et du Développement Durable). (2016). *Contribution nationale déterminées au niveau National. Convention cadre des Nations Unies sur le changement climatique.* https://www4.unfccc.int/sites/ndcstaging/PublishedDocuments/Mali%20First/Mali_revised%20NDC.pdf

NASA. (2022). *Worst drought on record parches horn of Africa.* https://earthobservatory.nasa.gov/images/150712/worst-drought-on-record-parches-horn-of-africa. Accessed on March 31, 2023.

Nerini, F., Broad, O., Mentis, D., Welsch, M., Bazilian, M., & Howells, M. (2016). A cost comparison of technology approaches for improving access to electricity services. *Energy, 95*, 255–265.

Ogundari, I., & Otuyemi, F. A. (2021). Project planning and control analysis for suburban photovoltaic alternative electric power supply in Southwestern Nigeria. *African Journal of Science Technology and Innovation Development, 13*(1), 31–49.

Okoye, V., Sands, J., & Asamoah Debrah, C. (2010). *The Accra pilot bus-rapid transit project: Transport-land use research study.* Millennium Cities Initiative, The Earth Institute at Columbia University.

Olatomiwa, L., Mekhilef, S., Huda, A., & Ohunakin, O. (2015). Economic evaluation of hybrid energy systems for rural electrification in six geo-political zones of Nigeria. *Renewable Energy, 83*, 435–446.

Omilola B. (2014). *Inclusive green growth in Africa: Rationale, challenges and opportunities* (Policy Brief). UNDP.

Ouédraogo, M., Partey, S. T., Zougmoré, R. B., Nuyor, A. B., Zakari, S., & Traoré, K. B. (2018). *Uptake of climate-smart agriculture in West Africa: What can we learn from Climate-Smart Villages of Ghana, Mali and Niger?* (CCAFS Info Note). CGIAR Research Program on Climate Change, Agriculture and Food Security (CCAFS).

Owusu, A., & Asumadu-Sarkodie, S. (2016). A review of renewable energy sources, sustainability issues and climate change mitigation. *Cogent Engineering, 3*, 1. https://doi.org/10.1080/23311916.2016.1167990

Pan-Africa. (2021). *Driving a green and sustainable post-covid-19 recovery in Africa: Recommendations for Policy Actors.*

Project Design Document. (2019). Partial substitution of coal by Jatropha fruits and biomass residues in the production of portland cement. Version 6.1. SOCOCIM industries.

Rumea, T., & Islam, S. (2020). Environmental effects of COVID-19 pandemic and potential strategies of sustainability. *Heliyon*, 6(9), e04965.

Sarr, B. (n.d.). *Moins de taxes pour plus de solaire? Pluralité et poids des droits fiscaux et taxes sur les matériels énergétiques solaires au Sénégal depuis l'entrée en vigueur en 2000 du TEC de l'UEMOA.* Du soleil pour tous. https://scienceetbiencommun.pressbooks.pub/soleilpourtous/chapter/moins-de-taxes-pour-plus-de-solaire-pluralite-et-poids-des-droits-fiscaux-et-taxes-sur-les-materiels-energetiques-solaires-au-senegal-depuis-lentree-en-vigueur-en-2000-du-tec-de-lue/. Accessed on May 9, 2022.

Schoch, M., & Lakner, C. (2020). *The number of poor people continues to rise in Sub-Saharan Africa, despite a slow decline in the poverty rate.* World Bank.

Tesfa, D., Tiruneh, S., Gebremariam, A., Azanaw, M., Engidaw, M., Kefale, B., Abebe, B., Dessalegn, T., & Tiruneh, M. (2023). The pooled estimate of the total fertility rate in sub-Saharan Africa using recent (2010–2018) Demographic and Health Survey data. *Frontiers in Public Health, Section Children and Health*, 10.https://doi.org/10.3389/fpubh.2022.1053302

UNCTAD. (2020). *Au Sénégal le commerce électronique renforce la lutte conte le COVID-19.* https://trade4devnews.enhancedif.org/fr/news/au-senegal-le-commerce-electronique-renforce-la-lutte-conte-le-covid-19. Accessed on May 9, 2022.

UNECA. (2016). *Greening Africa's Industrialization, Economic Report on Africa.* Addis Ababa.

U.N.G. Assembly, Transforming Our World. (2015). *The 2030 Agenda for Sustainable Development. Resolution Adopted by the General Assembly on 25 September 2015, United Nations.* http://www.un.org/ga/search/view_doc.asp

United Nations Department of Economic and Social Affairs—UNDESA. (2021). *Global population growth and sustainable development* (UN DESA/POP/2021/TR/NO. 2, Population Division, New York).

United Nations Environment Programme. (2022). Emissions gap report 2022: The closing window—Climate crisis calls for rapid transformation of societies. Nairobi. https://www.unep.org/emissions-gap-report-2022

Vivre un développement durable. (2012). *SOCOCIM envisage de substituer près de la moitié de sa consommation de charbon par du Jatropha.* https://www.vivredurable.net/spip.php?article76

World Bank. (2022). *Putting Africans at the heart of food security and climate resilience.* https://www.worldbank.org/en/news/immersive-story/2022/10/17/putting-africans-at-the-heart-of-food-security-and-climate-resilience. Accessed on March 31, 2023.

Würtenberger, L., Bunzeck, I. G., & van Tilburg, X. (2011). *Initiatives related to climate change in Ghana: Towards coordinating efforts.* Climate & Development Knowledge Network (CDKN).

Yahaya, N., Hussaini, M., & Bashir, A. (2020). Population growth and environmental degradation in Nigeria. *Academic Journal of Economic Studies, 6*(1), 31–35.

CHAPTER 9

Digitalization of What We Eat and How We Think in Africa Post-COVID-19

Korbla P. Puplampu and Samuel M. Mugo

INTRODUCTION

The agricultural system in Africa, as in other parts of the world, occupies a central place in the political and socio-economic affairs of society. A robust system of agricultural organization is the foundation of a healthy economy. The system extends from agricultural production to marketing, and consumption, and interlinks to many other relevant social institutions. The educational system, one such institution, is central in the production and dissemination of the knowledge that can sustain agricultural organization. Given that several African countries occupy the lower levels of the human development index, there is an increasing interest in how technology and innovation can transform the African development agenda

---

K. P. Puplampu (✉)
Department of Sociology, Grant MacEwan University, Edmonton, AB, Canada
e-mail: puplampuk@macewan.ca

S. M. Mugo
Department of Physical Sciences, Grant MacEwan University, Edmonton, AB, Canada

© The Author(s), under exclusive license to Springer Nature Switzerland AG 2023
K. P. Puplampu et al. (eds.), *Sustainable Development, Digitalization, and the Green Economy in Africa Post-COVID-19*, International Political Economy Series, https://doi.org/10.1007/978-3-031-32164-1_9

(Arthur et al., 2020; UNDP, 2022). However, the COVID-19 global pandemic revealed three major lessons for African development. First, it swept away any modicum of recovery for African countries after the 2018 global financial crisis. Second, the pandemic laid bare the implications of inequality for global development, specifically the attainment of the Sustainable Development Goals (SDGs) by 2030 (Zeufack et al., 2022). Finally, COVID-19 reinforced the role of technological changes, especially digitalization and innovation to shore up problems in agricultural and educational systems in Africa.

In Africa, as in some parts of the world, food shortages or high prices of food can easily unleash political chaos. This is because the agricultural sector contributes to economic employment and input to agricultural and allied businesses. For example, the sector employs about 54 percent of workers in direct and indirect employment with that figure rising to over 70 percent in some African countries (Gwagwa et al., 2021). Contemporary systems of agricultural organization including value chain dimensions have changed the labor dynamics of the agricultural sector in different forms and critical areas of study in Africa especially in the context of COVID-19 (Grote et al., 2021; Nchanji et al. 2021; Puplampu & Essegbey, 2020). Equally significant is the systems of education that produce the necessary and required knowledge to sustain agricultural organization systems (Jacquet et al., 2022; Puplampu & Mugo, 2020; Swanepoel et al., 2020). Against this background, African governments, in alignment with global initiatives like the SDGs, continue to focus on the agricultural and educational systems with relevant policy and institutional initiatives. From the global framework, the key document is the United Nations-sponsored sustainable development goals (SDGs) (United Nations, 2015).

The 17 SDGs apply to both the global North and global South and a relationship between people and the environment, broadly defined and specifically around the notion of 5Ps (people, planet, prosperity, peace, and partnership), a relationship that reveals and calls for synergies to attain the desired goals (Tremblay et al., 2020). Focusing on the people-related aspects of the SDGs, SDG 1 (no poverty), SDG 2 (zero hunger), SDG 3 (good health and well-being), SDG 4 (quality education), SDG 5 (gender equality), SDG 6 (clean water and sanitation) are significant. In terms of prosperity, SDG 7 (affordable and clean energy), SDG 8 (work and economic growth), SDG 9 (innovation and infrastructure), and SDG 10 (reduced inequalities) are illustrative. Meanwhile, SDG 16 (peace) and

SDG 17 (partnerships) wrap up the essential aspects of the SDGs that are central to an analysis of agricultural and educational systems in Africa. Any successes in the agricultural and educational sectors of any society would require close relations with several SDGs. Improved outcomes in agriculture would revolve around the people, prosperity, peace and partnership goals, planet related goals such as SDGs 11 (sustainable cities and communities), 12 (responsible consumption and production), 13 (climate action), 14 (life below water), 15 (life on land). Similarly, the success of any educational system requires a viable interaction among the people, prosperity, peace, and partnership dimensions of the SDGs. As such, a holistic evaluation of the role of agricultural and educational systems in the African development agenda is essential.

From the African continental agricultural perspective, two specific policies must be identified. First, the almost decade-old campaign that declared 2014 as the Year of Agriculture and Food Security that drew on the earlier high-profile and politically endorsed 2003 Comprehensive Africa Agriculture Development Program (CAADP) as part of the 2003 Maputo Declaration (African Union, 2003, 2014). The second, the African Union Agenda 2063 with thematic priority areas on inclusive growth and sustainable development (AUC, 2015). Agenda 2063 specifically highlights the role of science, technology, innovation, and indigenous knowledge as part of the arsenal in the modernization of the agricultural sector to make it profitable and attractive to the continent's young people (AUC, 2015: 3). For the educational sector, notable continental policy initiatives include not only the broader African Union Agenda 2063, but also the Science Technology and Innovation Strategy for Africa (STISA 2024), and the Continental Education Strategy for Africa (CESA 16–25) (AUC, 2014, 2015, 2016). Educational systems, particularly higher education will be the sites for sustained investment with the stated purpose to catalyze "education and skills revolution and actively promote science, technology, research and innovation, to build knowledge, human capital, capabilities and skills to drive innovations and for the African century" (AUC, 2015: 4).

A recurring theme in both the global and continental policy positions is the role of technological changes via globalization and digitalization. In the case of technological changes, the result has been the compression of time and space, with specific outcomes for the role of the state and its relationship with non-state actors and society at large. While most studies focus on either agricultural or educational studies, there are few studies that integrate both agricultural and educational systems as part of the broader analysis of tertiary agricultural education (TAE) (Kabasa et al., 2015; Kraybill et al., 2022; Spielman et al., 2008). TAE addresses the nature of the relationship between agriculture and education, with a focus on agricultural training systems and programs in institutions of higher education. The digitalization of agriculture, and of education in a post-COVID-19 context is a valuable approach in Africa and is consistent with globalization.

This chapter utilizes the process of digitalization to study the relationship between agricultural and educational systems in Africa. With a focus on the people and prosperity aspects of the SDGs, what they eat through agriculture, how they think, through higher education, the chapter argues that digitalization has the potential to break down boundaries, can foster and generate novel ways of agricultural education and cross-national knowledge transfer to catalyze development in Africa post-COVID-19. However, digitalization as part of surveillance capitalism cannot be a neutral entity in the development process. Therefore, the challenges and pitfalls of digitalization and surveillance capitalism will be addressed, and viable options presented. To demonstrate the argument, the study is divided into three main sections. The first section will situate digitalization and surveillance capitalism, agriculture, and education in an appropriate theoretical framework. Section two will examine the tertiary agricultural institutions landscape in Africa with a focus on specific institutions. The third section will analyze the relationship between tertiary agricultural education and trends in digitalization, sketch out challenges before proceeding to policy options and concluding remarks.

Digitalization of Agriculture and Higher Education: A Theoretical Overview

The theoretical situatedness of TAE revolves around the role of education in agricultural development. It is a role that is central to modernization theorists in the creation of a knowledgeable or required human capital based on science and technology. Classical modernization theories in the early postcolonial period formulated technology as the missing link in the transformation of agrarian and traditional societies to industrial-based and technological societies on their way to modernity. It is therefore postulated that while technology would transform agricultural systems with the introduction of new production and marketing techniques, educational institutions would create new knowledge to empower farmers, for example, in their agricultural operations. The role of technological change in agriculture finds expression in the Green Revolution in Indian agriculture in the 1960s. The new forms of technology led to increases in agricultural output, but also exposed small holder farmers to expensive agricultural inputs sourced and controlled by big corporations and had negative environmental consequences due to monocropping and the use of agro-chemicals (Giles & Stead, 2022: 43).

Although the technological transformation from the Green Revolution did not live up to expectations in terms of equity and empowerment, the dramatic contemporary breakthroughs in communication and information technologies and digitalization have unique possibilities for African agriculture. Digitalization comes across as "creating leapfrogging opportunities in communications" with subsequent transformations and opportunities in various sectors of the economy, including agriculture and education (OECD & ACET 2020: 11). Digitalization technology, and technological processes occupy a central place in the role of agriculture and higher educational systems in the development discourse. In agriculture, technological innovations and value chain considerations improve productivity and consumers embrace new agricultural products (Puplampu & Essegbey, 2020: 41), just as technology also contributes to learning systems (Puplampu & Mugo, 2020: 150). The central aspect of technology in both agriculture and education is the generation of new forms of knowledge driven by digitalization and innovation.

Digitalization and innovation are by nature and character not neutral in agricultural and educational systems and outcomes. Rather they are premised on the architecture of what Zuboff (2019: 8; italics in original) calls surveillance capitalism, which is the behavioral data, that, within the context of machine-learning systems can be "fabricated into *prediction products*" that have a temporal dimension of "what you do now, soon, and later... these prediction products are traded in a new kind of marketplace for behavioral prediction...." Google pioneered surveillance capitalism and the concept is key in the role of technology in digitalization. For instance, it demonstrates the processes whereby the predictive behavior can be commodified. Indeed, the relationship and implications for innovation in the current age of the internet of things (IoTs) is the subject of debate between technological optimists and technological pessimists, especially in the case of the global South (Avgerou, 2008, 2010; Giles &

Stead, 2022; Hackfort 2021; Kraemer et al., 2009; Prause et al., 2021; Thompson, 2008).

The key focus in the technocentric model or optimists is on the nature and character of the technology and its role in policy discussions in agriculture, regardless of time and space. This emphasis, informed by several assumptions underpinned discussions on technology transfer and draws from the classical work of Rogers (1995) on diffusion processes in the transfer or physical movement of tools or physical processes from the global North to the global South. One assumption is that the material endowments within technology or information systems "are adequately independent from the social circumstances that give rise to them to be transferable, more or less intact, into any other society" (Avgerou, 2010: 4). There is an assumption here that technology is neutral in nature and thus value-free. Another assumption is that technology and innovation would flow freely from the global North to the global South. Analysts, bringing these attributes to bear on, for example, the case of digitalization of agriculture, argue that digital transformation is a potential game changer that would significantly affect food production, distribution, and consumption (Klerkx & Rose, 2020: 4). The idea of the potential game changer metaphor in theorizing the relationship between technology and agriculture was also at play in the Green Revolution (Prause et al., 2021).

The techno-pessimists are not against the use of technology in agriculture. Rather, they raise critical questions about the motivation of various actors in the digital reorganization of agriculture and systems of learning, specifically its situatedness in colonialism as well as global capitalism and point out omissions in the emerging discourse (Chukwuere, 2017; Giles & Stead, 2022; Klerkx & Rose, 2020; Msila, 2021). At stake is the thorny problem of social inequality in terms of access to resources in the organization of both agricultural and educational systems. The assumption here is that technology may contribute to technological concentration and a digital divide. What is at stake for techno-pessimists is the argument that technology is value-laden, not a disembodied entity and its impact is not neutral. The digital divide, which is about the differential access to technology does not simply disappear because of new forms of technology or innovation since access to technology cannot be taken for granted. An emerging shift on the key actors and owners of digital technology development to include African grown technologies may further realign the techno-pessimissits and techno-optimists discourse. This is because the distrust dimension of techonology seems to depend on several factors, including who owns the technology and for whom.

Notwithstanding the debate between the techno-optimists and the techno-pessimists, there are areas of convergence in their respective stances. First, both highlight the role of technology, but proceed on a different set of assumptions. While the proponents assume that technology is a rational product and neutral, the opponents point to constraining social factors. Second, both proponents and opponents present technology as an external phenomenon to African agricultural and educational systems. Missing from both perspectives are two main issues: first the policy and institutional framework and capacity; and second human agency and resistance (Srinivasan, 2019). It is therefore important to situate the debate on digitalization in African agriculture and education in a wider policy and institutional framework that considers how various countries or regions employ technology to address local needs in a way that has significant implications for social change in agriculture and education, and ultimately, social development.

In bringing the foregoing to bear on TAE, the attention is on tertiary or higher educational institutions such as universities, technical universities, and agricultural colleges. The main areas of attention in a study of TAE in Africa are institutional capacity in the production of the required human capital, an outcome that is contingent on the nature of the curriculum and academic faculty. The curriculum is a central part of the education of learners and defines the pedagogical approach. Curriculum is the course of study that includes goals for student learning (skills, knowledge, and attitudes); and the instructional material they study, its sequence, evaluation and assessment techniques in a way that improves the learning experience (Barrier et al., 2019: 34; Villet, 2022: 230).

While the teacher is key in operationalizing the curriculum as part of knowledge creation, the operationalization is also dependent on the philosophical orientation of the educational system.

There are two philosophical orientations, the traditional status-quo approach, and the transformative approach. The former approach is closely tied to the colonial context and the circumstances that led to the creation of universities in Africa (Puplampu, 2006). In that environment, African universities were modeled on the university structure of their colonizer. The result was the curriculum inhibited did not pay serious attention to the creation of knowledge to address issues in the relationship between the social and natural environments (Villet, 2022: 230). Notably, the status-quo approach, it is important to note, gave rise to a curriculum that was not anchored in the political and socio-economic circumstances of the country, even though universities on the dawn of postcolonial rule assumed a pivotal role in the national development agenda (Green, 1997).

The transformative approach acknowledges the historical origins of African universities and the failure of the postcolonial state to transform institutions for national development and consistently mentions the role of the curriculum and, by extension, how that frames the relationship between educators and learners. The transformative approach therefore requires African universities to embark upon changes in the higher education curriculum, adopt innovative teaching and learning practices that would spark the imagination of learners and leading them on a journey of deep reflection and subsequent learning with the hope that the learning process would make it possible to solve existing political and socio-economic problems (Villet, 2022: 232). As an approach, it recognizes academic faculty as one major actor, who together with learners, would operationalize the curriculum. The overriding issue is how the relationship between educators and learners, against, the democratizing impulses of digitalization, will inform not only the creation of knowledge, but the utilization of new forms of knowledge to enhance the human capital required for agricultural development and national development. Furthermore, it is useful to bear in mind that digitalization is subject to commodified relations, hence its role in the business of producing transformative knowledge in tertiary agricultural education would not be problem-free. To examine the on-folding dynamic relationship calls for some remarks on digitalization and the tertiary agricultural education landscape in Africa.

DIGITALIZATION AND AFRICAN UNIVERSITIES: THE LANDSCAPE OF TERTIARY AGRICULTURAL INSTITUTIONS

Digitalization has changed and transformed several aspects of the African society spawning new economic opportunities, especially in the case of education and agriculture to enhance the human capital potentials for the region's youth, especially in post-COVID-19 Africa (AUC/OECD, 2021; Daum, 2021; Langthale et al., 2020). The Africa Union (2014) *Science, Technology and Innovation Strategy for Africa (STISA) 2024* identified universities on the continent as sites for building excellence to inform social transformation. While there is recognition that African universities are yet to attain the capacity to create and transfer knowledge, digitalization efforts underway in several universities are essential parts of capacity improvement (AfDB & KOAFEC, 2019). The same source identified the variations in access to computers across the continent with good access at schools in Egypt, Mauritius, Morocco, and Rwanda, and not in Angola, Ghana, Liberia, and Sierra Leone (AfDB & KOAFEC, 2019: 58). Consequently, even though universities continue to be lead institutions when it comes to innovation, the innovation capacity in many African universities, apart from those in South Africa, are limited (AfDB & KOAFEC, 2019: 70).

In any case, the extent of digitalization in respective African countries has implications for the state of digitalization in their universities. For universities, the key aspect of digitalization is in the business of knowledge production, especially the knowledge that is transformative and elevates the role of the university as the site of national and continental development. The state of internet connectivity in Africa and the regional disparities informed the nature of the National Research and Education Networks (NREN), which researchers use to gauge the level of national support for research, and the subsequent classificatory systems as Matured, Connecting, Starting, to No Activity (Internet Society, 2017: 28). The Matured NRENs have made significant strides in digitalization with a favorable regulatory regime, well established synergies, including with universities and research institutions by 2016. The countries in this category are Algeria, Egypt, Kenya (TAE), South Africa (TAE), and Uganda (TAE). The Connecting NRENs countries have established physical networks among their universities and research institutions and geared towards initiating international networks. These include countries such as Cote d'Ivoire, Mozambique, Nigeria, and Rwanda (National Digital Policy). As implied, the Starting NRENs have not yet built any strong physical networks between academic and other sites of interconnectivity of institutions. Thus, there is a lag in the institutional framework. Some countries in this category include Benin (TAE), Cameroon, Democratic Republic of Congo, Gabon, Lesotho, and Malawi. Finally, the No Activity category is home to countries that do not have NREN activities on the ground. The specific countries range from Angola, Cape Verde, Central African Republic, Chad, Comoros, to Republic of Congo.

In terms of universities, an essential part is therefore the digitalization of the learning system, specifically information and communication technologies (ICTs) in teaching and learning about different aspects of the agricultural system, including value chain and agri-business. At issue is the fact that agricultural knowledge can best be attained from the intersections of several knowledge systems, especially the innovation ecosystem in an institutional setting like the university. Makerere University's Artificial Intelligence (AI) and Data Science research facility has been a resounding success on various fronts (Srinivasan, 2019). The lab has been central in the crops research involving AI, specifically in the identification and diagnosis of viral crop diseases in cassava plants, findings that mitigate the spread of diseases and enhance the digitalization of agricultural production (Srinivasan, 2019: 207).

Beintema et al. (2022) identified several features of the institutionalization of TAEs in Africa. First, they are mostly public institutions, standalone entities like colleges of agriculture or embedded as Faculties of agriculture and natural resources within the university. In this regard, TAE is part of the national innovation or research infrastructure in several African countries. Second, there are significant variations in the number of TAE institutions across the African continent, but with disproportionate numbers in Nigeria, Kenya, and South Africa (Beintema et al., 2022: 87–89). Third, African universities, like their counterparts in other regions, have been the focus of institutional restructuring in the last three decades and as part of the globalization of higher education (Puplampu & Wodinski, 2016). One premise of the restructuring was to introduce the market ethos in running the academy in terms of the selection of and enrollment in courses. However, the emerging private universities in Africa have stayed away from introducing courses and offering degree on TAE compared to business and other areas of study (Beintema, 2022: 87). This is because private universities seek a higher return on their investment and focus on knowledge areas that generate such returns (Tettey, 2006). Finally, the TAE system in Africa is poised to play a dominant role in the emerging landscape of disruptive technology and the knowledge development regime on the continent (Puplampu & Mugo, 2020).

According to Kraybill and Osiru (2022) existing TAE institutions in Africa provide insights to the possibilities these institutions can have on the communities they serve and the larger development agenda. The four existing institutions to be analyzed are the Jomo Kenyatta University of Agriculture and Technology (JKUAT) in Kenya, Gulu University (GU), Uganda, University of Abomey-Calavi (UAC), Benin, and the University of Venda (UNIVEN), South Africa. The history of the Jomo Kenyatta University of Agriculture and Technology (JKUAT) began in

1981 with the establishment of Jomo Kenyatta College of Agriculture and Technology in Juja, around Nairobi, as a joint venture between the Governments of Kenya and Japan. The College assumed the status of a university in 1994 and has satellite campuses in other parts of Kenya and neighboring East African countries such as Rwanda and Tanzania (Kraybill & Osiru, 2022: 241). As a tertiary agricultural institution, JKUAT offers programs in agriculture and natural resources and other areas like health sciences, engineering and technology, pure and applied sciences, and development with its biotechnology and energy and environment institute.

JKUAT, as part of its transformation, embarked upon several institutional initiatives, including reaching out to both external and internal agents or institutions, rethinking priorities, and changes in mindset (Kraybill & Osiru, 2022: 243). For example, in terms of external and internal agents, the institution sought strategic partnership with academic institutions on the African continent (South Africa) and in Europe and North America. Rethinking priorities was about ways of communicating organizational goals to maximize buy-in from faculty and staff. The central theme in all the initiatives was to better position the university in "addressing problems of food security" (243) and also serving as a site "for training, research and problem-solving" (Kraybill & Osiru, 2022: 244).

Gulu University, another public institution, is based in northern Uganda, opened its doors in 2002 with a focus on agriculture and environmental science. Located in Gulu with a transformative agenda against the backdrop of post-conflict reconstruction, Gulu University focused on the idea of community engagement forms of learning. Consequently, the university is "outward-looking and developmental in its orientation to a much greater extent than most African universities. It connects with the region's problems and concerns through its work-study program, which embeds students in the surrounding region for extended periods of time" (Kraybill & Osiru, 2022: 245). The forms of learning were intentionally based on knowledge co-creation and bolstered by funding from the Government of Uganda, the institution has expanded in terms of enrollment and programs including partnership with foreign universities like the Earth University in Costa Rica (Hulela et al., 2022: 128).

Kraybill and Osiru (2022) identify the University of Abomey-Calavi (UAC), which is part of the National University of Benin, as a third notable TAE in Africa. The university was established in 1970 and has two campuses with a total of six Faculties including agronomic sciences, arts and humanities, science and technology, and technology and teacher training. The transformation of the UAC was premised on leadership, specifically, the election of their top administrators who "launched a modernization process with the goals of increasing the relevance of the university's degree programmes for employment and increasing the quality and quantity of research conducted" (245). The program changes also included curriculum review and other pedagogical initiatives.

The final illustrative institution is the University of Venda (UNIVEN), a public university in South Africa, was established in apartheid-era South Africa in 1981 and upon the transition to democratic rule in 1994 shifted its focus to science and technology (Kraybill & Osiru, 2022). By 2002, University of Venda has become a comprehensive university with a single campus location of Thohoyandou in the Limpopo Region of South Africa (Kraybill & Osiru, 2022). Its transformational variables included the external and internal contexts and changes in mindset. In terms of the former, UNIVEN benefited from the infusion of resources from the South African government, including infrastructural support which was augmented by a strategic-minded institutional leadership. In the case of the latter, UNIVEN also embarked on improved communication strategies and an orientation on enlarging the spheres of diversity, relevance, and excellence (Kraybill & Osiru, 2022: 247). The cumulative result has been "research output per researcher increased 783% from 2008 to 2015, based on research output units defined by South Africa's National Research Foundation" (Kraybill & Osiri, 2022: 247). There are several issues at stake in the interface between digitalization and TAE in Africa. In view of the complex relationship among people, planet, prosperity, peace, and partnership dimensions of TAE, the subsequent analysis will focus on common threads around institutional capacity and the policy regime as part of a holistic approach to analyzing the role of higher education in the national development project.

DIGITALIZATION OF WHAT WE EAT AND HOW WE THINK IN AFRICA: ANALYSIS AND CRITIQUE

The complex relationship between agriculture and education in the African development agenda calls for a holistic analytical approach and so the fundamental issue is to analyze the relationship against the backdrop of digitalization and surveillance capitalism. An initial entry point is the two related aspects of the SDGs framework, first, the people and planet relationship and, second, the partnership debate. The key areas in the people and planet relationship are institutional capacity in terms of training and human capital, faculty research and teaching relations, and the implications for teaching and student learning in agricultural education. The digitalization and transformation aspects of the people and planet nexus can be examined in two different ways: the national context and African universities. One key aspect of digital technology is its transferability and universality into a social environment. Srinivasan (2019: 197–198) therefore points to the potential of technological innovations that can impact the power grid in several African countries. There is an emerging space for off-the-grid startups such as Greenlight Planet (in Eastern and Western African countries such as Kenya, Tanzania, Uganda and Nigeria) and M-KOPA (Ghana, Kenya, Nigeria, Uganda) (EEP Africa, 2021; M-KOPA, 2021). The result in all of these trends is that technological innovations affect the people and planet relations dimensions of the SDGs and African development, making it possible to preserve agricultural lands that would be essential in agricultural production systems, even as the technological innovations are also central in energy marketing or transporting and ultimately patterns of consumption.

According to Puplampu and Essegbey (2020: 46), technological changes in addressing agriculture and climate change concerns, "improve the quality of agricultural produce and products for consumers" especially in the context of "national, regional and global value-chain operations." Perhaps, financial services to farmers are the most developed aspect of digitalized agriculture in Africa, illustrated by the case of M-Pesa in Eastern Africa, Esoko (West and East Africa) to DrumNet (Kenya), providing digitalized services to farmers in areas such as real-time prices of agricultural goods, input supplies, and cash transfers (Abdulhamid, 2020; Ndung'u 2018; Yonazi et al., 2012). The technological possibilities in the interface between farmers and the market provide predictability for farmers as well as flexibility in credit systems.

Central to the people and planet relation aspects of digitalization of agricultural organization is the knowledge-producing infrastructure. The National Research Education Networks (NREN) found that Africa is at the bottom, at 67 percent compared to the global average of 71 percent (Zeleza & Okanda, 2022: 7). The NREN picture at the continental level has relevance for an understanding of TAE in Africa. The TAEs in Kenya, South Africa, and Uganda discussed earlier also reflected the fact that these three countries also happen to have the most Matured NRENs on the continent, suggesting that a bold national digitalization approach will rub off on universities and improve their capacity in the national context. For example, the strides in AI at Makerere University in Uganda demonstrate the digital ethos in the country. The innovative work from Makerere University's AI and Data Science lab can be attributed to the work of Gregg Zachary and Ernest Mwebaze (Srinivasan, 2019). The science group at Makerere adopted the ethical approach of creating technology to solve local problems. In other words, African countries have taken the view echoed by the Africa-based technology journalist Toby Shapsak that technology's capability to solve problems can best be better appreciated in an environment that has several problems that require solutions (Srinivasan, 2019: 197). So for example, the researchers pioneered Mcrops, a software to identify and diagnose crop diseases in cassava plants (Srinivasan, 2019: 207). These cases illustrate that the potential for researchers in African universities to bring their innovative findings to address specific issues in their communities cannot be disputed.

The second concern is to stress the interdisciplinary dimensions of TAE and that calls for a network approach to tertiary agricultural education in Africa (Nakayiwa & Lyman, 2022). This approach seeks to bring together institutions with the same or different capacities that have common policy objectives and "leverage their comparative advantages and maximize economies of scale in order to access resources for research and outreach, while also establishing nodes of specialization with viable regional academic programmes" (Nakayiwa & Lyman, 2022: 227). The Regional Universities Forum for Capacity Building in Agriculture (RUFORUM) is a valuable networking approach with African universities such as the University of Ghana, University of Dar Es Salaam, Tanzania, University of Cape Town, South Africa, and Addis Ababa University in Ethiopia (Nakayiwa & Lyman, 2022: 230). The important question is the extent to which RUFORUM can leverage these partnerships to deepen the quality of tertiary university education in Africa. For example, the strides at Makerere University and other TAE institutions on the continent could showcase intra-African consolidation, a process that, drawing on digitalization, can benefit and improve student learning.

However, a point worth stressing is that many African universities have intensified their efforts at digitalization, especially in the context of the response to COVID-19 global pandemic (Mhlanga, 2022; Osabwa, 2022; Zeleza & Okando, 2022). The major problems are data cost, internet speed, and internet reliability, even as there are growing efforts of institutional supports including contributions to the cost of data, provision of a device, and significantly some "institutions [have] adopted innovative ameliorative measures, ranging from negotiating zero-rated access with technology companies or reduced subscription prices to educational context, to providing free dongles to students without remote connections" (Zeleza & Okando, 2022: 14). An overriding lesson was the need to build and maintain digital capacities in the first place, since that is one way to minimize the digital divide among and within countries as well as the need for universities to rethink modes of educational delivery while maintaining quality and improving access (Mhlanga, 2022; Osabwa, 2022).

Furthermore, there have been concerted efforts to employ information technology in curricula improvement in several African universities, even as a technological infusion in curriculum per se does not guarantee equitable or improved learning outcomes. South Africa is in the Matured category of the NREN and most universities in the country have internet bandwidth comparable to European universities (Czerniewicz et al. 2014: 124). The country's performance in digitalizing higher education notwithstanding, in view of the apartheid legacy, students in South African universities have been contesting the curriculum (Luckett, 2016). Thus, digital technology alone cannot be the missing link in curriculum changes that can maximize the nature of learning outcomes. This is because technology is not neutral in terms of outcomes. Outcomes are contingent on a range of other factors, including faculty training, the terms of their rewards, and the cost of technology. Policy initiatives therefore must focus on renewal and incentivize the professoriate, be intentional with research investment, and the production and transfer of knowledge to impact the community.

The second analytical focus is the partnership question that interrogates the age-old issue of foreign aid and its impact on people and the planet relations, in terms of institutional capacity in African universities. There are two significant partnership initiatives worthy of further analysis. First, the role of Chinese technological companies in Africa and second, the role of global digital giants like Google and Meta. China has a long history in the African development program dating back to the early postcolonial era, beginning with Prime Minister Zhou Enlai's historic visit to Ghana in 1964. Against this historical backdrop, the Forum on China-Africa Cooperation (FOCAC) in 2000 was the deepening, not the beginning, of China's role on the African continent. One area of the deepening relationship is in digitalization and the prominent role of two Chinese telecommunications companies, Huawei and Zhongxing Telecommunications Equipment Corporation (ZTE) in Africa (Cooke, 2012; Pawlicki, 2017). It is therefore not surprising that in 2010, Huawei donated computers and other information and technology products to universities in Ghana and Uganda, entered into partnership agreements with universities in Kenya as part of an exchange arrangement for IT professionals between African countries and China (Ehizuelen, 2018: 571–572; Li, 2016: 189–190; NEPAD and UN, 2015: 54–55).

These partnerships must be celebrated since they offer a framework for technology transfer and human capital development in digitalization in African universities and are thus essential in creating knowledge forms for agricultural education (Agbebi, 2018; Ehizuelen, 2018; Li, 2016). The Huawei training centers will only augment the skills of labor when working for Huawei or another IT company. While the employment opportunities for those working in the IT field will contribute to poverty alleviation, the issue is the link between the IT industry and, in this case, TAE . Donations to universities need to complement local capacity-building efforts towards knowledge creation, technology transfer, and human capital development (Puplampu & Mugo, 2020). This is because the chances for technology transfer are minimal when local actors are not active in critical areas of the technological systems, especially if such controls are in the hands of Huawei or Chinese nationals or expertise from Europe (Ehizuelen, 2018: 571; Reed, 2013). At issue is the nature of the aid package. For example, the partnership that Japan forged with the JKUAT had the potential to research transfer and capacity, which is quite different from the donation of computers by China to universities in Ghana and Uganda.

The persistent problem is the skills gap between what students are learning and what they are expected to accomplish in the labor market, a relationship that is of utmost importance in TAE. Hence, the need for TAE institutions to "stay abreast of the evolving competencies required in agricultural food systems if they are to succeed in training highly-sought-after and valued graduates capable of creating employment opportunities for themselves and others" (Hulela et al., 2022: 127). As mentioned earlier, Gulu University in Uganda embarked up curriculum changes and incorporated entrepreneurial principles and other pedagogical initiatives from the Earth University in Costa Rica. There is an increasing realization that ICT partnerships must be integrated into teaching and learning through significant changes in the curriculum, a recognition that has been the subject of other donor assistance programs (Zschocke et al., 2013).

Partnership agreements must elevate the training or capacity of local or national institutions, address the digital divide and the related cost, as well as access problems for citizenry. One hallmark of a digitized society is that services, including public services can be accessed online, especially in the case of educational institutions. It is necessary to possess the appropriate skills to participate in the burgeoning knowledge society, the increasing and changing nature of jobs in the service economy associated with the internet of things (Hanson, 2020; Hanson & Puplampu, 2018; Hanson & Tang, 2020). In other words, a singular focus on technology transfer and human capital development must go beyond the establishment of training centers for operators (Sutherland, 2016: 186). The point is how digitalization would help in any attempt at improving agricultural and educational institutions in Africa.

The second aspect of the partnership dimension is the activities of global digital giants in Africa. As Srinivasan (2019: 192–193) states "Apple, Amazon, Google, Facebook, Microsoft, and many others [including Chinese technology companies] are moving all over the continent, setting up shop in urban hubs such as Johannesburg and Cape Town (in the south), Nairobi and Kigali (in the eastern and central region), and Accra, Lagos, and Abuja (in the west)." By their nature, the global digital giants are profit-seeking entities and while that, by itself, is not necessarily negative, the question is whether their motivations and activities will dovetail into producing knowledge relevant to agricultural educational systems in Africa. Put differently, the issue is the implications of the activities of technology giants for African universities in the areas of agriculture and education.

Consequently, the question is not the nature of Google and other tech giants, rather it is the role they seek to play in Africa. Gwagwa et al. (2021: 3–4) draw attention to Google's AI open-source library, TensorFlow, that is used to monitor crops for disease. A technology start-up company in Kenya is using TensorFlow to recognize species and diseases in crops with a high degree of accuracy. The South African company, Aerobotics, uses aerial imagery and machine-learning algorithms across several industries, for example in agriculture, to address early pest detection and control (Aguera et al, 2020: 23). Furthermore, a Kenyan company, Apollo

Agriculture, utilizes AI to enhance agricultural services, specifically to "interpret satellite data, soil data, farmer behavior, and crop yield models. The data interpretation algorithms are targeted at detecting plant pests and diseases and give farmers access to customized financing, seed, and fertilizer packages" (Gwagwa et al.: 4).

The foregoing illustrations point to the motivations and eventual outcomes of the role of technology giants in improving agricultural educational systems in Africa. While it is obvious that Google's AI in a smartphone will help the farmer, the argument is that Google needs to work rather closely with tech companies based on the African continent to development context-relevant technology that can support agricultural education. A partnership that is supported by capable internal actors will be one aspect of ensuring optimal outcomes, as was the case in the Makerere University AI and Data Science lab. There is unstated skepticism about the motives of Google and other technology giants in their rush to establish a foothold in Africa. The skepticism is fueled by the suspicion that Google is attempting to address their algorithmic bias problem with respect to their AI architecture. In 2015, Google photos labeled phenotypical Africans as "gorillas" highlighting the technological biases that result from a lack of horizontal co-creation for knowledge ecosystems (BBC, 2015). The contention is that technological context matters, more so in the case of agricultural and educational systems. Even though Africa seems to be a booming digital market with teeming youthful and savvy digital natives, the major ICT drivers and beneficiaries are the global tech giants like Facebook and Google. The issue is that these "organizations, through their software, are the gateway to the internet in Africa, while Chinese firms have also benefited on the hardware side" (Ademuyiwa & Adeniran, 2020: 13).

Policy Options and Conclusion

This chapter addressed the challenges of digitalization for what we eat and how we think in Africa. In effect, the role of TAE institutions in the context of digitalization and institutional capacity in knowledge production and dissemination. Anchored by the notion of diffusion and technology transfer, the chapter surveyed the landscape of TAE institutions and their digitalizing imperatives in line with relevant aspects of the SDGs. The chapter explored how digitalization can enable the emergence of policy and institutions and human capital development in Africa.

There are several lessons from the historical and contemporary role of technology and development assistance. First, technology is not neutral in terms of outcomes and that gives rise to technology winners and losers. Second, technology requires appropriate policy and institutions and that has implications for institutional advancement. Third, the nature of the technology, if predominantly geared towards production or consumption, cannot be ignored. Fourth, the relationship between the source, in terms of partnership, and the host of the technology is not problem-free in terms of policy, programming, and actual utilization of the technology. Finally, technology and development, to be sustainable, should focus on human capital development, especially with a lens on equity.

The dynamics of tertiary agricultural education, like any aspect of the development process, will be based on political considerations. The problem is how to balance short-term political and policy expediency with a focus on long-term public policy outcomes for the larger society in an era of digitalization. The challenges and policy options should focus on two main issues: the policy and institutional context of African digitalization; higher education and trends on research and innovation in African universities, including the role of the African diaspora. Enacting policies and establishing institutions is not the only requirement to shore up digitalization in Africa. Equally important is to ensure that policies and institutions can discharge their mandate. This suggests that the African state, regardless of neoliberal pronouncements, must adopt a consistent and proactive stand towards building policy and institutional capacity. Developing policies and institutions are critical for the digital age. Hence, even if foreign donors offer some opportunities for human capital development, "African governments through policy measures and actions should play an active role in steering these investments towards the intended outcomes" (Agbebi, 2018: 536). The policy and institutional context for digitalization in Africa in agriculture and education would need a rethinking, with clear and specific emphasis on long-term benefits that should include Africa-based ICTs. Perhaps, a renewed focus on the role that South Africa's MTN, global technology and communication company with operations in several African countries and the Middle East, would be a useful beginning (Bick et al., 2011; Sutherland, 2015).

The second policy challenge is the state of higher education, including science education within the respective regions in Africa, an issue that has implications for human capital development and digitalization

(Puplampu & Mugo, 2020). African universities continue to experience increases in enrollment, which is a clear testament to the value of higher education. However, the universities experience chronic underfunding, learning experiences are compromised and that suggests a capacity problem. These problems occur when local innovations in mobile financial systems like M-Pesa have attracted the attention of global digital companies like Huawei, Google, IBM, and Microsoft. The strides in financial mobile transfers and related iHub activities that dot the many parts of Africa today are commendable (Abdulhamid, 2020; Chironga et al., 2017; Choi et al., 2019; Srinivasan, 2019).

These trends call for responses to questions such as "terms of engagement between the technological giants and their local counterparts on issues such as intellectual property rights, patent protection and knowledge co-creation" (Hanson et al., 2020: 296). This is because ICT companies through their worldwide investments in research and development, can leverage successes with respect to digitalization in addressing the state of TAE institutions in Africa. That implies African political leaders must address increases in enrollment and resource constrains that impact the research capabilities of their universities. It is remarkable that in cases where institutions have enough and the required resources, they are able to make meaningful research outcomes as mentioned in the case of Uganda's Makerere University AI and Data lab (Hanson et al., 2020: 299). This is the basis to continue enlarging the mandate of the African Centers of Excellence idea so that such learning centers can occupy a central stage in knowledge creation and dissemination for the benefit of regional communities and the continent with universities playing a central role in systems of innovation (Zeleza, 2017).

There are enormous opportunities for partnership and the cross-fertilization of ideas for research collaboration and innovation (Ehizuelen, 2018). The argument is for African universities to find more creative ways to engage with African academics in the diaspora, especially diasporic networks (Tettey, 2016). Working with the African diaspora in a context of partnership, is based on several assumptions. Partnership requires that the actors in the relationship relate to and treat each other as free and equals and that working relationships are geared towards mutually beneficial outcomes. These assumptions often break down when issues of commodification are at the heart of any transaction. Development is not an apolitical enterprise. Therefore, while there are universal and homogenized technologies and standards in contemporary telecommunication, there is a need to tailor practices and engineer innovative knowledge to the local context for positive and impactful outcomes. Partnership has underlining structural considerations. These considerations, if not adequately addressed will reinforce the digital divide not only between the global North and the global South, but also within African countries and their universities. Indeed, neoliberal globalization and digitalization present opportunities and hindrances and that realization is essential in discussions on the digitalization of what we eat and how we think in Africa post-COVID-19.

REFERENCES

Abdenur, A. E. (2014). China and the BRICS development bank: Legitimacy and multilateralism in South-South cooperation. *IDS Bulletin*, 45(4), 85–101. https://doi.org/10.1111/1759-5436.12095

Abdulhamid, N. A. (2020). Disruptive technology, mobile money, and financial mobilization in Africa: M-pesa as Kenya's solution to global financial exclusion? P. Arthur et al. (Eds.), *Disruptive technologies, innovation and development in Africa* (pp. 187–202). Palgrave MacMillan https://doi.org/10.1007/978-3-030-40647-9_9

Africa Capacity Building Foundation (ACBF). (2019). *Africa capacity report 2019—Fostering transformative leadership for Africa's development*, Harare, ACBF

African Development Bank (AfDB) & Korea-Africa Economic Cooperation (KOAFEC). (2019). *Unlocking the potential of the fourth industrial revolution in Africa*. African Development Bank.

African Union. (2003, July). Assembly of the African Union. *Second Ordinary Session*, 10–12. (Assembly/AU/Decl.4-11 (II)). African Union.

African Union (AU). (2014). *2014 year of agriculture and food security in Africa, marking 10th anniversary of the adoption of CAADP*. Department of rural economy and agriculture (Briefing Note). African Union.

African Union (AU). (2020). *The digital transformation strategy for Africa (2020–2030)*. Available at: https://au.int/sites/default/files/documents/38507-doc-dts-english.pdf (accessed 29 June 2021).

African Union Commission (AUC). (2014). *Science, technology and innovation strategy for Africa 2024*. AUC.

African Union Commission (AUC). (2015). *Agenda 2063, The Africa we want, popular version*. AUC.

African Union Commission (AUC). (2016). *Continental education strategy for Africa (CESA) CESA 2016–2025*. AUC.

African Union Development Agency (AUDA-NEPAD). (2019). *African innovation outlook III*. AUDANEPAD.
African Union, Economic Commission for Africa; African Development Bank and United Nations Development Programme (AU/ECA/AfDB and UNDP). (2016). *MDGs to agenda 2063/SDGs transition report 2016: Towards an integrated and coherent approach to sustainable development in Africa*. AU/ECA/AfDB and UNDP.
Agbebi, M. (2018). China in Africa's telecom sector: Opportunities for human capital development? A Case of Huawei in Nigeria, *Human Resource Development International*, 21(5), 532–551. https://doi.org/10.1080/13678868.2018.1512232
Aguera, P., Berglund, N.,Chinembiri, T., Comninos, A., Gillwald, A., & Govan-Vassen, N. (2020). Paving the way towards digitalising agriculture in South Africa. Research ICT Africa.
Arthur, P. (2020). Disruptive technologies, democracy, governance and national elections in Africa: Back to the future? P. Arthur et al. (Eds.), *Disruptive technologies, innovation and development in Africa* (pp. 17–38). Palgrave MacMillan. https://doi.org/10.1007/978-3-030-40647-9_2
Arthur, P., Hanson, K. T., & Puplampu, K. P. (Eds.). (2020). *Disruptive technologies, innovation and development in Africa*. Palgrave MacMillan https://doi.org/10.1007/978-3-030-40647-9
Avgerou, C. (2008). Information systems in developing countries: A critical research review. *Journal of Information Technology*, 23, 133–146. https://doi.org/10.1057/palgrave.jit.2000136
Avgerou, C. (2010). Discourses on ICT and development. *Information Technologies and International Development*, 6(3), 1–18. http://eprints.lse.ac.uk/35564/
AU & Commission Organization of Economic Cooperation and Development (AUC, OECD). (2021). Africa's development dynamics 2021: Digital transformation for quality jobs. *AUC, Addis Ababa/OECD Publishing, Paris,*. https://doi.org/10.1787/0a5c9314-en
Barrier, J., Quéré, O., & Vanneuville, R. (2019). The making of curriculum in higher education power, knowledge, and teaching practices. *Revue d'anthropologie des connaissances*, 13(1), 33–60.
Beintema, N., Lynam, J., & Nakayiwa, F. (2022). Trends in tertiary agricultural education capacity in Africa. In D. Kraybill, J. Lyman, & A. Ekwamu (Eds.), *Transforming tertiary agricultural education in Africa* (pp. 85–105). RUFORUM and CABI.
Bick, G., Luiz, J., & Townsend, S. (2011). MTN South Africa: one group, one vision, one brand. *Emerald Emerging Markets Case Studies*, 1(1). https://doi.org/10.1108/20450621111126765

British Broadcasting Corporation (BBC). (2015). Google apologizes for photos app's racist blunder. https://www.bbc.com/news/technology-33347866

Chironga, M., Grandis, H. D., & Zouaoui, Y. (2017). *Mobile financial services in Africa: Winning the battle for the customer*. McKinsey and Company https://www.mckinsey.com/industries/financial-services/our-insights/mobile-financial-services-in-africa-winning-the-battle-for-the-customer

Choi, J., Dutz, M., & Usman, Z. (2019). *The future of work in Africa—Harnessing the potential of digital technologies for all: A companion to the world development report 2019 on the changing nature of work*. World Bank Group.

Chukwuere, J. E. (2017). From decolonisation to digitalisation of education in South Africa. *Ponte Academic Journal, 73*(12), 232–241.

Cooke, F. L. (2012). The globalization of Chinese telecom corporations: Strategy, challenges and HR implications for the MNCs and host countries. *The International Journal of Human Resource Management, 23*(9), 1832–1852. https://doi.org/10.1080/09585192.2011.579920

Czerniewicz, L., Deacon, A., Small, J., & Walji, S. (2014). Developing world MOOCs: A curriculum view of the MOOC landscape. *Journal of Global Literacies: Technologies and Emerging Pedagogies, 2*(3), 122–139.

Daum, T., Adegbola, Y. P., Adegbola, C., Daudu, C., Issa. F., Kamau, G., Kergna, A., Mose, L., Ndirpaya, Y. Oluwole, F., Zossou, R., Kirui, O., & Birner, R. (2021) *Mechanization, digitalization, rural youth: Stakeholder perceptions on mega-topics for African agricultural transformation* (Hohenheim Working Papers on Social and Institutional Change in Agricultural Development. 010–2021). University of Hohenheim. https://490c.uni-hohenheim.de/en/75736

EEP Africa. (2021). EEP *Africa Trust Fund, Annual Report*, EEP Africa. https://www.eepafrica.org

Ehizuelen, M. M. O. (2018). Education and skills development in China-Africa cooperation. *Frontiers of Education in China, 13*, 553–600. https://doi.org/10.1007/s11516-018-0030-0

Giles, D. B., & Stead, V. (2022). Big Data won't feed the world: Global agribusiness, digital imperialism, and the contested promises of a new Green Revolution. *Dialectical Anthropology, 46*, 37–53.

Green, A. (1997). *Education, globalization and the nation state*. St. Martin's Press.

Grote, U., Fasse, A., Nguyen, T. T., & Erenstein, O. (2021). Food security and the dynamics of wheat and maize value chains in Africa and Asia. *Frontiers in Sustainable Food Systems, 4*, 617009. https://doi.org/10.3389/fsufs.2020.617009

Gwagwa, A., Kazim, E., Kachidza, P., Hilliard, A., Siminyu, K., Smith, M., & Shawe-Taylor, J. (2021, December 10). Road map for research on responsible artificial intelligence for development (AI4D) in African countries: The case study of agriculture. Patterns 2. https://doi.org/10.1016/j.patter.2021.100381

Hackfort, S. (2021). Patterns of inequalities in digital agriculture: A systematic literature review. Sustainability, 13, 12345. https://doi.org/10.3390/su132212345

Hanson, K.T. (2020). Automation of knowledge work and Africa's transformation agenda: Threats, opportunities, and possibilities. In Arthur et al. (Eds.), Disruptive technologies, innovation & development in Africa (pp. 273–292). Palgrave Macmillan.

Hanson, K. T., & Puplampu, K. P. (2018). The internet of things and the sharing economy: Harnessing the possibilities for Africa's sustainable development goals. In K. T. Hanson, K. P. Puplampu, & T. M. Shaw (Eds.), From millennium development goals to sustainable development goals: Rethinking African development (pp. 133–151). Routledge.

Hanson, K.T., & Tang, V.T. (2020). Perspectives on disruptive innovations and Africa's services Sector. In Arthur et al. (Eds.), Disruptive technologies, innovation & development in Africa (pp. 255–271). Palgrave Macmillan.

Hanson, K.T., Shaw, T.M., Puplampu, K.P., & Arthur, P. (2020). Digital Transformation: A Connected and "Disrupted" Africa. In Arthur et al. (Eds.), Disruptive technologies, innovation & development in Africa (pp. 295–305). Palgrave Macmillan.

Hulela, K., Mukuni, J., Abreh, M. K., Kasozi, J. A., & Kraybill, D. (2022). Transformative curricula and teaching practices to meet labour market needs in tertiary agricultural education in Africa. In D. Kraybill, J. Lyman, & A. Ekwamu (Eds.), Transforming tertiary agricultural education in Africa (pp. 126–134). RUFORUM and CABI.

Internet Society. (2017). Internet for education in Africa: Helping policy makers to meet the global education agenda sustainable development goal 4. Internet Society. https://www.internetsociety.org

Jacquet, I., Wang, J., Zhang, J., Wang, K., & Liang, S. (2022). An understanding of education in supporting cotton production: An empirical study in Benin. West Africa. Agriculture, 12, 836. https://doi.org/10.3390/agriculture12060836

Kabasa, J. D., Kirsten, J., & Minde, I. (2015). Implications of changing agri-food system structure for agricultural education and training in Sub-Saharan Africa. Journal of Agribusiness in Developing and Emerging Economies, 5(2), 190–199. https://doi.org/10.1108/JADEE-03-2015-0016

Klerkx, L., & Rose, D. (2020). Dealing with the game-changing technologies of agriculture 4.0: How do we manage diversity and responsibility in Food

System Transition Pathways? *Global Food Security*, *24*, 100347. https://doi.org/10.1016/j.gfs.2019.100347

Kraemer, K. L., Dedrick, J., & Sharma, P. (2009). One laptop per child: Vision vs reality. *Communications of the ACM*, *52*(6), 66–73.

Kraybill, D., Lyman, J., & Ekwamu, A. (Eds.). (2022). *Transforming tertiary agricultural education in Africa*. RUFORUM and CABI

Kraybill, D., & Osiru, M. (2022). A case study of transformation in four African universities. In D. Kraybill, J. Lyman, & A. Ekwamu (Eds.), *Transforming tertiary agricultural education in Africa* (pp. 240–250). RUFORUM and CABI.

Langthaler, M., & Bazafkan, H. (2020). *Digitalization, education and skills development in the global South: An assessment of the debate with a focus on Sub-Saharan Africa* (ÖFSE Briefing Paper, No. 28). Austrian Foundation for Development Research (ÖFSE), Vienna. https://www.oefse.at/publikationen/briefing-papers/detail-briefing-paper/publication/show/Publication/digitalization-education/

Li, A. (2016). Technology transfer in China-Africa relation: Myth or reality. *Transnational Corporations Review*, *8*(3), 183–195. https://doi.org/10.1080/19186444.2016.1233718

Li, S. (2017). *Mediatized China-Africa relations: How media discourses negotiate the shifting of global order*. Palgrave Macmillan.

Luckett, K. (2016). Curriculum contestation in a post-colonial context: A view from the south. *Teaching in Higher Education*, *21*(4), 415–428. https://doi.org/10.1080/13562517.2016.1155547.

Ma, L., Chung, J., & Thorson, S. (2005). E-government in China: Bringing economic development through administrative reform. *Government Information Quarterly*, *22*, 20–37.

Mhlanga, D., Denhere, V., & Moloi, T. (2022). COVID-19 and the key digital transformation lessons for higher education institutions in South Africa. *Education Sciences.*, *12*, 464. https://doi.org/10.3390/educsci12070464

M-KOPA. (2021). *M-KOPA 2021 impact report*. https://www.m-kopa.com

Msila, V. (2021). Digitalization and decolonizing education: A qualitative study of University of South Africa (UNISA) leadership *International Journal of Information and Education Technology*, *11*(11), 553–560 https://doi.org/10.18178/ijiet.2021.11.11.1564

Nakayiwa, F., & Lyman, J. (2022). Network approaches to transforming tertiary agricultural education in Africa. In D. Kraybill, J. Lyman, & A. Ekwamu (2022) (Eds.). *Transforming tertiary agricultural education in Africa* (pp. 227–239). RUFORUM and CABI.

Nchanji, E. B., Lutomia, C. K., Chirwa, R., Templer, N., Rubyogo, J. C., & Onyango, P. (2021, March). Immediate impacts of COVID-19 pandemic on bean value chain in selected countries in sub-Saharan Africa. *Agricultural*

Systems *Agricultural Systems,* 188, 103034. https://doi.org/10.1016/j.agsy.2020.103034

NEPAD and UN. (2015). *Infrastructure development: Within the context of Africa's cooperation with new and emerging development partners.* AUDA-NEPAD Agency

Ndung'u, N. (2018). *Next steps for the digital revolution in Africa: Inclusive growth and job creation lessons from Kenya.* Brookings Institute, Africa Growth Initiative, (Working Paper 20).

OECD/ACET. (2020). *Quality infrastructure in 21st century Africa.* Prioritising, Accelerating and Scaling up in the Context of Pida (2021–30).

Osabwa, W. (2022). Coming to terms with Covid-19 reality in the context of Africa's higher education: Challenges, insights, and prospects. *Frontiers in Education.,* 7, 643162. https://doi.org/10.3389/feduc.2022.643162

Pawlicki, P. (2017). *Challenger multinationals in telecommunications: Huawei and ZTE,* European Union Trade Institute. *Background Analysis,.*

Prause, L., Hackfort, S., & Lindgren, M. (2021). Digitalization and the third food regime. *Agriculture and Human Values,* 38, 641–655. https://doi.org/10.1007/s104-020-10161-2

Puplampu, K. P. (2006). Critical perspectives on higher education and globalization in Africa. In A. A. Abdi et al. (Eds.), *African education and globalization: Critical perspectives* (pp. 31–52). Rowman and Littlefield.

Puplampu, K. P., & Essegbey, G. O. (2020). Agricultural research and innovation: Disruptive technologies and value chain development in Africa. In Arthur et al. (Eds.), *Disruptive technologies, innovation & development in Africa* (pp. 39–61). Palgrave Macmillan.

Puplampu, K. P., & Mugo, S. M. (2020). Disruptive technology and knowledge development: African universities, human capital and educating for global citizenship. In P. Arthur et al. (Eds.), *Disruptive technologies, innovation and development in Africa* (pp. 147–169). Palgrave MacMillan. https://doi.org/10.1007/978-3-030-40647-9_7

Puplampu, K. P., & Wodinski, L. (2016). Study abroad programs, international students, and global citizenship: Colonial-colonizer relations in global higher education. In R. C. Mizzi, T. S. Rocco, & S. Shore (Eds.), *DIsrupting adult and community education: Teaching, learning, and working in the periphery* (pp. 293–306). State University of New York Press.

Reed, J. (2013, July 30). Africa's big brother lives in Beijing. *Foreign Policy.* https://foreignpolicy.com/2013/07/30/africas-big-brother-lives-in-beijing/

Rogers, E. M. (1995) *Diffusion of innovation* (4th ed.). The Free Press.

Spielman, D. J., Ekboir, J., Davis, K., & Ochieng, C. M. O. (2008). An innovation systems perspective on strengthening agricultural education and training in sub-Saharan Africa. *Agricultural Systems,* 98(1), 1–9. https://doi.org/10.1016/j.agsy.2008.03.004

Srinivasan, R. (2019). *Beyond the valley: How innovators around the world are overcoming inequality and creating the technologies of tomorrow*. The MIT Press.

Sutherland, E. (2015). MTN: A South African mobile telecommunications group in Africa and Asia. *Communication, 41*(4), 471–505. https://doi.org/10.1080/02500167.2015.1100645

Sutherland, E. (2016). China and Africa: Alternative telecommunication policies and practices. *The African Journal of Information and Communication (AJIC), 17*, 165–195.

Swanepoel, F., Stroebel, A., Mentz-Coetzee, M. (2020). Education driving agriculture-led economic and social transformation in Africa. In M. Ndulo & N.Assié-Lumumba (Eds.), *Education and development* (pp. 79–107). Palgrave Macmillan. https://doi.org/10.1007/978-3-030-40566-3_5

Tchao, E. T., Keelson, E., Aggor, C., & Amankwa, G. A. M. (2017). e-Government Services in Ghana—Current State and Future Perspective. *2017 International Conference on Computational Science and Computational Intelligence* (CSCI) (pp. 624–631). Las Vegas, NV https://doi.org/10.1109/CSCI.2017.108

Tettey, W.J. (2006). Globalization, information technologies, and higher education in Africa: Implications of the market agenda. In A. A. Abdi et al. (Eds.), *African education and globalization: Critical perspectives* (pp. 93–115). Rowman and Littlefield.

Tettey, W. J. (2016). Regenerating scholarly capacity through diaspora engagement: The case of a Ghana diaspora knowledge network. In A. Chikanda, J. Crush, & M. Walton-Roberts (Eds.), *Diasporas, development and governance. Global migration issues* (Vol. 5, pp. 171–186). Springer.

Thompson, M. (2008). ICT and development studies: Towards development 2.0. *Journal of International Development, 20*(6), 821–835.

Thompson, M., & (UNDP). (2015). *Sustainable development goals*. United Nations Development Program.

Tremblay, D., Fortier, F., Boucher, J-F., Riffon, O., & Villeneuve, C. (2020). Sustainable development goal interactions: An analysis based on the five pillars of the 2030 agenda. *Sustainable Development, 28*, 1584–1596. https://doi.org/10.1002/sd.2107

United Nations Development Programme (UNDP). (2003). *Human development report 2003 millennium development goals: A compact among nations to end human poverty*. Oxford University Press.

United Nations Development Programme (UNDP). (2022). *Uncertained times, unsettled lives: Shaping our future in a transforming world*. United Nations Development Programme.

United Nations Educational, & Science and Cultural Organization (UNESCO). (2016). *UNESCO: Science report towards 2030*. UNESCO.

Villet, C. B. (2022). Curriculum, learning and teaching. In Association of African Universities. (Ed.), *Materials on african regional and continental integration in higher education* (pp. 225–238). African Union, Africa-EU Partnership, & European Union.

Wang, R. Bar, F., & Hong, Y. (2020). ICT aid flows from China to African countries: A communication network perspective *International Journal of Communication*, *14*, 1498–1523

Yonazi, E., Kelly, T., Halewood, N., & Blackman, C. (2012). (Eds.). *Transformational use of information and communication technologies in Africa*. AfDB Temporary Relocation Agency (Tunis): The World Bank and the African Development Bank, with the support of the African Union.

Zeleza, P. T. (2017). Positioning universities as engines of innovation for sustainable development and transformation. *Journal of Higher Education in Africa*, *15*(2), 1–22. https://doi.org/10.2307/26640368.

Zeleza, P.T., & Okanda, P. M. (2022). Enhancing the digital transformation of African Universities. *Journal of Higher Education in Africa*, *19*(1), 1–28. https://www.jstor.org/stable/10.2307/48645900

Zeufack, A. G., Calderon, C., Kabundi, A., Kubota, M., Korman, V., Raju, D., Girma Abreha, K., Kassa, W., Owusu, S. (2022, April). *Africa's Pulse*, 25, World Bank. https://doi.org/10.1596/978-1-4648-1871-4

Zschocke T., Beniest J., Yayé A. D., Chakeredza, S. (2013) Readiness to use e-learning for agricultural higher education in Sub-Saharan Africa. Results from a survey of faculty members *Journal of Agricultural Informatics*, *4*(1), 37–47 http://www.magisz.org/journal

CHAPTER 10

The African State, Sustainable Development, Digitalization, Green Economy in Africa Post-COVID-19

Korbla P. Puplampu, Kobena T. Hanson, Timothy M. Shaw,
and Peter Arthur

INTRODUCTION

It has become a common practice for various actors to assign labels to trends and possibilities on the African continent in terms of development, especially since the dawn of the current millennium. Three such labels are illustrative. First, *The Economist* (2000), the London-based influential business magazine, in a 2000 cover named Africa as "the hopeless continent". As if on cue, Tony Blair, the then British Prime Minister in 2001

K. P. Puplampu (✉)
Department of Sociology, Grant MacEwan University, Edmonton, AB, Canada
e-mail: puplampuk@macewan.ca

K. T. Hanson
Independent Development Evaluation, African Development Bank, Abidjan, Côte d'Ivoire
e-mail: k.hanson@afdb.org

© The Author(s), under exclusive license to Springer Nature Switzerland AG 2023
K. P. Puplampu et al. (eds.), *Sustainable Development, Digitalization, and the Green Economy in Africa Post-COVID-19*, International Political Economy Series, https://doi.org/10.1007/978-3-031-32164-1_10

opined that: "The state of Africa is a scar on the conscience of the world. But if the world as a community focused on it, we could heal it. And if we don't, it will become deeper and angrier" (cited in *Independent*, 2004). In response, Blair established the Commission for Africa (2005) to offer him some policy guidance on the region when Britain assumed the presidency of the Group of Eight (G8) industrialized countries in 2005.

Second, the African Union in 2001 launched the New Partnership for African Development (NEPAD), as a continent-wide development initiative based on the spirit of the UN-Millennium Development Goals (MDGs) (2000–2015), especially MDG 8 which called for global partnership on development (UNDP, 2003). African leaders and their external partners proclaimed NEPAD as the beginning of an African Renaissance and the Twenty-First century as belonging to Africa (NEPAD, 2001). Third, in 2011, The Economist, which a decade earlier declared Africa "the hopeless continent", conveyed a different message as "Africa Rising" (*The Economist*, 2011). Similarly, in 2015, Tony Blair, out of political office in 2007, named Africa as the "most exciting continent on the planet because of its opportunities" (Blair, 2015). What is remarkable about these shifting labels or terminologies is that they are based on different readings of the human condition on the African continent, a condition that can best be analyzed from the complex interaction between historical and contemporary issues from the internal, continental Africa context, and external forces. The labels raise several questions. For instance, the "Africa Rising" narrative invites several questions such as Africa is rising from what and into what? Africa is rising based on what? The labels, however, offer a useful analytical entry point in discussing the development challenges and possibilities on the African continent.

This chapter seeks to synthesize, against the backdrop of sustainable development, the role of the UN Agenda 2030 and the African Union

T. M. Shaw
Global Governance and Human Security Program, University of Massachusetts, Boston, MA, USA
e-mail: Timothy.Shaw@umb.edu

P. Arthur
Department of Political Science, Dalhousie University, Halifax, NS, Canada
e-mail: peter.arthur@dal.ca

Agenda 2063, the increasing significance of digitalization and the natural resources infused discourse on the green economy in Africa. These policy frameworks and their potential impact on African countries cannot be considered as inevitable. Discussions on the role of natural resources in Africa's development have been part of the African reality since the beginning of time, but specifically in the postcolonial period. The contributors to this volume therefore approach the role of development policy and institutions in a nuanced manner, demonstrating that global and continental policy frameworks that underpin the notion of Africa Rising do require human agency to attain the stated goals. The changing fortunes of the continent's economy during and after the global pandemic, reveal the precarious nature of the African economy and whether the government can strengthen its role and satisfy the needs of, for example, the teeming youth looking for employment.

Indeed, contributors to the volume engage with different aspects and processes of digitalization on the continent and stress the fact that the leapfrogging implications of the processes involve myriad factors. Thus, even though there is a discernible and flourishing digitalization thrust on the continent, there are questions about the regulatory framework and the digital divide. The remaining issue is the dearth of a homegrown innovation infrastructure on the continent. For example, the depth of innovation in many African universities has not risen to a critical mass and MTN is the only communication company with roots in an African country. It is because of this that according to Atiase et al. (2020), Do-it-Yourself tech hubs in Africa are challenging the dominance of traditional universities as sites of knowledge production. Although the period from 2010 saw dozens of innovation hubs (iHubs) emerge across the African continent (Friederici, 2019a), they are not anchored into a wider national or continental digital ecosystem. Moreover, as Friederici (2019b: 194) has observed, despite the "enthusiasm, in practice hubs are small organizations with a relatively simple functional setup. A hub usually consists of a Wi-Fi–connected space with hot desks and meeting rooms, used for laptop-based work or for training and mentorship sessions, networking events, presentations, and small innovation competitions like hackathons". These concerns and omissions continue, even as policymakers present digitalization as the next frontier in the development agenda.

The argument then becomes that without a well-resourced homegrown digital architecture, the region will continue to rely on foreign technological assistance, often dominated by global tech giants like Google and Meta. In other words, iHubs, while necessary, are not sufficient in reaping the benefits of digitalization on the continent, even though digitalization has the potential in advancing the African development from several angles. Several studies in this volume reveal that potential, for example, in governance (Arthur), extractives (Hanson & Arthur), the transition towards the green economy (Puplampu et al.; Kedir et al.), agricultural and educational systems (Puplampu & Mugo). The fundamental question is how Africa can arrive at 2030 based on sustainable development, digitalization, natural resources management, and the green economy. In the following section, we sketch out some salient pointers that can aid in creating and establishing resilient policies and institutions necessary and sufficient for a digital transformation in Africa.

POLITICAL LEADERSHIP AND SOCIAL CHANGE

Social change cannot occur in a vacuum, and it also cannot occur based on hope. Social change requires a focus on the relationship between political leadership and human development. Political leadership in Africa has been the basis of several studies (Arthur, 2018). Two notable forms of evaluating African leaders have been the African Peer Review Mechanism and the Mo Ibrahim Leadership Prize and these forms, while not problem-free, do demonstrate the significance of leadership (African Union, 2021; Ibrahim, 2022). The major point of debate is the quality of political leadership in Africa because of the various attempts at circumventing presidential term limits and variations in the transfer of power and the democratic quality of leaders across the continent (Reyntjens, 2020). A related area of focus and of immense significance to this study is the impact of political leadership on human development. The longevity of African political leaders, many of whom lack the necessary character and skills, has resulted in most of them undertaking policies that have no positive and meaningful impact on the human development of their nations (Hanson et al., 2018). This has contributed to the increasing disillusionment and general disenchantment of African people of their leaders. Therefore, the argument is that the existing political leadership cannot "inspire any confidence in the ability of political leaders to shepherd the 'Africa Rising' narrative, since they have not shown any deference to their nation's constitution; an embodiment of the rule of law in any country" (Hanson et al., 2018: 168). Similarly, Friedman (2018) argues that African leaders often seem unwilling or unable to ensure stronger and deeper democracies.

However, the case of Rwanda under Paul Kagame cautions us against strict interpretations of political longevity and the ambivalence of being a developmental state and an authoritarian 'ethnocracy' (McDoom, 2022). Rwanda occupies a contradictory binary such that, on one hand, the country is hailed by development practitioners as the best exemplar of a developmental state in Africa with effective state institutions that deliver on their core mandates for the citizenry. On the other hand, the country has had one leader for over two decades and boasts of being stable, but in a context of repression and likened to an authoritarian or surveillance state. In addressing this dilemma, McDoom (2022: 537) introduces the idea of securocratic state building, which first refers to "the preeminent role played by security actors and their commitment to coercion to assure the state's security and … developmental ambitions. The term refers, second, to the regime's developmental but non-doctrinaire ambitions". Rwanda, thus, provides a different trajectory for African development, a trajectory that is developmental oriented, but in a context of coercion. The trade-off between development and coercion though leaning towards human development, from the current membership in the low human development category, would be instructive in the long run (UNDP, 2022: 279).

A contrary or comparative country to Rwanda is Botswana. Unlike Rwanda, Botswana has maintained a developmental-focused state machinery, but in a context of the trappings of constitutional government. Botswana, therefore, showcases stability on democratic principles and practices and credentials as a developmental state and in the medium human development category (UNDP, 2022: 278). Perhaps, Botswana's natural resources, specifically diamonds, might have alerted the country to the fact that to better manage its diamond wealth for national development and escape the resource curse, the country had to establish capacity-infused public institutions (Puplampu, 2014). These institutions together with political leadership have been the basis of Botswana's relative stability and strides in human development compared to Rwanda and most importantly other mineral-rich African countries like Nigeria (UNDP, 2022: 279).

The foregoing remarks reinforce the importance of political leadership in social transformation. Regardless of the type of political leadership, the major duty of any political leader is transforming the lives of the citizens. For all intents and purposes, Africa needs leaders that are interested in serving the public as opposed to themselves. However, it is also obvious that leaders derive their legitimacy from the society they lead. This is the exact point Friedman (2018) makes when he suggested that the onus of deciding and determining what is best for them lies with the decisions that citizens themselves make. Aside from their role in the electoral process, Friedman (2018) asserts that collective action in the form of various groups and individuals working together to realize broader political objectives should be at the forefront of the development process. Herein lies the importance of not only citizens, but also, civil society groups in influencing public policy and decision-making in African countries.

FUTURE CHALLENGES, YOUTH, AND CIVIL SOCIETY

At the heart of sustainable development is the relationship between the present and future generation, relative to available resources. The expectation is that future generations can also have access to resources available to the present generation. In addition to the natural resource endowments in Africa, another critical source of resource is civil society, particularly the youth. The youth in Africa and issues of digitalization and the green economy are, for several reasons, of utmost importance. First, the changing fortunes of the economy would have a direct impact on their economic welfare and prospects of the youth. Youth unemployment is a product of several factors, but two are critical for the current study, the large percentage of African youth, about 43 per cent are under the age of 15 and find themselves in an environment of no sustained economic growth, because of the absence of the required financial "investments to build more resilient economies and societies" (Fox & Gandi, 2021: 2). In the context of over-skilling and under-skilling, as well as the slow growth of the large formal sector, the need to pay attention to micro, small and medium enterprises (MSMEs) and improvements in informal systems cannot be overemphasized, especially if these systems are grounded in the digital economy (Fox & Gandi 2021; Hanson, Tang & Mutula in this volume). The MSME sector is an active and vibrant force for economic growth and the vanguard in innovation, job creation and employment, entrepreneurship, reducing poverty, boosting national gross domestic product (GDP), and increasing public revenue in several African countries (Amoah & Amoah, 2018; Muriithi, 2017; Quartey et al., 2017).

Radebe (2019) in a study on the barriers to youth employment and entrepreneurship in South Africa, identified the lack of education and finance as well as general social attitudes towards youth entrepreneurship and suggested the need for changes in education in both formal and informal settings. Thus, the policy option is enhancing education in entrepreneurship and related social attitudes. From an educational point of view, the African economy depends, directly or indirectly, on agriculture and a closer integration between agricultural and educational systems should be part of the mix of policy options (Puplampu & Mugo this volume). Such an integration will address deficiencies in agricultural education, provide improved skills to enhance productivity, and create more jobs in the agricultural value chain.

The underlying problem is that rewards from agriculture are minimal compared to other areas of the economy, a situation that is compounded by structural factors. The result is the hands-off approach towards agriculture by many young people. Based on this analysis, Geza et al. (2021) called for integrated agricultural-based policy interventions that are sensitive to context and promote a more meaningful participation by the youth in future discussions on food systems. It is obvious that labour market regulations are also at play in youth unemployment. That is why Awad (2019) stressed the need for urbanization to also factor job creation opportunities, especially in the global supply chain and other forms of international trade and other pragmatic policies once policymakers acknowledge the prevailing level of youth unemployment in Africa (Awad, 2019; Berhe, 2021; Fox & Gandhi, 2021; Radebe, 2019).

Second, as the proverbial digital natives, African youth are at the centre of digitalization on the continent and leaders in emerging businesses in the digital economy. Azu et al. (2021) contend that digitalization has the potential to reduce youth unemployment in West Africa if robust attention is paid to digital technologies and job creation opportunities in both the short and long term. To Porter et al. (2020), the gender dimension of digitalization also deserves equal if not more attention if the vision of female empowerment is to be attained. This is because their study in Ghana, Malawi, and South Africa shows that use of digital technologies such as the phone, are "embedded within a broader context of social connections, norms and responsibilities, [and] intersects with themes extending from education and entrepreneurship to sexuality and safety" (Porter et al., 2020: 181). The gender digital divide is generally most visible in the global South where only 19 per cent of women are using the internet, which is 12 percentage points lower than men), whereas in Africa, 24 per cent of women have internet access compared to 35 per cent for men. On the other hand, in the Arab region, 56 per cent for women compared to 68 per cent men have access to internet (ITU, 2023a: 8). Hence, it is urgent and necessary, in view of the low access to internet and its gender dimensions, to address the situation in which the African region is not making much progress towards gender parity (ITU, 2023b: 6).

One useful program that can address the gender digital divide and contribute to SDG 5 (gender equality and empower all women and girls) is the African innovation and research network (OPEN Air, 2020). Open AIR, a truly collaborative and interdisciplinary project, intentionally straddles and integrates both formal and informal sectors in several African countries with a specific focus on commercial and social enterprise objectives and working with technology hubs in universities on the African continent (University of Cape Town and University of Johannesburg in South Africa, Strathmore University in Kenya, the Nigerian Institute for Advanced Legal Studies, the American University in Cairo, Egypt) and the University of Ottawa in Canada (Open AIR, 2020: 5). By drawing on researchers from disciplines such as law, economic, management, political science, and public policy, the program pursues outcomes in the development of mobile digital applications, agricultural products, and the production and distribution of entertainment products (Open AIR, 2020: 7).

Third, it is important for the youth, as any other group in the civil society, to engage in social change from a democratic governance perspective (Arthur, in this volume; Ndjié et al., 2019). At the heart of governance are issues of fairness, accountability, and the dynamics of decision-making. Governance is a clear reflection of state-society relations, which if properly nurtured and embedded in a digitalized environment can help in reducing or minimizing the incidence of corruption and other negative factors driving youth unemployment in Africa. The overriding issue is how to ensure that governance indicators such as government effectiveness, regulatory quality, the rule of law, and voice produce the desired outcomes for the citizenry (Ndjié et al., 2019). Bringing all these considerations into a digital framework, it is important for the youth to transcend their use of communication technologies beyond consumption and lifestyle activities on social media platforms and recognize its significance as key in the production of goods and services.

Fourth, possibilities for inter-cultural communication and understanding in an age of the internet also raise questions about decolonization, the role of the internet in the discourse on human rights, cybercrime, and the value of electronic evidence in the court of law (Chirwa & Ncube, 2023). Put differently, the strides made in financial inclusion through M-Pesa, the digitalization, and digital income do not minimize continuing problems in migration of Africans, with the emergence of nationalist parties and leaders, especially in Europe. These leaders, with an eye on the domestic front, often operate within the trappings of formal democratic institutions, and are unilateralists in orientation. The changing landscape of migration in the context of COVID-19 is likely to have negative consequences for the employment prospects of the diaspora and their remittance capabilities in Africa, but bearing in mind the fact that ebb and flow of remittances will depend on the location of the diasporic community and their relationship to the homeland (Bisong et al., 2020; Mbiba & Mupfumira, 2022). The argument is that COVID-19 has impacted the economic situation world-wide and post-COVID-19 recovery efforts are yet to be robust and restore the economic situation back to pre-pandemic levels. Without consistent income, Africans in the diaspora might not be able to send remittances on the earlier scale of magnitude. Thus, there is an increasing need to focus on remittances and financial development in Sub-Saharan Africa post-COVID-19 (Acheampong et al., 2021). These trends are emerging when it is becoming increasingly clear that global economic problems, as illustrated by the COVID-19 pandemic, require global solutions. At the same time, several African governments have imposed or proposing to impose taxes on money transfers in the national context to improve their fiscal capacity but remain oblivious to the activities of religious organizations in the democratic governance in Africa, since some of the leaders of some of these religious organization operate as franchises and could easily pass as transnational corporations. Furthermore, in the cultural realm, is the creative and dance forms and other entertainment industries (Nwankwo, 2018; Shipley, 2013). Countries such Nigeria and Ghana are yet to deepen the range and digital dimensions of creative capacities in films and dance forms respectively. The Azonto dance form, which is part of the urban dance scene in Ghana has the potential to become a global phenomenon that will be of interest to diasporic youth if properly integrated into a broader national and continental arts agenda.

Fifth, transnational organized crime (TOC) is a pervasive global issue and Africa is not immune. There are growing concerns around money laundering, human trafficking, smuggling of illicit drugs and conflict minerals, deep sea piracy, and their link to terrorism and extremism, pose serious threats to Africa. According to the 2021 Organized Crime Index, TOC increased across Africa during the COVID-19 pandemic and shows no signs of abating. Africa today ranks as the continent with the second highest levels of criminality globally, impeding its realization of the UN-SDGs (UP, 2022); and subjecting over two-thirds of its populace to high criminality, acute vulnerability, and low resilience (ISS, 2021).

The Democratic Republic of Congo (DRC) has the highest criminality, followed by Nigeria, Kenya, South Africa, Libya, and Mozambique (ISS, 2021). The intricate mix of alienation, fundamentalism, and the proliferation of small arms continue to destabilize the Sahel with its high population growth rates and vulnerability to climate change as well as in East Africa (Shaw, 2015). There are threats from multiple sources, from the earlier Lord's Resistance Army (LRA) out of northern Uganda; Boko Haram in northern Nigeria (Oriola et al., 2021); to Al Qaeda in the Maghreb—Burkina Faso, Mali, Libya, and Central African Republic (CAR) to Al-Shabaab in East Africa, and Africa needs to seriously focus on security issues. In West and Central Africa, drugs (Guinea-Bissau), deep sea piracy (Ghana, Benin, Nigeria), and illicit minerals respectively are wreaking havoc. Illicit and conflict minerals from Gabon, Cameroon, DRC together with Chad and CAR have become fertile funding grounds for terrorists.

The entanglement of illicit economies and organized crime call for efforts to prevent and counter these criminal activities. Gaps such as institutional fragility; weak capacity; absence of institutional cooperation between law enforcement and anti-corruption agencies; a culture of distrust and unilateralism among countries and law enforcement agencies on land and at sea; lack of judicial uniformity; deficits in the legislative, executive, and judicial branches, all hinder the fight against TOC (UP 2022: 10). What is more concerning is the apparent growing collaboration in some nations among TOC groups and elements of government, including intelligence services and high-level business figures, a relationship that represents an existential threat to economic growth and democratic institutions.

While ongoing efforts such as the West African Commission on Drugs (WACD) are meaningful (Shaw, 2015), they require greater political will and regional collaboration. Several other initiatives such as the Enhancing Africa's response to transnational organized crime (ENACT) project, implemented by the Institute for Security Studies (ISS), in partnership with INTERPOL and the Global Initiative Against Transnational Organized Crime (GI-TOC), all aim to reduce the impact of transnational organized crime on development, governance, security and the rule of law in Africa. Together, these and other efforts at national, regional, and continental levels, both demonstrate Africa's growing agency (Hanson et al., 2018), new regionalisms, and forms of cooperation.

Sixth, in an increasingly multipolar world order, in which a variety of state and non-state actors are operating at several levels (Hanson, 2015; Hettne, 2005), Africa is engendering its own regionalisms, which are less exclusively state and economic and more inclusive around emerging issues (Shaw et al., 2011), and involve state and non-state actors: from the Maputo Corridor and Kgalagadi trans-frontier peace-park to the Nile Basin Initiative/Dialogue (Hanson et al., 2012). A result of this new regionalisms is that Africa is now characterized by its own emerging pattern of "hubs-and-spokes" that encompass airlines (e.g., Ethiopian, Kenya, Rwanda), cable TV and Internet servers plus websites (MNet and iAfrica), financial centres (Johannesburg Stock Exchange), FinTechs, dynamic MSMEs, think tanks, and universities, both private and state-funded (Hanson, 2015; Shaw, 2000) all of which are transforming the African reality. So, as Africa seeks to truly leverage digitalization, these actors need to advance their own varieties of 'servicification' (Hanson & Tang this volume) applying fit-for-purpose technologies to innovations and related services. Indeed, the above constitutes a snapshot of challenges African scholars and analysts must interrogate to further our understanding of digitalization and the African condition.

Conclusion

This chapter reiterates the notion of sustainable development by showing that social change must pay equal attention to the balance between human beings and available natural resources. Technological challenges, especially the onset of digitalization, present considerable opportunities, and challenges. Equally significant is the emerging discourse on the green economy. The result is a multiprong and theoretically complex approach to Africa's development trajectory. Africa, like the rest of the world, was confronted with a global pandemic in March 2020 and its lingering effects continue to have ramifications for social and economic development. What the global pandemic revealed was the collective dimensions of the global community and a common theme of social inequality.

Given its enduring nature, social inequality can only be mitigated or disrupted by sound planning and political leadership. Political leadership and sound planning are sporadic on the African continent and yet these valuable attributes must attain a critical mass for any meaningful social transformation. Thus, attempts at outlining robust policies and creating institutions must be necessary and sufficient for dealing with emerging developmental challenges. The authors point out not only the challenges, but also the changes required to position the continent more strategically to reach the goals outlined in UN *Agenda 2030* and significantly the African Union's *Africa We Want* by 2063.

References

Acheampong, A. O., Appiah-Otoo, I., Dzator, J., & Agyemang, K. K. (2021). Remittances, financial development and poverty reduction in Sub-Saharan Africa: Implications for post-COVID-19 macroeconomic policies. *Journal of Policy Modeling, 43*(6), 1365–1387. https://doi.org/10.1016/j.jpolmod.2021.09.005

African Union. (2021). *The Africa governance report 2021 Africa's governance futures for the Africa we want*. African Union and African Peer Review Mechanism.

Amoah, S. K., & Amoah, A. K. (2018). The role of small and medium enterprises (SMEs) to employment in Ghana. *International Journal of Business and Economics Research, 7*(5), 151–157.

Arthur, P. (2018). The African state and development initiatives: The role of good governance in the realization of the MDGs and SDGs. In Hanson et al. (Eds.), *From millennium development goals to sustainable development goals: Rethinking African development* (pp. 11–31) Routledge.

Atiase, V. Y., Kolade, O., & Liedong, T. A. (2020). The emergence and strategy of tech hubs in Africa: Implications for knowledge production and value creation, *Technological Forecasting and Social Change, 161*, 120307.

Awad, A. (2019). Economic globalization and youth unemployment—Evidence from African countries. *International Economic Journal, 33*(2), 252–269. https://doi.org/10.1080/10168737.2019.1604787

Azu, N. P., Jelivov, G., Aras, O. N., & Isik, A. (2021). Influence of digital economy on youth unemployment in West Africa. *Transnational Corporations Review, 13*(1), 32–42. https://doi.org/10.1080/19186444.2020.1849936

Berhe, M. W. (2021). Empirical analysis of urban youth unemployment in Ethiopia. *African Development Review, 33*, 104–116. https://doi.org/10.1111/1467-8268.12514

Bisong, A., Ahairwe, P. E., & Njoroge, E. (2020). *The impact of COVID-19 on remittances for development in Africa* (Discussion Paper No. 269). The European Centre for Development Policy Management (ECDPM). www.ecdpm.org/dp269

Blair, T. (2015). *Africa is the most exciting continent on the planet.* https://institute.global/policy/africa-most-exciting-continent-planet Retrieved March 23

Chirwa, D., & Ncube, C. (Eds.). (2023). *The internet, development, human rights and the law in Africa.* Routledge.

Commission for Africa. (2005). *Our Common Interest—An Argument.* Penguin Books.

Fox, L., & Gandi, D. (2021). *Youth employment in sub-Saharan Africa Progress and Prospects* (Africa Growth Initiative (AGI): The Brookings Institute, AGI Working Paper No. 28).

Friederici, N. (2019a). Innovation hubs in Africa: What do they really do for digital entrepreneurs? In N. D. Taura, E. Bolat, & N. O. Madichie (Eds.), *Digital entrepreneurship in Sub-Saharan Africa.* Palgrave Studies of Entrepreneurship in Africa. Palgrave Macmillan. https://doi.org/10.1007/978-3-030-04924-9_2

Friederici, N. (2019b). Hope and Hype in Africa's digital economy. In M. Graham (Ed.), *Digital economies at global margins* (pp. 193–215). MIT Press and IDRC.

Friedman, S. (2018). *Power in action: Democracy, citizenship and social justice.* Wits University Press.

Geza, W., Ngidi, M., Ojo, T., Adetoro, A. A., Slotow, R., & Mabhaudhi, T. (2021). Youth participation in agriculture: A scoping review. *Sustainability, 13*, 9120. https://doi.org/10.3390/su13169120

Hanson, K. T. (Ed.). (2015). *Contemporary regional development in Africa.* Ashgate.

Hanson, K. T., Kararach, G., & Shaw, T. M. (Eds.). (2012). *Rethinking development challenges for public policy: Insights from contemporary Africa.* Palgrave Macmillan.

Hanson, K. T., Puplampu, K. P. & Shaw, T. M. (2018). Crystallizing the Africa rising narrative with sustainable development. In Hanson et al. (2018) (Eds.), *From millennium development goals to sustainable development goals: Rethinking African development* (pp. 167–177). Routledge.

Hettne, B. (2005). Beyond the new regionalism. *New Political Economy, 10*(4), 543–571.
Ibrahim, Mo (2022). Africa's past is not its future: How the continent can chart its own course *Foreign Affairs, 101*(6), 146,148–150,152–157
Independent. (2004). *Africa: A scar on the conscience of the world*. https://www.independent.co.uk/news/world/africa/africa-a-scar-on-the-conscience-of-the-world-52775.html Retrieved March 23, 2023
International Telecommunication Union (ITU). (2023a). *Handbook on mainstreaming gender in digital policies*. International Communication Union.
International Telecommunication Union (ITU). (2023b). *Global Digital Regulatory Outlook 2023 Policy and regulation to spur digital transformation*. International Communication Union.
ISS. (2021). Organised crime rises in Africa as criminal groups take advantage of COVID-19. Online. Available at: https://issafrica.org/about-us/press-releases/organised-crime-rises-in-africa-as-criminal-groups-take-advantage-of-covid-19. Accessed 30 March 2023.
Mbiba, B., & Mupfumira, D. (2022). Rising to the occasion: Diaspora remittances to Zimbabwe during the COVID-19 pandemic. *World Development Perspectives, 27*, 100452. https://doi.org/10.1016/j.wdp.2022.100452
McDoom, O. S. (2022). Securocratic state-building: The rationales, rebuttals, and risks behind the extraordinary rise of Rwanda after the genocide. *African Affairs, 121*(485), 535–567. https://doi.org/10.1093/afraf/adac031
Muriithi, S. (2017). African small and medium enterprises contributions. *Challenges and Solutions, European Journal of Research and Reflection, 5*(1), 1–13.
New Partnership for Africa Development (NEPAD). (2001). *NEPAD policy document*. New Partnership for Africa Development.
Ndjié, A. A., Ondoa, H. A., & Tabi, H. N. (2019). Governance and youth unemployment in Africa. *Labor History, 60*(6), 869–882, https://doi.org/10.1080/0023656X.2019.1645320
Nwankwo, A. O. (2018). Harnessing the potential of Nigeria's creative industries: Issues. *Prospects and Policy Implications, Africa Journal of Management, 4*(4), 469–487. https://doi.org/10.1080/23322373.2018.1522170
Open African Innovation Research (Open AIR). (2020). *Scaling innovation: How open collaborative models help scale Africa's knowledge-based enterprises*. Open AIR Network.
Oriola, T. B., Onuoha, F., & Oyewole, S. (Eds.). (2021). *Boko Haram's terrorist campaign in Nigeria: Contexts, dimensions and emerging trajectories*. Routledge.
Porter, G., Hampshire, K., Abane, A., Munthali, A., Robson, E., De Lannoy, A., Tanle, A., & Owusu, S. (2020). Mobile phones, gender, and female

empowerment in sub-Saharan Africa: Studies with African youth. *Information Technology for Development, 26*(1), 180–193. https://doi.org/10.1080/02681102.2019.1622500

Puplampu, K. P., et al. (2014). The capacity question, leadership and strategic choices: Environmental sustainability and natural resources management in Africa. In T. K. Hanson (Ed.), *Managing Africa's natural resources: Capacities for development* (pp. 162–184). Palgrave Macmillan.

Quartey, P., Turkson, E., Abor, J. Y., & Iddrisu, A. M. (2017). Financing the growth of SMES in Africa: What are the constraints to SME financing within ECOWAS? *Review of Development Finance, 7,* 18–28.

Radebe, T. N. (2019). The challenges/barriers preventing the South African youth in becoming entrepreneurs: South African overview. *Journal of Economics and Behavioral Studies, 11*(4(J)), 61–70. https://doi.org/10.22610/jebs.v11i4(J).2921

Reyntjens, F. (2020). Respecting and circumventing presidential term limits in Sub-Saharan Africa: A comparative survey. *African Affairs, 119*(475), 275–295. https://doi.org/10.1093/afraf/adz029

Shaw, T. M. (2015). Afterword: 'African agency' to maximize the continent's policy choices after a decade of the BRICS: Beyond dependency? In K.T. Hanson (Ed.), *Contemporary Regional Development in Africa*. Ashgate.

Shaw, T. M. (2000). New regionalisms in africa in the new millennium: Comparative perspectives on renaissance, realisms and/or regressions. *New Political Economy, 5*(3), 399–414.

Shaw, T. M., Grant, J. A., & Cornelissen, S. (2011). Introduction and overview: The study of new regionalisms at the start of the second decade in the twenty-first century. In T. Shaw, J. A. Grant, & S. Cornelissen (Eds)., *Ashgate research companion to regionalisms* (pp. 3–30). Ashgate.

Shipley, J. W. (2013). Transnational circulation and digital fatigue in Ghana's Azonto dance craze. *American Ethnologist, 40,* 362–381. https://doi.org/10.1111/amet.12027

The Economist (2011, December 3). *Africa Rising* (Vol. 401), 8762.

The Economist. (2000, May 13). *The Hopeless Continent* (vol. 355), 8170.

United Nations Development Programme (UNDP). (2003). *Human development report 2003 millennium development goals: A compact among nations to end human poverty*. Oxford University Press.

United Nations Development Programme (UNDP). (2022). Human development report, 2021–2022. *Uncertain times, Unsettled lives Shaping our future in a transforming world*. United Nations Development Programme.

UP (University for Peace). (2022). *Illicit economies & organized crime in Africa* (White Paper). Available at: https://www.upeace.org/files/Publications/Illicit%20Economies%20and%20Organized%20Crime%20in%20Africa-White%20Paper.pdf

INDEX

A
ACBF. *See* African Capacity Building Foundation
AfCFTA, 32, 144, 169. *See also* African Continental Free Trade Area
AfDB. *See* African Development Bank
African Capacity Building Foundation, 14, 18, 19, 26, 30, 32, 33, 105, 115, 126, 129, 132
African Continental Free Trade Area, 32, 144, 169. *See also* AfCFTA
African Development Bank, 4, 16, 18, 28, 31, 126, 175, 176, 180, 207
African Mining Vision (AMV), 8, 72, 77, 78, 83, 84, 87, 88, 92, 106
African Peer Review Mechanism, 47, 53, 230
African Union (AU), 3, 7, 14, 16, 19, 21, 25, 26, 32, 33, 47, 77, 86, 106, 126, 187, 201, 228, 230
Agenda 2063, 3, 6, 7, 11, 14, 16, 21, 22, 115, 201, 229

New Partnership for African Development (NEPAD), 22, 214, 228
Agenda 2030. *See* UNSDGs
Agenda 2063. *See* African Union (AU)
agricultural
   association, 215
   education, 6, 7, 10, 185, 189, 199–206, 210–212, 214–217, 233. *See also* tertiary institutions
   organization, 10, 199, 200, 204, 211
   production, 15, 199, 208, 211
   sector, 15, 21, 74, 177, 178, 186, 187, 190, 200, 201, 203
   systems of, 10, 200, 204
   transformation, 15, 204
AI. *See* artificial intelligence
APRM. *See* African Peer Review Mechanism

New Partnership for African
   Development (NEPAD), 228
artificial intelligence, 16, 72, 80, 107,
   115, 141, 208, 212, 215, 216

B
big data, 72, 78, 91, 107, 114, 115,
   127, 142, 155
block chain, 115
Botswana, 22, 27, 49, 79, 82, 102,
   128, 131, 132, 137, 231
   Pula Fund, 131, 132, 138. *See also*
      Sovereign Wealth Fund(s)

C
CAADP. *See* Comprehensive Africa
   Agriculture Development
   Program
   Maputo Declaration, 201
capacity building, 15, 16, 19, 20, 22,
   25–27, 30, 32, 214
   innovation, 15, 16
   natural resources governance/
      management, 76
capacity development, 9, 19, 25, 32,
   33, 102, 170
   digitalization, 25, 32
   in extractives sector, 112
China, 22, 28, 29, 91, 137, 140, 184,
   213, 214
civil society, 26, 27, 33, 45, 58, 72,
   77, 106, 143, 232, 234. *See also*
   civil society organizations
civil society organizations, 53, 83, 84
clean energy, 5, 101, 176, 184, 200
Comprehensive Africa Agriculture
   Development Program, 201
COVID-19, 3, 4, 6, 8, 11, 13, 14,
   16, 18–20, 22, 24, 25, 27, 30,
   31, 33, 41–43, 49–59, 61, 127,
   133, 135, 138, 139, 153–156,
   161, 164, 167, 178, 180, 187,
   189, 200, 212, 235, 236
   WHO, 18, 51. *See also* World
      Health Organization

D
democracy, 47–49, 53, 55, 57, 138
digital
   ecosystem, 6, 7, 22, 27, 229
   preparedness index. *See* DPI
   technology, 8, 19, 28, 72, 76, 78,
      85–87, 92, 107–112, 114,
      115, 117, 118, 128, 134, 135,
      141, 155, 156, 160, 161, 211,
      213, 233
   trade in services, 9, 155, 156, 161,
      169. *See also* servicification
digital economy, economies, 160, 161
digitalization
   Fourth Industrial Revolution (4IR),
      16, 108, 113
   green economy, 6, 7, 10, 134, 135,
      137, 138, 142, 143, 232
   green technology, 15
   innovation, 5, 15–20, 23, 31, 32,
      108, 110, 115, 156, 200, 203
   of governance, 6, 7, 9, 27, 102
   surveillance capitalism, 10, 202,
      203, 210
   technological advances, 127, 134,
      135, 161
digital preparedness index, 28, 31
disruptive innovation, 108, 115
disruptive technology, 5, 208. *See also*
   innovation
DPI. *See* digital preparedness index
Dutch disease, 75, 104, 105

E
economy, economies, 4–10, 15, 20,
   23, 27, 30, 32, 46, 71, 75, 88,

90, 102–104, 106, 108, 112, 113, 115, 116, 126–128, 133–135, 137–144, 153–160, 165–167, 169, 176, 177, 183, 188–191, 203, 212, 229, 230, 232, 233, 236, 237
education. *See also* educational
  agricultural, 7, 10, 185, 200–206, 210–212, 214–217, 230, 233
  systems, 7, 10, 200–205, 215, 216, 230, 233
educational, 7, 10, 28, 104, 155, 199–205, 213, 215, 216, 230, 233
EITI. *See* Extractive Industries Transparency Initiative
energy transition, 5, 187, 188
environmental sustainability, 21, 92, 108, 127, 135, 136, 139
extractive, 8, 9, 71, 73, 75–78, 90, 101–112, 114–118, 126, 138, 230
  natural resources, 6, 71, 74, 114, 116, 117
  sector, 9, 73, 76, 101–103, 105–107, 112, 115–118
Extractive Industries Transparency Initiative, 8, 72, 77, 83, 92, 105, 106

F
FAO, 178, 182. *See also* Food and Agriculture Organization
FDI. *See* foreign direct investment
financialization, 23
  digital market economy, 23
Food and Agriculture Organization, 178, 182
foreign direct investment, 169
Fourth Industrial Revolution (4IR), 16, 84, 108, 113
  digitalization, 108

G
5G, 25, 27, 168
Generation 5. *See* 5G
GHG, 139, 177, 179, 182
global
  approach, 4
  biodiversity, 141
  capitalism, 204
  community, 3, 13, 14, 127, 131, 238
  digital giants, 213, 215
  ecosystem, 177
  financial crisis, 3, 129, 200
  pandemic, 3, 6, 8, 13, 14, 18, 21, 24, 30, 33, 41, 127, 134, 200, 212, 229, 238
  warming, 6, 184
globalization, 14, 22, 129, 201, 202, 208, 219
global North, 3, 13, 16–18, 21, 30, 86, 112, 134, 137, 154, 200, 204, 219
Global Reporting Initiative, 106. *See also* GRI
global South, 3, 8, 13, 16, 17, 21, 73, 103, 107, 126, 134, 154, 200, 203, 204, 219, 234
global value chains, 9, 118, 156. *See also* GVCs
good governance
  characteristics and attributes, 44
  elements and principles, 42
  natural resource governance, 6, 8, 11, 72, 73, 83, 84, 86–91, 93, 116
  natural resource management, 4, 7, 104, 115, 127–129, 144
  public policy, 42, 46, 50
Google, 203, 213, 215, 216, 218, 230
governance. *See also* transitional governance

Africa's extractives, 9, 102
challenges, 8, 9, 42, 52, 61, 72, 73, 84, 102, 115
implications of impact of COVID-19, 19, 42
initiatives, 9, 30, 43, 47, 72, 76, 78, 92, 102, 106, 108
green
economic policies, 6, 44, 154, 177, 178, 187, 191. *See also* economy, economies
digitalization, 6
economic policies and strategies, 159, 187
energy policies, 179
growth, 5, 10, 175–177, 181, 187
industrialization, 144, 176
policies, 177, 191
challenges of, 155, 175
green economy, economies, 154, 156–159, 177, 180, 183, 186, 191
policies, 157
transformation, 158
greenhouse gas emissions. *See* GHG
GRI, 106. *See also* Global Reporting Initiative
GVCs, 9, 118, 156, 159, 160. *See also* global value chains

H
HDI. *See* human development index
higher education, 6, 201–203, 205, 206, 208, 210, 213, 217, 218
human development index, 18, 137, 199
human resources, 15, 118, 126

I
ICT. *See* Information, Communication Technology

Information, Communication Technology, 22, 23, 25–27, 90, 91, 108, 109, 116, 136, 142, 168, 169, 215, 216, 218
innovation, 6, 14, 15, 17–19, 21, 23–25, 28, 61, 72, 87, 91, 92, 107, 109, 112, 115, 127, 161, 169, 176, 177, 182, 191, 199–201, 203, 204, 207, 208, 211, 217, 218, 229, 232, 234, 237
internet of things, 16, 72, 78, 80, 81, 85, 107, 110, 203, 215
IoT. *See* internet of things

K
Kagame, Paul, 231
Rwanda, 231
Kenya, 19, 23–25, 27, 30, 47, 52–54, 76, 79, 85, 114, 158, 168, 176, 180, 208, 209, 211, 214, 215, 236, 237
Kimberley Process Certification Scheme, 8, 72, 77, 83, 92, 106
KPCS. *See* Kimberley Process Certification Scheme

L
LIA, 133
Libreville Declaration, 176
Libya Investment Authority. *See* LIA; Sovereign Wealth Fund(s)

M
Makerere University, 208, 212, 216, 218
MDGs. *See* Millennium Development Goals
micro, small and medium enterprises, 7, 9, 154–156, 159, 160, 164, 165, 169, 232

Millennium Development Goals, 17, 21, 228
mining sector, 77–79, 110, 136, 138, 140, 141
MSMEs. *See* micro, small and medium enterprises
Multinational Corporations (MNCs), 235

N
National Research and Education Networks, 207, 211–213
natural resource
  conflict, 75
  extractives, 6–8, 71, 72, 74, 76
  governance, 6, 8, 11, 72, 73, 83, 84, 86–89, 91, 93, 116
  management, 4, 7, 104, 115, 127–129, 144
  value chains, 118
  renewable and non-renewable, 90, 191
Natural Resource Charter, 106
natural resource management, 4, 7, 104, 115, 127–129, 144
Natural Resources Governance Institute, 106
New Partnership for African Development (NEPAD), 22, 214, 228
  African Peer Review Mechanism (APRM), 53
non-governmental organizations (NGOs), 86, 106
Norway, 128, 130, 131
  sovereign wealth fund (SWF), 4, 6, 7, 9, 88, 127–131, 133, 137, 142
NREN. *See* National Research and Education Networks
NRGI. *See* Natural Resources Governance Institute

NRM. *See* natural resource management

O
oil and gas industry, 80, 82, 114

P
political leadership, 8, 15, 42, 60, 61, 129, 166, 230–232, 238
post-COVID-19, 6, 8–11, 15, 16, 18, 20–22, 25–27, 30, 31, 42, 56, 58, 59, 61, 127, 128, 138, 160, 161, 202, 206, 219, 235
poverty alleviation, 18, 57, 214
production, 10, 203, 234
Publish What You Pay, 106
PWYP. *See* Publish What You Pay

R
rare earth elements (REE), 126, 136, 139, 140, 143
renewable energy, 134, 136, 157, 158, 175–177, 180, 184, 188, 189
  Kenya, 180
resource curse, 76, 92, 103–105, 126, 137, 138, 142, 231
resource paradox, 126. *See also* resource curse
Rwanda, 23–25, 27, 52, 61, 109, 135, 181, 207, 209, 231, 237
  Paul Kagame, 231

S
SAPs. *See* structural adjustment policies
SDGs. *See* Sustainable Development Goals; UNSDGs
SDLO. *See* Sustainable Development License to Operate

Senegal, 10, 22, 27, 49, 52, 53, 61, 168, 178, 181, 182, 187–190
services sector, 9, 74, 155, 156, 159, 169
servicification, 9, 156, 159, 164, 167–169, 237
  digital trade in services, 9, 155, 156, 161, 169
SLO. *See* Social License to Operate
small and medium enterprises, 191
SMEs. *See* small and medium enterprises
  micro, small and medium enterprises (MSMEs), 7, 9, 155, 156, 159, 160, 164, 169, 232, 237
Social License to Operate, 107, 116
South Africa
  COVID-19, 4, 25
  global supply of manganese, 5
  Omicron, 4
  tax administration, 25
Sovereign Wealth Fund(s)
  Kuwait Investment Fund, 128
  Norway, 128, 131
  Singapore, 128
SSA. *See* sub-Saharan Africa
structural adjustment policies, 18, 46, 47
sub-Saharan Africa, 5, 41, 49, 73–75, 104, 164, 168, 182–186, 235
sustainable development, 5–7, 9, 10, 21, 102, 105, 107, 112, 115, 127, 128, 130, 133, 134, 137, 140, 142–144, 156, 158, 159, 177, 179, 183
Sustainable Development Goals, 3, 5, 7, 14, 17, 20–22, 103, 117, 127, 134, 141, 142, 169, 200–202, 211, 216
  Agenda 2030, 3, 7
Sustainable Development License to Operate, 116
SWF. *See* Sovereign Wealth Fund(s)

T
technological, 14, 15, 17, 19, 29, 90, 91, 108, 112, 113, 116, 127, 140, 141, 167, 179, 180, 200–204, 211, 213, 214, 216, 218, 230, 237
  innovation, 14, 15, 19, 91, 112, 127
  transformation, 108, 109, 117, 202, 203
tertiary institutions, 202, 209
transitional governance, 7
transnational governance, 72, 76, 78, 86, 92

U
Uganda, 27, 51, 53, 88, 126, 132, 158, 207–209, 211, 212, 214, 218, 236
UNSDGs, 115, 157

W
WEF. *See* World Economic Forum
World Bank, 18, 23, 43, 44, 46, 51, 107, 126, 137, 156, 159, 160, 165, 176–178, 185, 186, 203
World Economic Forum, 85, 108, 112, 160
World Health Organization, 18, 51
  COVID-19, 18, 51. *See also* WHO

Z
Zimbabwe, 22, 27, 126, 136, 137, 143

Printed in the United States
by Baker & Taylor Publisher Services